# JEWELRY&GEMS
## THE BUYING GUIDE
How to Buy Diamonds,
Colored Gemstones, Pearls,
Gold & Jewelry

with Confidence and Knowledge

Antoinette L. Matlins, PG
& Antonio C. Bonanno, FGA, PG, ASA

GEMSTONE PRESS
Woodstock, Vermont

*Distributed by*

VAN NOSTRAND REINHOLD
NEW YORK

Copyright 1993
by Antoinette B. Leonard Matlins

1984, First Edition, Hardcover, Published by Crown Publishers, Inc., New York as *The Complete Guide To Buying Gems.*
1985, First Edition, Hardcover, Second Printing
1987, Second Edition, Softcover, Revised, Updated, Expanded, Published by GemStone Press, South Woodstock, Vermont as *Jewelry & Gems: The Buying Guide.*
1988, Second Edition, Softcover, Second Printing
1989, Second Edition, Softcover, Third Printing
1989, Second Edition, Softcover, Fourth Printing
1990, Second Edition, Softcover, Fifth Printing
1992, Second Edition, Softcover, Sixth Printing
1993, Third Edition, Hardcover and Softcover, Revised, Updated, Expanded.
Published by GemStone Press, Woodstock, Vermont.

Library of Congress Cataloging-in-Publication Data
Matlins, Antoinette Leonard.
    Jewelry & gems.
    Bibliography: p.
    Includes index.
    1. Jewelry-Purchasing. 2. Precious stones- Purchasing. 1. Bonanno, Antonio C. II. Title.
III. Title: jewelry and gems.
TS756.M28        1987                736'.2                87-23807
ISBN 0-943763-11-8 (pbk.)
            -12-6(HC)
Cover photograph by Sky Hall, Long Beach, CA
Book design by Rachel Kahn

10 9 8 7 6 5 4 3 2 1

Manufactured in the United States of America

GemStone Press
A Division of LongHill Partners, Inc.
Route 4, Sunset Farm Offices, P.O. Box 237
Woodstock, Vermont 05091
Tel: (802) 457-4000
Fax: (802) 457-4004

To Ruth Bonanno,
who had nothing—and everything—
to do with it

# Contents

## Price Guides

Diamond price guides, pages 94–97
Colored gem price guides, pages 150–156
Pearl price guide, page 152
Opal price guides, pages 155–156

# Special Charts and Tables

# Color Photograph Sections

## GEMSTONES
(first color section)

Rare & Distinctive Fancy Natural Color Diamonds
Red & Pink Gemstones to Warm Any Heart
Blue Gemstones Offer Heavenly Choices
Yellow & Orange Gems to Brighten the Day
Green & Blue-Green Gems Offer Rich & Uncommon Alternatives
Opals—A Fiery World of Color
Ornamental Stones & Decorative Art
Popular Diamond Shapes

## JEWELRY
(second color section)

Platinum—Rarest & Purest of Precious Metals
Gold—A Favorite from Ancient Times
Gold—A Favorite in the Present
Pearls—Freshwater, Baroque & Natural
Fine Jewelry Design—Art You Can Wear
(two pages)
Popular Diamond Ring Styles for Her & for Him

# Acknowledgments

Although we are closely related (father and daughter), my co-author and I found that in many cases we had different people to thank and different reasons for thanking them. For this reason, we have decided to express our gratitude separately.

I first thank my father, who shared with me in this task, who inspired me as a child and filled me with awe and wonder, and who gave so generously of his knowledge. In addition, I want to thank my husband, Stuart Matlins, for his support, encouragement, and willingness to suffer many hours of loneliness as I labored through the days and nights; and my wonderful daughter, Dawn Leonard-Huxoll, for her love, support and independence, without which I would never have found the time or focus to attempt this undertaking.

*Antoinette Leonard Matlins, PG*

I thank Dr. William F. Foshag, Edward P. Henderson, and James H. Benn, all of the United States National Museum, whose generosity and patience started me as a young teenager in this field; Miss Jewel Glass, Dr. Hugh Miser, Dr. Clarence Ross, Joseph Fahey, all of the United States Geological Survey; Dr. Frank Hess, of the United States Bureau of Mines; and Dr. Hatton Yoder, of the Geophysical Laboratory of the Carnegie Institution, for their interest and help as my interest and thirst for knowledge grew.

*Antonio C. Bonanno, FGA, MGA, PG*

Together, we would like to express our appreciation to the following for their help in creating this Third Edition:

Karen Bonanno Ford DeHaas, FGA, PG
Kathryn L. Bonanno, FGA, PG
Kenneth E. Bonanno, FGA, PG
and
Rachel Kahn and Wendy Kilborn, sparkling assets at GemStone Press, who have become members of our family!

# Preface
## to the Third Edition

In the years since the first edition of this book was published, over 100,000 copies have been printed. In the meantime, many changes have occurred in the jewelry and gem world.

Based on my experience working with clients in acquiring and selling gems and jewelry, I believed from the start that there was a need for this book—one that explained in simple terms what people should know before buying or selling gems and jewelry. But there weren't many who seemed to share my belief that this was a worthwhile pursuit, that enough people would want such a book, or that it could help people derive greater pleasure and satisfaction from buying and owning gems. It is gratifying to see from the sales figures that I was right. Many people—consumers, collectors, people working in the jewelry trade, students, investors—were looking for this book. And the many thousands of letters, phone calls, and in-person comments we've received telling us how thorough and helpful it is, are the best "reviews" we could ever hope for. Thank you for taking the time to let us know, and for sharing with us your own experiences and suggestions. We know now that the tremendous effort that went into writing *Jewelry & Gems: The Buying Guide* was worthwhile.

Among the letters and calls were many requests for information that was not included in previous editions—on gold and platinum, on design and re-design, on how to read gemstone reports issued by respected laboratories, and on several new gems, including the discovery both of a new tourmaline in Brazil—which occurs in some of the most exciting colors ever seen in any gem—and of *green* tanzanite. This new edition is expanded to include these areas. It also addresses throughout the text important new developments in the areas of treatments, enhancements, synthetic and imitation materials, changes in professional practices and Federal Trade regulations. Price guides for diamonds, colored gemstones, and pearls are also updated.

The primary purpose of this book remains the same: to make the purchase of gems and jewelry less confusing and more pleasurable—whether the purchase is a gift, to commemorate an important event or moment, as a memento from a visit to an exotic gem-producing nation, or simply for appreciation of the stones' innate beauty. This book covers:

- The fundamentals of how to look at gems
- Factors that affect value
- Types of fraud and misrepresentation, and how to protect yourself from them
- Questions to ask your jeweler before buying a specific stone
- Yellow gold, white gold, and platinum, and how to decide which is right for you
- Settings, design, and re-design
- How to select a reputable jeweler or appraiser

. . . and much more!

We have written it to help you know what to look for. We want you to fully understand the factors that affect the quality, beauty, durability, and price of any gem you select: a sparkling colorless diamond, a rich red ruby, a vivid green emerald, an intense blue sapphire, a shimmering pearl.

We also want to open your eyes to the whole spectrum of magnificent gems and jewelry alternatives available today: gems you may not yet have heard about; gems in colors you never imagined; gems you may know about, but whose colors may surprise you; gems that may be less well known, but equally exciting. Perhaps you'd treasure one of the lovely pink, blue, or cognac-colored diamonds now coming from Australia, or a rich ruby-colored spinel from a recent discovery in Tanzania, or a "red emerald" from a newly discovered deposit in Utah; maybe a shimmering lilac kunzite, or peachy-pink morganite; or a brilliant green garnet, neon-colored tourmaline, or purple sapphire.

Whatever your color choice, whatever your budget, there are more gemstones available, and more interesting designs, than ever before. There are even new cuts, some creating a much larger look for the stone. In short, it's a very exciting time to be thinking about buying gems and jewelry for any occasion. Knowing what's available today, and seeking some of the exciting newcomers, will enrich the entire experience.

As we pointed out in our first edition, however, deriving lasting pleasure from your purchase depends on taking the right precautions to ensure that you get what you think you're getting. It's absolutely essential to protect yourself against fraud and misrepresentation, whether it's intentional or unintentional.

That's why we have also included in this edition the latest information about what you must look out for. This is a time of intense competition, international trade with countries with different cultural attitudes and ethical standards, and new technologies making it easier and cheaper to "improve" gems and to produce imitations. An abundance of imitation material is being sold as genuine (*to jewelers as well as consumers*), and numerous new treatments can conceal and enhance gemstones. Many of these treatments are considered acceptable trade practices, but many are not. In the United States, the American Gem Trade Association mandates disclosure of gemstone treatment; the International Colored Gemstone Association is also working toward making disclosure mandatory around the world. Nonetheless, enhancement often is not disclosed.

For all these reasons, prospective purchasers must be cautious when buying both diamonds and colored gemstones. With diamonds, for example, visible black inclusions can be made to virtually disappear with the use of lasering techniques, and visible cracks can be *filled* with a near colorless substance (see chapter 6) that makes them difficult to detect even with magnification. There is nothing wrong with these treatments themselves—for those who want a larger diamond than they could afford otherwise, a filled or lasered stone may be an attractive alternative—as long as the treatment is disclosed, and the price is right. *But problems do arise when there is failure to disclose—sometimes even to the jeweler—and the diamond is misrepresented as a result.*

With colored gems you need to be doubly cautious of treatments, imitations, and mistaken identification. Let's look at a relatively new product on the market—diffusion-treated blue sapphires (see chapter 13). This treatment produces a beautiful blue color in sapphire, but the blue color is only on the *surface* of the stone. As long as the buyer knows this at the time of purchase, there is no problem. However, sometimes diffused sapphire is sold *without disclosure,* or without the buyer being fully aware of what the term "diffused blue" really means. We also know of cases where diffusion-treated blue sapphires have been mixed with other blue sapphires and inadvertently sold without disclosure.

This is not the only problem today where colored gemstones are concerned. We are seeing inexpensive synthetic sapphires and rubies arriving alongside *genuine* stones mixed in parcels coming from foreign countries. The market is flooded with very sophisticated ruby, sapphire, and emerald *doublets* (an inexpensive fake made by fusing two pieces of material together). Some of the most convincing doublets are now made by fusing a piece of genuine material to a piece of synthetic or imitation material. We are even seeing doublets made to imitate the new "Paraiba" tourmaline—by fusing genuine green tourmaline to the top of appropriately colored glass! These can easily be mistaken for genuine. We are also seeing an increase in the number of inexpensive natural gems being substituted for much more expensive gems of similar color (such as "apatite," an inexpensive, soft stone, being substituted for "Paraiba" tourmaline).

To help you deal with such practices, chapters that cover some of the most frequently encountered types of fraud and misrepresentation are included in this book. We want to stress, however, that the purpose is not to give you false confidence, nor is it to frighten or discourage you from buying gems and jewelry with confidence. Our primary purpose in covering this material is to make you less vulnerable to the allure of *bargains* and to make you aware of the importance of buying only from knowledgeable, reputable jewelers.

Furthermore, please understand that, while information provided here may enable you to spot some fakes or detect some treatments, no book can make you an expert. Be sure to follow the advice we offer regarding questions to ask, what to get in writing, and how to check it out to be sure of your purchase. To further pursue the field of gem identification, treatment, and enhancement, see our book *Gem Identification Made Easy*, which is a non-technical book for the layperson (Gemstone Press, P.O. Box 237, Woodstock, VT 05091, (800)962-4544, $29.95 plus $3.50 shipping/handling).

On the subject of gemstone investment, we want once again to underscore the need for extreme caution. When we wrote the chapter on gem investment, "A Word About Investment," for the first edition of this book, we did not recommend gems for the average investor.

However, at that time we discussed some investment pros and cons because, whether or not we thought it wise, "investment" was a word the public was applying all too frequently to gem and jewelry purchases.

Subsequent developments—including major fraudulent international gemstone investment schemes—necessitate continued caution, and so we still do not recommend gems as an investment for the average buyer.

Gemstone investment can be profitable, but we cannot emphasize too strongly the need to exercise extreme caution. In light of our concern about the growing potential for renewed speculation, we would like to refer any reader seriously considering gem investment to my chapter "Gemstones" in the Encyclopedia of Investments (Warren, Gorham and Lamont, New York City, 1989). It is much broader in scope than the investment chapter in this book and was written for the serious investor, not the average consumer. A copy of the article, including updates, may be obtained from GemStone Press, P.O. Box 237, Woodstock, VT 05091 ($10.00 including postage/handling).

Whatever your interest in gems, we hope they give you the pleasure and joy they have given us throughout the years. And we hope that this book will add new "facets" to your understanding and appreciation.

Antoinette Leonard Matlins
South Woodstock, Vermont
January 1993

# Introduction

Throughout history, gems have been a much sought-after commodity. Their beauty, rarity, and inherent "magical powers" have made them the symbol of kings, the symbol of power, the symbol of wealth, and in more recent history, the symbol of love. Every civilization, every society, grandly exhibits mankind's fascination with and desire to possess these beautiful gifts of nature.

As the growth of the American jewelry business attests, we are no different from our ancestors. We too share the fascination, appreciation, and desire to possess beautiful gems. If history serves as a sound indicator of taste, we can rest assured that the lure of gems will be just as great in future generations. At least once in a lifetime nearly every American has an occasion to buy or receive a gem.

The experience of purchasing a gem can be a magical one. It can be filled with excitement, anticipation, and pleasure—and it is to that end that this book is dedicated. The purpose of this book is to provide a basic but complete consumer's guide to buying a gem, whether it be for one's own personal pleasure, for a gift, or for investment. It is designed and written for a wide market—husbands, wives, or parents buying gems as gifts for loved ones for some special occasion; young couples looking for an engagement ring to last a lifetime; tourists, business travelers, and service men and women traveling throughout the world hoping to pick up real bargain gems while they are near the mines; investors looking for a hedge against inflation; or those information regarding fraudulent practices, provide lists of relevant questions that should be asked of a jeweler. It will not make you a gemologist, but it will make you a smart shopper who will be able to derive pleasure from what can become a truly exciting, interesting, and safe experience.

From the time I was a small child, I had the pleasure of being surrounded by beautiful gems and had a unique opportunity to learn the gem business. Having a father who was a well-known gemologist, appraiser, and collector, I was able to spend hours marveling at stones—those in his own private collection as well as those brought to him to be professionally appraised.

Dinner conversation usually centered on the day's events at my father's office. Sometimes he would thrill us with an account of a particularly fine or rare gem he had had the pleasure of identifying or verifying. But too often the subject would turn to some poor, unknowing consumer who had been victimized. It might have been a soldier who thought he had purchased genuine sapphires while in Asia, and learned sadly that they were either glass or synthetic; or a housewife who bought a "diamond" ring at an estate sale, only to learn that the stone was a white sapphire or zircon. It might have been a doctor who thought he had purchased a fine, natural "canary" diamond as a gift for his wife, who learned to his dismay that the beautiful bright yellow color was not natural at all, but the result of special treatment, and not worth anywhere near what he had paid for it. But occasionally, my father would have a wonderful story to share. One in particular illustrates especially well how complex the gem business can be. One day an average-looking elderly woman came into my father's office with a green stone she wanted identified and appraised. She had already taken the stone to a well-known jeweler who also had an excellent reputation as a gemologist-appraiser. The jeweler told her that the stone was a tourmaline worth only a few hundred dollars. She was very disappointed, since it was a family heirloom that she had believed for many years was a fine emerald. Her own mother had assured her of the fact. When she questioned the jeweler about its being an emerald, he laughed and told her that was impossible. He was the expert, so she accepted his appraisal, as most people would.

Many months later, at the insistence of a friend who knew of my father's reputation from the curator of the Smithsonian's gem collection, she sought my father's opinion. In fact, it was a genuine emerald, and one of the finest my father had ever seen. He could barely contain his excitement about the stone. It was worth about $60,000 even then, which was about twenty-five years ago. Fortunately, the woman learned its true identity and value before it was too late.

My first response upon hearing the story was anger at the "dishonest" jeweler, but, as my father explained, he was not dishonest. Dad actually went to see this man, because he knew his reputation was good. The jeweler discussed the stone with my father, and it became clear that he genuinely believed it to have been a tourmaline. Based upon the woman's "ordinary" appearance and the absence of any eye-visible characteristics so typical of an emerald, he drew the immediate conclusion that the stone could only be a green tourmaline. His experience with emeralds was limited to those of lesser quality, with their telltale inclusions. His limited experience, combined with his impression of the woman, led him to make an assumption regarding the identity of the stone without even performing any definitive test. He made an incorrect identification of this unusually fine stone, but certainly he was not acting dishonestly in hopes of picking up a steal.

This anecdote illustrates the danger consumers frequently face when they come to buy gems. They are vulnerable not only to intentional fraud but also to unintentional misrepresentation resulting from a jeweler's lack of experience and knowledge. The very person on whom one would naturally rely—the jeweler—sometimes lacks sufficient knowledge about the gems he is selling. Fortunately, such educational institutions as the Gemological Institute of America (in New York and Los Angeles) our school—Columbia School of Gemology, near Washington, D.C., and an increasing number of colleges, universities, and associations across the country offering gemology courses are helping to rectify this situation. More and more, reputable jewelers are concerned with increasing their own knowledge and that of their salespeople, not only to protect their valued customers, but also to protect themselves!

Another incident that occurred just a few years ago proves how rewarding education can be. A former student of my father's was visiting in a midwestern city. She decided to go to some pawnshops to kill time and in one shop discovered a beautiful diamond-and-emerald ring. The pawnbroker told her that the diamonds were unusually fine quality, which her examination confirmed. The ring was also beautifully designed, with outstanding workmanship. The question she had was whether the emerald was genuine or synthetic. As she examined the stone, she began to suspect it was genuine. But she didn't have the right equipment with her to be sure. The $500 price was appropriate for the diamonds and the gold setting alone, indicating that the pawnbroker believed the emerald was synthetic. But since the visitor liked the ring, and the price was fair, she was willing to take a chance that it might in fact be genuine. Upon her return to Washington she brought the ring to my father's lab, where they proceeded immediately to examine the emerald. It was genuine. Its value was many times what she had paid; it could easily have sold for over $30,000 at a retail jewelry store. She sold it for a very handsome profit. The student profited because of her knowledge; the pawnbroker lost an opportunity because of his lack of it.

As the result of my father's long experience in the gem business, and my own professionally in the last twelve years, I have felt for some time that a book about gems—written just for the consumer—was desperately needed. The cost of gems is greater than ever before, and projections indicate that prices will continue to rise. Thus, in a market where jewelers and gem dealers are often not as knowledgeable as they should be, where the price of gems continues to rise, and where consumers consider ever more frequently buying gems for investment, the gem buyer must become more informed. A consumer cannot learn to be an expert in gems through reading a single book; a gemologist is, after all, a highly trained, skilled professional. What we can provide here is some basic information that can make buying gems a more pleasurable, less vulnerable experience.

*Jewelry & Gems: The Buying Guide* covers everything you, the consumer, need to know before buying any of the most popular gems. I hope you will find as much pleasure as I have found in getting to know gems, and that your future purchases will be happy ones.

*Antoinette Leonard Matlins*
New York City
October 1980

# 1

# Getting to Know Gems

# 1

# Becoming Intimate with Gems

Gems should never be bought as a gamble—the uneducated consumer will always lose. This is a basic rule of thumb. The best way to take the gamble out of buying a particular gem is to familiarize yourself with the gem. While the average consumer can't hope to make the same precise judgments as a qualified gemologist, whose scientific training and wealth of practical experience provide a far greater data base from which to operate, the consumer can learn to judge a stone as a "total personality" and learn what the critical factors are—color, clarity (also referred to in the trade as "perfection"), cut, brilliance, and weight—and how to balance them in judging the gem's value. Learning about these factors and spending time in the marketplace looking, listening, and asking questions before making the purchase will prepare you to be a wise buyer more likely to get what you really want, at a fair price.

Try to learn as much as you can about the gem you want to buy. Examine stones owned by your family and friends, and compare stones at several different jewelry stores, noting differences in shades of colors, brilliance, and cut. Go to a good, established jewelry store and ask to see fine stones. If the prices vary, ask why. Let the jeweler point out differences in color, cut, or brilliance, and if he can't, go to another jeweler with greater expertise. Begin to develop an eye for what constitutes a fine stone by looking, listening, and asking good questions.

Five key questions to ask yourself initially before you consider buying any stone are:
1. Is the color what you desire?
2. Is the shape what you want?
3. Does it have liveliness, or "zip"?

3

4. Do you like it and feel excited by it?
5. Can you afford it?

If you answer yes to all five questions, you are ready to examine the specific stone more carefully.

## The Six Key Steps in Examining a Stone

1. *Whenever possible, examine stones unmounted.* They can be examined more thoroughly out of their settings, and defects cannot be hidden by the mounting or side stones.
2. *Make sure the gem is clean.* If buying a stone from a retail jeweler, ask that it be cleaned for you. If you are not someplace where it can be cleaned professionally, breathe on the stone in a huffing manner in order to "steam" it with your breath and then wipe it with a clean handkerchief. This will at least remove the superficial film of grease.
3. *Hold the unmounted stone so that your fingers touch only the girdle.* Putting your fingers on the table (top) and/or pavilion (bottom) will leave traces of oil, which will affect color and brilliance.

   The *careful* use of tweezers instead of fingers is recommended only if you feel comfortable using them. Make sure you know how to use them and get the permission of the owner before picking up the stone. It is easy for the stone to pop out of the tweezers and to become damaged or lost, and you could be held responsible.
4. *View the gem under proper lighting.* Many jewelers use numerous incandescent spotlights, usually recessed in dropped ceilings. Some use special spotlights that can make any gemstone—even glass imitations—look fantastic.

   Fluorescent lights may also *adversely* affect the appearance of some gems. Diamonds will not show as much fire under fluorescent lighting, and colored gems, such as rubies, look much better in daylight or under incandescent light.

   The light source should come from above or behind you, shining down and through the stone, so that the light traveling through the stone is reflected back up to your eye.
5. *Rotate the stone in order to view it from different angles.*
6. *If using a loupe, focus it both on the surface and into the interior.* To focus into the interior, shift the stone slowly, raising

or lowering it, until you focus clearly on all depths within it. This is important because if you focus on the top only, you won't see what is in the interior of the stone.

# How to Use a Loupe

A loupe (pronounced *loop*) is a special type of magnifying glass. The use of the loupe can be very helpful in many situations, even for the beginner. With a loupe you can check a stone for chips or scratches or examine certain types of noticeable inclusions more closely. Remember, however, that even with a loupe, you will not have the knowledge or skill to see or understand the many telltale indicators that an experienced jeweler or gemologist could spot. No book can provide you with that knowledge or skill. Do not allow yourself to be deluded or let a little knowledge give you a false confidence. Nothing will more quickly alienate a reputable jeweler or mark you faster as easy prey for the disreputable dealer.

The loupe is a very practical tool to use once you master it, and with practice it will become more and more valuable. The correct type is a 10X, or ten-power, "triplet" which can be obtained from any optical supply house. The triplet-type is recommended because it corrects two problems other types of magnifiers have: the presence of traces of color normally found at the outer edge of the lens; and visual distortion, also usually at the outer edge of the lens. In addition, the loupe must have a black housing around the lens, not chrome or gold, either of which might affect the color you see in the stone.

The loupe *must* be 10X because the Federal Trade Commission in the United States requires grading to be done under 10-power magnification. Any flaw that does not show up under 10X magnification is considered nonexistent for grading purposes.

With a few minutes' practice you can easily learn to use the loupe. Here's how:

1. Hold the loupe between the thumb and forefinger of either hand.
2. Hold the stone or jewelry similarly in the other hand.
3. Bring both hands together so that the fleshy parts just below the thumbs are pushed together and braced by the lower portion of each hand just above the wrists (the wrist portion is actually a pivot point).
4. Now move the hands up to your nose or cheek, with the

loupe as close to the eye as possible. If you wear eyeglasses, you do not have to remove them.

5. Get a steady hand. With gems it's very important to have steady hands for careful examination. With your hands still together and braced against your face, put your elbows on a table. (If a table isn't available, brace your arms against your chest or rib cage.) If you do this properly you will have a steady hand.

A 10x Triplet Loupe

How to hold a loupe when examining a stone.

Practice with the loupe, keeping it approximately one inch (more or less) from the eye, and about an inch from the object being examined. Learn to see through it clearly. A 10x loupe is difficult to focus initially, but with a little practice it will become easy. You can practice on any object that is difficult to see—the pores in your skin, a strand of hair, a pinhead, or your own jewelry.

Play with the item being examined. Rotate it slowly, tilt it back and forth while rotating it, look at it from different angles and different directions. It won't take long before you are able to focus easily on anything you wish to examine. If you aren't sure about your technique, a knowledgeable jeweler will be happy to help you learn to use the loupe correctly.

# What the Loupe Can Tell You

With practice and experience (and further education if you're really serious), a loupe can tell even the amateur a great deal. For a gemologist it can help determine whether the stone is natural, synthetic, glass, or a doublet (a composite stone, to be discussed later) and reveal characteristic flaws, blemishes, or cracks. In other words, the loupe can provide the necessary information to help you know whether the stone is in fact what it is supposed to be.

For the beginner, the loupe is useful in seeing:

1. *The workmanship that went into the cutting.* For example, is the symmetry of the stone balanced? Does it have the proper number of facets for its cut? Is the proportion good? Few cutters put the same time and care into cutting glass as they do into a diamond.

2. *Chips, cracks, or scratches on the facet edges, planes, or table.* While zircon, for example, looks very much like diamond because of its pronounced brilliance and relative hardness, it chips easily. Therefore, careful examination of a zircon will often show chipping, especially around the table edges and the girdle. Glass, which is very soft, will often show scratches. Normal wear can cause it to chip or become scratched. Also, if you check around the prongs, the setter may even have scratched it while bending the prongs to hold the stone.

    In such stones as emeralds, the loupe can also help you determine whether or not any natural cracks are really serious, how close they are to the surface, how deep they run, or how many are readily visible.

3. *The sharpness of the facet edges.* Harder stones will have a sharp edge, or sharper boundaries between adjoining planes or facets, whereas many imitations are softer and under the loupe the edges between the facets are less sharp and have a more rounded appearance.

4. *Bubbles, inclusions, and flaws.* Many flaws and inclusions that cannot be seen with the naked eye are easily seen with the loupe. But remember, many are not easily seen unless you are very experienced. The presence of inclusions is not as serious in colored stones as in diamonds, and they don't usually significantly reduce the value of the stone. However, the *kind*

of inclusions seen in colored stones can be important. They often provide the necessary key to positive identification, determine whether a stone is natural or synthetic, and possibly locate the origin of the stone, which may significantly affect the value. With minimal experience, the amateur can also learn to spot the characteristic bubbles and swirl lines associated with glass.

The loupe can tell you a great deal about the workmanship that went into cutting a gem. It can help a professional decide whether a gem is natural, synthetic, a doublet, or glass. It can provide the clues about the gem's authenticity, its durability, and its point of origin. But spotting these clues takes lots of practice and experience.

When you use a loupe, remember that you won't see what the experienced professional will see, but with a little practice, it can still be a valuable tool which might save you from a costly mistake.

# 2

# Looking for A Gem That's
# A "Cut Above"

One of the most important things to learn is how to look at a gem, even if you won't see all that a gemologist will. Let's begin by making sure you understand the terms you will be hearing and using to describe what you want—especially terms pertaining to the stone's "cut" and the names for the parts of a cut stone.

It's important to be familiar with a few general terms that are commonly used when referring to faceted stones. The parts of a stone can vary in proportion and thus affect its brilliance, beauty, and desirability. This will be discussed later in greater detail.

*Girdle.* The girdle is the edge or border of the stone that forms its perimeter; it is the edge formed where the top portion of the stone meets the bottom portion—its "dividing line." This is the part usually grasped by the prongs of a setting.

*Crown.* The crown is also called the *top* of the stone. This is simply the upper portion of the stone, the part above the girdle.

*Pavilion.* The pavilion is the bottom portion of the stone, the part from the girdle to the "point" at the bottom.

*Culet.* The culet is the lowest part or point of the stone. It may be missing in some stones, which can indicate damage, or, particularly with colored stones, it may not be part of the original cut.

*Table.* The table is the flat top of the stone and is the stone's largest facet, often called the face. The term *table spread* is used to describe the width of the table facet, often expressed as a percentage of the total width of the stone.

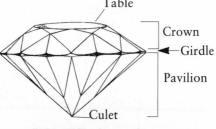

Parts of a faceted stone

9

# The Cut of the Stone

The most important—and least understood—factor which must be evaluated when considering any gem is the *cutting*. When we talk about cut, we are not referring to the shape, but to the care and precision used in creating a finished gem from the rough. There are many popular shapes for gemstones. Each shape affects the overall look of the stone, but if the stone is cut well its brilliance and value endures no matter what shape it is. For the average consumer, choosing a shape is simply a matter of personal taste. Some of the most popular shapes are pictured. New shapes are discussed in chapter 4.

## Classic Shapes

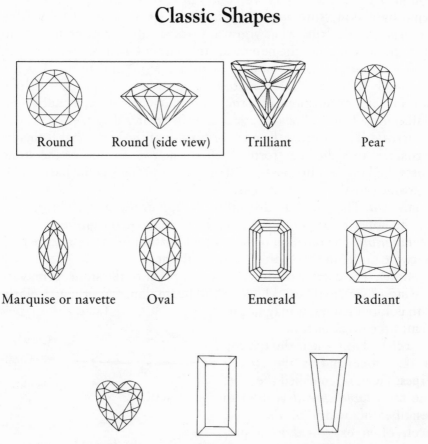

Round    Round (side view)    Trilliant    Pear

Marquise or navette    Oval    Emerald    Radiant

Heart    Baguette    Tapered baguette

## *Make* Makes a Big Difference

The shape of the stone may affect the personality it displays, but it is the overall cutting that releases its full beauty. A term used by professionals to describe the overall quality of the cutting is *make*. Having a "good make" is especially important in diamonds. A diamond with an "excellent make" will sell for much more than one with a "fair make." The difference in price between a well-cut and poorly cut diamond can be as much as 50 percent, or more. Even more important, careless cutting, or cutting to get the largest possible stone from the rough, can sometimes result in faults that may make a stone more fragile and vulnerable to breakage. Such stones should sell for much less, although the fault may not be visible without careful examination by an expert. Here we will discuss cutting in a general way. It will be discussed in greater detail later.

## How to Know If a Stone Is Well Cut

The precision of the cutting dramatically affects the beauty and value of any stone. This is especially true in *faceted* stones, those on which a series of tiny flat planes (facets or faces) have been cut and polished. (Nonfaceted stones are called *cabochons;* these are discussed in part 3.) By following some general guidelines and tips for looking at faceted gemstones, you can better determine both the quality of the stone and the quality of the cut.

The first thing to keep in mind is that in any stone, if the basic material is of good quality, the way it is cut will make the difference between a dull, lifeless stone and a beautiful, brilliant one. In diamonds, the cutting and proportioning are the greatest influence on the stone's brilliance and fire. In colored gems, the perfection of the cut is not as important as it is with diamonds, but proportioning remains critical because it will significantly affect the depth of color as well as the stone's brilliance and liveliness.

Look at the stone face up, through the top (table). This is the most critical area to view, since this is the one most often noticed. If looking at a diamond, does it seem to sparkle and dance across the whole stone, or are there dead spots? In a colored gem, does the color look good from this direction? Is the table centered and symmetrical?

A quick way to check the symmetry of a round diamond is to look at the table edges. The lines should be straight, regular, and parallel to one another. The table edges should form a regular octagon, with the edges meeting in sharp points. If the lines of the table are wavy, the overall symmetry is not good, and the symmetry of the adjoining facets will also be affected.

| Table centered but not symmetrical | Table off-center and asymmetrical | Table centered and symmetrical–the ideal |

Next, look at the stone from the side. Note the proportion of the stone both above and below the girdle.

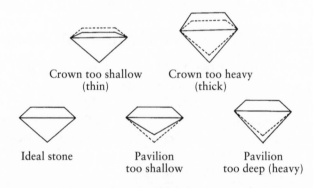

Crown too shallow (thin)    Crown too heavy (thick)

Ideal stone    Pavilion too shallow    Pavilion too deep (heavy)

The stone's proportion—whether it is too thin or too thick—will have a marked affect on its overall beauty. With colored stones, the relative terms of thickness or thinness vary greatly due to the inherent optical properties of different gems. As a general guide when considering colored stones, keep in mind these three points:

1. If the stone appears lively and exhibits an appealing color when viewed through the table, no matter how the proportion appears (thick or thin), it is usually correct and acceptable proportioning for that particular stone.
2. The depth of color (tone) will become darker as the stone is cut thicker, particularly if the bottom portion (pavilion) is deep and broad.

3.  A stone's depth of color will become lighter as the stone is cut thinner. This is especially important when considering a pastel colored stone. A pastel stone should always have fairly deep proportioning.

The effects of cut and proportioning will be discussed in greater detail in parts 2 and 3, as the factors affecting cut and proportioning are somewhat different for diamonds and colored gems. It is an important first step, however, to become aware of general views and to begin to have a feeling about what looks "right."

## Before Beginning

As you shop for any fine gem or piece of jewelry, keep in mind the importance of visiting fine jewelry stores to look at stones and compare them. Many of the factors discussed in the following chapters will become clearer when you have actual stones before you to examine, and you will gain a deeper understanding and appreciation for the gem you are considering. Knowledgeable jewelers will also be happy to take time to help you understand quality and cost differences.

Also keep in mind the importance of buying only from a well-trained, reputable jeweler. Remember, you are not an expert. The information provided here should help you begin your search more confidently and gain insights that will make the experience more fun, more challenging, and more fulfilling. But perhaps just as important, we hope it will help you make a wiser decision about the jeweler with whom you decide to do business, and about his or her knowledge, professionalism, and integrity. If so, this book will have provided a valuable service and, perhaps, saved you from a costly mistake.

# 2

# Diamonds

# 3

# The Magic of Diamonds

The diamond has been one of the most coveted gems in history. Uncut diamonds adorned the suits of armor of the great knights; cut diamonds have adorned the crowns of kings and queens throughout the ages. Today the diamond is internationally recognized as a symbol of love and betrothal and is the recipient of increasing interest as a source for investment.

The diamond has been credited with many magical powers. At one time it was considered the emblem of fearlessness and invincibility; the mere possession of a diamond would endow the wearer with superior strength, bravery, and courage. It was also believed that a diamond could drive away the devil and all spirits of the night.

During the 1500s diamonds were looked upon as talismans that could enhance the love of a husband for his wife. In the Talmud a gem that, from its description, was probably a diamond was worn by the high priest and served to prove innocence or guilt. If an accused person were guilty, the stone grew dim; if innocent, it shone more brilliantly than ever.

The Hindus classed diamonds according to the four castes. The Brahmin diamond (colorless) gave power, friends, riches, and good luck; the Kshatriya (brown/champagne) prevented old age; Vaisya (the color of a "kodali flower") brought success; and the Sudra (a diamond with the sheen of a polished blade—probably gray or black) brought all types of good fortune. Red and yellow diamonds were exclusively royal gems, for kings alone.

Diamonds have been associated with almost everything from producing sleepwalking to producing invincibility and spiritual ecstasy. Even sexual prowess has been strongly attributed to the diamond. There is a catch, however, to all the mythical powers associated with

17

this remarkable gem. One must find the diamond "naturally" in order to experience its magic, for it loses its powers if acquired by purchase. However, when offered as a pledge of love or friendship, its potency may return—another good reason for its presence in the engagement ring!

# What Is Diamond?

Chemically speaking, a diamond is the simplest of all gemstones. It is plain crystallized carbon, the same substance, chemically, as the soot left on the inside of a glass globe after the burning of a candle, or the substance used in lead pencils.

The diamond differs from these in its crystal form, which accounts for the desirable properties that have made it so highly prized—its hardness, which gives it unsurpassed wearability, its brilliance, and fire. Nonetheless, while diamond is the hardest natural substance known, it *can* be chipped or broken if hit hard from certain angles; and if the girdle—the edge of the diamond that forms the perimeter—has been cut too thin, the girdle can chip with even a modest blow.

White (or, more correctly, colorless) diamonds are the most popular, but diamond occurs in every color in the rainbow. When color is prominent the gem is called a *fancy* or *master fancy diamond*.

# How to Determine the Value of a Diamond— The Four Cs

The factors used to determine the quality and value of a diamond are referred to as the "four Cs." In terms of their effect on the *value* of a diamond—in order of importance—we would list them as follows:

1. Color (body color)
2. Clarity (degree of flawlessness)
3. Cutting and proportions (often called the *make*)
4. Carat weight

In terms of *beauty,* we would place the *cutting* first. Each factor is a lesson in itself, and so we have devoted a chapter to each.

## Finding the Right Combination

Keep in mind, however, that the key to being happy with your diamond purchase is understanding how each of these four Cs affects beauty and durability, cost, and the stone *as a whole*. It may sound complicated at first, but when you begin looking at stones you'll see it really isn't. With a little experience, you'll decide which Cs are most important to you, and know what to look for to get the right combination—one that meets your emotional *and* financial needs.

We will begin with a discussion of diamond cutting and proportioning because it is the least well understood of the four Cs.

# 4

## The Importance of Cut & Proportion

It's important to distinguish exactly what "cut" means when referring to diamonds and other stones. *Cut* does not mean *shape*. The selection of shape is a matter of individual preference. No matter which shape is selected, its *cutting* must be evaluated. Differences in cutting can affect a diamond's beauty, durability, and cost, the latter by as much as 50 percent, or more.

The cutting and proportioning of a diamond—the stone's "make" —is especially important because of its effect on the *fire* (the lovely rainbow colors that flash from within) and *brilliance* (the liveliness, the sparkle) exhibited by the stone (see chapter 2). Proper cutting and proportioning release the full beauty that sets diamond apart from all other gems. A stone with an excellent make will be exciting, while a stone with a poor make will look lifeless—it will lack the sparkle and personality we identify with diamond. In addition, stones are often cut to make them appear larger. But a stone that looks much larger than another of the same weight will not be as beautiful as a smaller stone that is properly cut.

Differences in cutting can also affect the *durability* of a diamond. Some cutting faults weaken the stone and make it more susceptible to breaking or chipping.

Fine cutting requires skill and experience, and takes more time. For all these reasons, a well-cut diamond commands a premium and will cost much more than one that is cut poorly.

There are many popular shapes for diamonds. Each shape affects the overall look of the stone, but if the stone is cut well, beauty and value endure no matter which shape you choose. We will begin our discussion of diamond cutting using the round brilliant-cut, since this is the most popular shape.

A modern round brilliant-cut diamond has 58 facets—33 on the top, 24 on the bottom, plus the culet (the "point" at the bottom, which normally is another tiny facet). Round brilliant-cut stones that are small in size are referred to as "full-cut" to distinguish them from "single-cut" stones that have only 17 facets, or "Swiss cut" with only 33 facets. Older pieces of jewelry, or inexpensive pieces containing numerous stones, often contain these cuts instead of full-cut stones. They have less brilliance and liveliness than full-cuts, but with fewer facets they are easier and less expensive to cut. Jewelry containing single- or Swiss-cut stones should sell for less than jewelry with full-cuts.

When a round brilliant-cut diamond is cut well, its shape displays the most liveliness because it enables the most light to be reflected back up through the top. This means that round brilliant-cut diamonds will have greater brilliance, overall, than other shapes. However, shape is a personal choice, and other shapes can also be very beautiful. New shapes also appear, some of which compare very favorably to round stones for overall attractiveness.

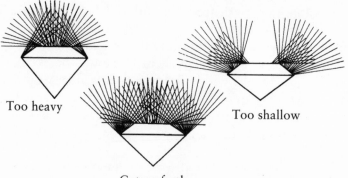

Too heavy

Too shallow

Cut perfectly

The importance of cut to brilliance

The above diagram provides an illustration, in its simplest terms, of the effect of proper cutting on fire and brilliance in a round brilliant-cut stone.

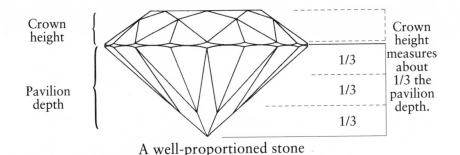

Crown height

Pavilion depth

Crown height measures about 1/3 the pavilion depth.

1/3

1/3

1/3

A well-proportioned stone

As a rule of thumb, if the top portion (crown) appears to be roughly one-third of the pavilion depth (distance from girdle to culet), the proportioning is probably acceptable.

## Types of Diamond Proportioning

The proportioning—especially the height of the crown in relation to the depth of the pavilion, and the width of the table facet in relation to the width of the stone—is what determines how much brilliance and fire the stone will have. Several formulas for correct proportioning have been developed for round diamonds. Stones that adhere to these very precise formulas are considered to have an "ideal" make and will cost more than other diamonds because of the extra time and skill required to cut them, and because more diamond "rough" is lost in the cutting.

There are several slightly differing formulas for cutting an "ideal" stone, but each results in an exceptionally beautiful stone. Generally speaking, diamonds that are cut with smaller tables exhibit more fire; those with larger tables exhibit more brilliance. The latter seems to be more in fashion today. But, as common sense may tell you here, both can't excel in the same stone. A larger table can create greater brilliance but will cause some reduction in fire; a smaller table area can increase fire but may reduce brilliance. The ideal would be a compromise that would allow the greatest brilliance and fire simultaneously. No one has come to agreement, however, on what the percentages should be, since some people prefer fire to brilliance, and vice versa. This is why there are several different types of proportioning found in diamonds, and "best" is usually a matter of personal preference.

In 1919 Marcel Tolkowsky developed what he thought would be the best combination of angles that would allow light to enter the stone and be reflected back in such a way to create the most vivid fire with the least loss of brilliance. The Tolkowsky cut provides the basis for the modern American ideal make. Today there are several variations of Tolkowsky's formula, all considered "ideal" and resulting in very beautiful diamonds.

When purchasing a round diamond, ask how the make would be graded: ideal, excellent, very good, good, fair, or poor. A diamond with a "fair" or "poor" make should sell for less than a diamond with a "good" make. A diamond with a "very good," "excellent," or "ideal" make will sell for more. (See chapter 8 for more information on grading the make.)

Your eye will be responsible for making the final determination. In general, when you look at a diamond that has a lot of brilliance and fire, the cutting and proportioning probably are acceptable. A stone that appears lifeless and seems to be "dead" or dark at the center probably suffers from poor cutting and proportioning. The more time you take to look at and compare diamonds of different qualities and prices, the better trained your eye will become to detect differences in brilliance and fire, lifelessness and dullness.

Diamonds exhibit somewhat different "personalities" depending upon the make. An "ideal" make will exhibit one personality, while another diamond with different proportioning will exhibit a different personality. A diamond cut with an ideal make will cost more, but that doesn't mean everyone will prefer stones cut to ideal proportions. A diamond doesn't have to be cut to "ideal" proportions to show strong fire and brilliance, to be beautiful or desirable. Many prefer a diamond with a wider table than is found in an "ideal." We have seen diamonds we liked even though the table exceeded 64 percent.

No matter what the proportions are, before making a final decision on a particular stone, ask yourself whether or not you think it is beautiful. If you like it, don't allow yourself to be overly influenced by formulas.

## Faulty Cuts

Many errors that affect the appearance and value of a diamond can occur in the cutting. Remember that some cutting faults will make a stone more vulnerable to breakage. We recommend avoiding such stones unless they can be protected by the setting.

There are several cutting faults to watch for in round diamonds. First, look carefully for a *sloping table* or a table that is not almost perfectly perpendicular to the point of the culet.

Second, the culet can frequently be the source of a problem. It can be chipped or broken, open or large (almost all modern cut stones have culets that come nearly to a point), or it can be missing altogether.

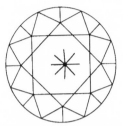

A brilliant-cut stone with a sloping table    Off-center culet

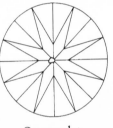
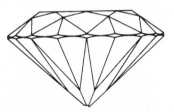

Open culet
(viewed from the bottom)

Broken or chipped culet

Third, repairs to chipped areas can result in misaligned facets, which destroy the stone's symmetry.

Sometimes, too, as a result of repair, an extra facet will be formed, often in the crown facets, but also on or just below the girdle. These extra facets may slightly affect the stone's brilliance.

Poor symmetry

Stone with extra facets

# Girdle Faults

The girdle is often the source of faults. *Bearded* or *fringed girdles* are common. A fringed girdle exhibits small radial cracks penetrating into the stone; these can result from a careless or inexperienced cutter. A bearded girdle is similar but not as pronounced a fault and can be easily repaired by repolishing, with minor loss in diamond weight.

The relative thickness of the girdle is very important because it can affect the durability as well as the beauty of the stone. Any girdle can be nicked or chipped in the course of wear, or by careless handling, but if the girdle is too thin it will chip more easily. Some chips can be easily removed by repolishing, with minimal diamond weight loss. If there are numerous chips, the entire girdle can be repolished. Chips or nicks in the girdle are often hidden under the prongs or concealed by the setting.

If the girdle is too thick, the stone may look smaller because a disproportionate amount of its weight will be in the girdle itself; such stones, for their weight, will be smaller in diameter than other stones of comparable weight.

extremely thin

thin

medium

slightly thick

extremely thick

The gradations of girdle thicknesses

The girdle can also be *wavy, rough,* or *entirely out-of-round.*

Wavy girdle        Out-of-round girdle

A *natural* may not be a fault. It's actually a piece of the natural surface of the diamond crystal. In cutting, a cutter may decide to leave part of the "natural" rough surface in order to get as large a diamond as possible from the rough stone. If this natural is no thicker than the thickness of the girdle and does not distort the circumference of the stone, most dealers consider it a minor defect at worst; if it extends into the crown or pavilion of the stone, it is a more serious fault.

Sometimes, if the natural is somewhat large but slightly below the girdle, it will be polished off. This produces an extra facet.

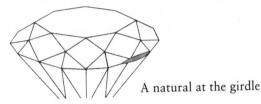

A natural at the girdle

# Other Popular Shapes

Unlike round diamonds, "fancy" shapes—all shapes other than round—have no set formulas, so evaluating the make of a fancy is more subjective. Table and depth percentage can vary widely among individual stones of the same shape, each producing a beautiful stone. Personal taste also varies with regard to what constitutes the "ideal" for shapes other than round. Nonetheless, there are certain visual indicators of good or poor proportioning—such as the "bow tie" effect—which even the amateur can learn to spot. There are recommended ratios for overall shape and symmetry, but a preferred shape is largely a personal matter. Ranges for what is "acceptable" or "unacceptable" have been developed. As you gain experience looking at specific shapes, you will be able to spot faults, and begin to determine what is within an "acceptable" range. Moderate deviation will not significantly affect the beauty or value of a stone; however, extreme deviations can seriously reduce a stone's beauty and value.

# Cutting Faults in Popular Fancy Shapes

One of the most obvious indicators of poor proportioning in fancy shapes is the *bow tie*, or *butterfly* effect, a darkened area across the center or widest part of the stone, depending upon the cut. The bow tie is most commonly seen in the pear shape or marquise but may exist in any fancy shape. Virtually all fancy shapes cut today will exhibit some minimal bow tie effect. Nonetheless, the presence or absence of a bow tie is an indicator of proper proportioning. In poorly proportioned stones there is a pronounced bow tie; the more pronounced, the poorer the proportioning. The less pronounced the bow tie, the better the proportioning. The degree to which the bow tie is evident is the first indicator of a good or poor make. A diamond with a pronounced bow tie should sell for much less than one without.

Marquise with a pronounced
bow tie, or butterfly

As with the brilliant-cut diamond, fancy shapes can also be cut too *broad* or too *narrow;* and the pavilion can be too *deep* or too *shallow.*

Personal taste will always play a role in fancy shapes—some prefer a narrow pear-shape, for example, while others might prefer a fatter pear. Whatever the shape you are considering, you must ask yourself whether or not you find the stone exciting. Does it have a pleasing personality? Does it exhibit good brilliance and fire? Is the entire stone brilliant, or are there "dead" spots? Are there any cutting faults that might make it more susceptible to chipping? Then you must make the choice.

Too broad    Too narrow    Culet too high

Culet too low    Open or misshapen culet

Pear-shaped stone, cut correctly

# New Shapes Create Excitement

Today we can choose from many shapes and cuts, ranging from the classics—round, oval, pear, marquise, emerald-cut, and heart shapes—to new shapes that appear as cutters continue to experiment with novel looks. Here are some of the most exciting:

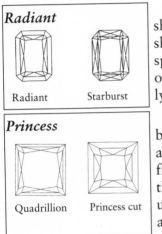

## Radiant

Radiant    Starburst

A rectangular or square brilliant cut, this shape is perfect for the person who likes the shape of an "emerald-cut" but wants more sparkle. The *starburst radiant* is a variation of the standard radiant, and exhibits a slightly different personality.

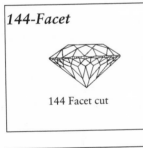

## Princess

Quadrillion    Princess cut

A square, brilliant cut which is ideal for bezel and channel settings (see chapter 21), or any setting in which you want the stone to be flush with the mounting. The *quadrillion* was the first trademarked "princess" and is cut to unique specifications which some believe creates the most beautiful of the square brilliant cuts, and which demands a slightly higher price than others of this general type.

## 144-Facet

144 Facet cut

This patented cut produces a diamond with 144 facets rather than 58, giving it unsurpassed brilliance and fire. An important feature of the 144-Facet is the girdle, which is more resistant to chipping than girdles produced by many other cuts. The 144 is an expensive cut, comparable in cost to an "ideal" make.

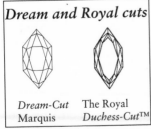

## Dream and Royal cuts

Dream-Cut    The Royal
Marquis    Duchess-Cut™

These cuts are a good choice for anyone who wants a large look on a limited budget. They are "thin" cuts, but unlike "spread" or "swindled" diamonds, which are usually lifeless, extra faceting and precision cutting help to produce unusual brilliance for their depth. A Dream-cut marquise (or, similarly, the "Duchess") will look much larger than a traditional marquise of the same weight. These cuts are available in shapes resembling the marquise, pear, and oval.

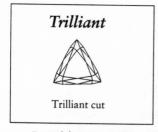

**Trilliant**

Trilliant cut

popular shape for use as a center stone, or for side stones, this triangular brilliant cut is also a thin cut, giving a large look for its weight. Extra facets and precision cutting produce high brilliance. When flanking either side of another diamond, trilliants produce a much larger diamond look, overall.

In addition to the new cuts discussed above, one of the newest cutting innovations is the *brilliant-cut baguette*, such as the *Princette*™ and *Bagillion*.™ They occur in a "straight" and "tapered" shape. These are gaining in popularity because they have greater brilliance than traditional baguettes. They can be used to flank diamonds or other stones in traditional settings, or used in very contemporary jewelry design with straight, clean lines.

## Early cuts enjoy renewed popularity

Interest in antique and period jewelry is growing rapidly and, as it does, the diamonds that adorn them are arousing renewed attention and gaining new respect. The way a diamond is cut is often one of the clues to the age of a piece. Older diamonds can be replaced or recut to modern proportions, but replacing or recutting stones mounted in antique or period pieces could adversely affect the value of the jewelry. To preserve the integrity of the piece, antique and period jewelry connoisseurs want "original" stones, or, if stones have been replaced, at least stones cut in the manner typical of the period. The market is becoming increasingly strong for diamonds with older cuts, and prices are also strengthening.

As these early cut diamonds receive more and more attention, a growing number of people are beginning to appreciate them for their distinctive beauty and personality, and for the romance that accompanies them. The romantic element—combined with a cost that is more attractive than new diamonds—is also making them an increasingly popular choice for engagement rings.

Some of the most popular early cuts are: the table cut, the rose cut, the "old-mine" cut, the "old-European" cut. (Prior to 1919, when America began to emerge as an important diamond cutting center, most diamonds were cut in Europe. Most "Old European" diamonds were cut prior to the first quarter of the 20th century).

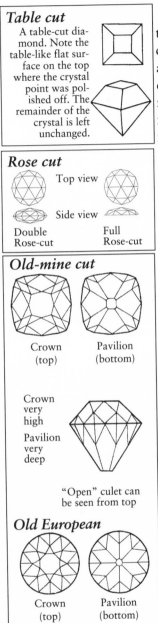

**Table cut**
A table-cut diamond. Note the table-like flat surface on the top where the crystal point was polished off. The remainder of the crystal is left unchanged.

**Rose cut**
Top view
Side view
Double Rose-cut
Full Rose-cut

**Old-mine cut**
Crown (top)
Pavilion (bottom)

Crown very high
Pavilion very deep

"Open" culet can be seen from top

**Old European**
Crown (top)
Pavilion (bottom)

The *table* cut illustrates man's earliest cutting effort. By placing the point of a diamond crystal against a turning wheel that held another diamond, the point could be worn down, creating a squarish, flat surface that resembled a *table top*. Today we still call the flat facet on the very top of the stone the *table* facet.

The *rose* cut is a sixteenth-century cut, usually with a flat base and facets radiating from the center in multiples of six, creating the appearance of an opening rose-bud. The rose cut appears in round, pear, and oval shapes.

The *old-mine* was a precursor to the modern round. This cut had a squarish or "cushion" shape (a rounded square or rectangular) and more facets than today's modern 58-facet stone. Proportions followed the diamond crystal, so the crown is higher and pavilion deeper than modern stones. The table is very small, and the culet is very large and easily seen from the top (resembling a "hole" in the diamond). These lack the brilliance of modern stones, but often exhibit tremendous fire. Old-mine cut diamonds are also seen in pear and oval shapes.

Appearing in the mid-1800s, the *old-European* is similar to the old-mine cut, but is round rather than squarish, with 58 facets. The crown is higher than modern cuts, but not as high as in the old mine cut; it has a deep pavilion, but not as deep as old-mines. The culet is still "open" but smaller than old-mines.

Old cuts can be very beautiful. The intense "fire" exhibited by some old-mine and old-European cuts can have tremendous allure. By today's standards, however, they lack brilliance, and a very large culet may detract from the stone's beauty.

## Are Diamonds with Old Cuts Valuable?

Old-mine-cut and old-European-cut diamonds are normally evaluated by comparison to modern-cut stones. Value is usually determined by estimating the color, clarity, and the weight the stone would *retain* if it were recut to modern proportions.

We don't suggest recutting old diamonds if they are in their original mountings. The overall integrity of the piece—and value—would be adversely affected by doing so.

If the setting has no special merit, the decision must be an individual one, based on whether or not the stone appeals to you. As we have said, some older cuts are very lovely, while others may look heavy, dull, or lifeless. An unattractive older cut may benefit from recutting and, although it will lose weight, it may have equal, or greater, value because of the improved make. In addition, recutting can sometimes improve the clarity grade of an older stone.

## A Word about Recutting Diamonds

There are many fine diamond cutters in the United States—New York City is one of the most important diamond cutting centers in the world for top quality diamonds—and many diamonds can be greatly improved by recutting. The cost is surprisingly low when one considers the benefit to the stone, and effect of recutting on the diamond's beauty and value (sometimes the clarity grade is also improved).

If you have an old-cut diamond which you don't care for, or a damaged diamond, your jeweler can consult with a diamond cutter—or refer you to one—to determine whether or not your stone can be improved by recutting and, if so, what risks and costs might be involved.

Normally the cost to recut a diamond ranges from approximately $125 per carat up to $250 per carat, depending upon the skill required and the labor involved. In rare instances the cost might be more. If the labor estimate to recut a stone is $150 per carat, recutting a two-carat diamond will cost $300.

A knowledgeable jeweler can help you decide whether or not a diamond should be recut, make arrangements for you, and help assure you that you've received the same stone back. For your own comfort and security, as well as the cutter's, we always recommend that prior to having a stone recut you obtain a diamond grading report or thorough appraisal so that you have a point of reference when the stone is returned.

## To What Extent Does Cutting & Proportioning Affect Value in Modern Diamonds?

Excellently cut and proportioned stones cost significantly more per carat than those that are not cut well. The following will give a very basic idea of how some of the most frequently encountered defects can affect a diamond's price.

- Table is not a reasonably accurate octagon—2 to 15 percent off
- Girdle is too thick—5 to 10 percent off
- Girdle is too thin—5 to 25 percent off
- Symmetry of crown facets off—5 to 15 percent on round, less on fancy cuts since defect is not so easily seen
- Asymmetrical culet—2 to 5 percent off
- Misaligned culet—5 to 25 percent off
- Stone too shallow—15 to 50 percent off
- Stone too thick—10 to 30 percent off
- Thin crown—5 to 20 percent off
- Thick crown—5 to 15 percent off

As you can see, there is a fairly wide range here, depending upon the severity of the error, and only an experienced professional can determine the extent to which the value of a given stone may be lessened. But a quick computation shows that a stone suffering from several errors (which is fairly common) could certainly have a significantly reduced price per carat.

**Remember:** The value of two diamonds with the same weight, color and clarity can differ dramatically because of differences in cutting.

# 5

# Body Color

Color is one of the most important factors to consider when selecting a diamond because one of the first things most people notice is whether or not the diamond is white, or, more accurately, *colorless*. It is also one of the most significant factors affecting value.

Color refers to the natural body color of a diamond. The finest—and most expensive—"white" diamonds are absolutely colorless. Most diamonds show some trace of yellowish or brownish tint, but diamonds also occur in every color of the rainbow. Natural colored diamonds are called "fancy" diamonds.

## How to Look at a Diamond to Evaluate Color

In white diamonds, color differences from one grade to the next can be very subtle, and a difference of several grades is difficult to see when a diamond is mounted. Keep in mind that it is impossible to accurately grade color in a mounted diamond. When looking at an unmounted stone, however, even an amateur can learn to see color differences if the stone is viewed properly.

Because of the diamond's high brilliance and dispersion, the color grade cannot be accurately determined by looking at the stone from the top, or face-up, position. It is best to observe color by examining the stone through the pavilion with the table down. Use a flat white surface such as a white business card, or a *grading trough,* which can be purchased from a jewelry supplier or through the Gemological Institute of America (GIA). Next, view the stone with the pavilion side down and the culet pointing toward you.

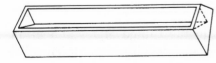
A grading trough, available in plastic for about $3, or in handy disposable folding white cardboard stand-up packs. Be sure to use a *clean* trough.

35

The following drawings show the best way to view loose diamonds.

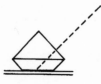

**Position 1.** Place table-side down and view the stone through the pavilion facets.

**Position 2.** Table-side down, view the stone through the plane of the girdle.

**Position 3.** Place the pavilion down with the culet pointing toward you. View the stone through the girdle plane.

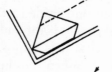

**Position 4.** Place table-down in a grading trough and view the stone through the girdle plane.

**Position 5.** Place pavilion-down in a grading trough, with the culet pointing toward you. View the stone through the pavilion facets.

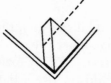

# What Is Body Color?

When we discuss body color we are referring to how much yellow or brown tint can be seen in a white (colorless) diamond. We are not referring to rare natural-colored diamonds, which are called "fancy" or "master fancy" in the trade.

Today, most colorless diamonds in the United States and in an increasing number of other countries are graded on an alphabetical scale beginning with the letter *D*—which designates the finest, rarest, most absolutely colorless diamond—and continuing down through the entire alphabet to the letter *Z*. Each letter after *D* indicates increasing amounts of yellowish (or brownish) tint to the body color. It's easy to understand the color grade, if you just remember: the closer the letter is to *D* the whiter the diamond; the closer the letter is to *Z*, the yellower (or browner) the diamond.

This grading system, with its letter designations, is part of a diamond-grading system introduced by the Gemological Institute of America (often referred to as GIA) and is used extensively in the diamond trade around the world. Grades *D-F* are exceptionally fine and diamonds in this range can be referred to as "colorless," although technically, *E* and *F* are not colorless since they possess a very slight trace of yellow; the tint is so slight, however, that the trade agrees they may be referred to as colorless.

Diamonds graded *D* color are becoming very rare, and a significant premium is paid for them. *E* color is also exceptionally fine, and increasingly rare. It is very close to *D* color, and almost indistinguishable from it except to the very experienced, but it costs significantly less per carat.

| | | |
|---|---|---|
| COLORLESS | **D** | Loose diamonds appear colorless. |
| | **E** | |
| | **F** | |
| NEAR COLORLESS | **G** | When mounted in a setting, these diamonds may appear colorless to the untrained eye. |
| | **H** | |
| | **I** | |
| | **J** | |
| FAINT YELLOWISH TINT | **K** | Smaller diamonds look colorless when mounted. Diamonds of $1/2$ carat or more show traces of color. |
| | **L** | |
| | **M** | |
| VERY LIGHT YELLOWISH TINT | **N** | |
| | **O** | |
| | **P** | |
| | **Q** | |
| | **R** | |
| TINTED LIGHT YELLOWISH | **S** | These diamonds show increasingly yellow tints to even the untrained eye, and appear very *"off-white."* |
| | **T** | |
| | **U** | |
| | **V** | |
| | **W** | |
| | **X** | |
| | **Y** | |
| | **Z** | |

# What Color Grade Is Most Desirable?

The colors *D, E, and F* can all be grouped as exceptionally fine and may be referred to as "colorless," "exceptional white," or "rare white" as they are often described by diamond dealers. *G* and *H* may be referred to as "fine white" or "rare white." These grades are all considered very good. *I* and *J* colors are slightly tinted white. *K* and *L* show a tint of yellow or brown, but settings can often mask the slight tint. Grades *M-Z* will show progressively more and more tint of color, and will have a definite yellowish or brownish cast; diamonds with a strong yellowish tint are often referred to as *cape* stones in the trade.

Grades *D-J* seem to have better resale potential than grades *K-Z*. This does not mean that diamonds having a more tinted color (grades below *J*) aren't beautiful or desirable. They can make lovely jewelry and, depending upon other quality factors and "overall personality," might be preferable on the whole to other diamonds with better color. Remember: color is important, but it's only one of *four* factors you must learn to weigh as you judge the whole stone.

# To What Extent Does the Color Grade Affect Value?

To an untrained eye, discerning the difference in color from *D* down to *H* in a *mounted* stone—without direct comparison—is almost impossible. Nevertheless, the difference in color greatly affects the value of the diamond. A one-carat, flawless, excellently proportioned *D*-color diamond might retail for $30,000 while the same stone with *H*-color might sell for only $12,000. The same stone with *K*-color might sell for only $7,500. And if the stone were not flawless, or well cut, it could sell for much less, as you will soon see.

In diamonds over one-carat, the whiter the stone, the more critical it becomes to know the exact color grade because of its effect on value. On the other hand, as long as you know for sure what color the stone is, and are paying the right price, choosing one that is a grade or two lower than another will reduce the cost per carat, and there will be little, if any, visible difference when the stone is mounted. Therefore, for the difference in cost, you might be able to get a larger diamond, or one with a better clarity grade, depending upon what is most important to you.

# Commonly Used Color-Grading Systems

The GIA and American Gem Society (AGS) grading systems are the most commonly used in the United States. GIA is the most widely used in the world.

Scandinavian diamond nomenclature (Scan D.N.) is often used in Scandinavian countries as well as a system developed by CIBJO. CIBJO stands for the International Confederation of Jewelry, Silverware, Diamonds, Pearls, and Stones. Participating member nations who use this scale include: Austria, Belgium, Canada, Denmark, Finland, France, Great Britain, Italy, Japan, the Netherlands, Norway, Spain, Sweden, Switzerland, the United States, and Germany.

Another system is applied by the Belgian "Hoge Raad voor Diamant," or Diamond High Council, abbreviated HRD.

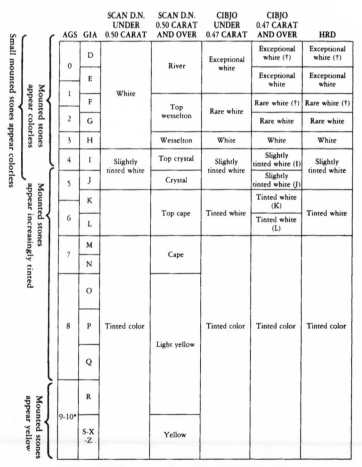

| AGS | GIA | SCAN D.N. UNDER 0.50 CARAT | SCAN D.N. 0.50 CARAT AND OVER | CIBJO UNDER 0.47 CARAT | CIBJO 0.47 CARAT AND OVER | HRD |
|---|---|---|---|---|---|---|
| 0 | D | White | River | Exceptional white | Exceptional white (†) | Exceptional white (†) |
| 0 / 1 | E | White | River | Exceptional white | Exceptional white | Exceptional white |
| 1 | F | White | Top wesselton | Rare white | Rare white (†) | Rare white (†) |
| 2 | G | White | Top wesselton | Rare white | Rare white | Rare white |
| 3 | H | White | Wesselton | White | White | White |
| 4 | I | Slightly tinted white | Top crystal | Slightly tinted white | Slightly tinted white (I) | Slightly tinted white |
| 5 | J | Slightly tinted white | Crystal | Slightly tinted white | Slightly tinted white (J) | Slightly tinted white |
| 6 | K | Slightly tinted white | Top cape | Tinted white | Tinted white (K) | Tinted white |
| 6 | L | Slightly tinted white | Top cape | Tinted white | Tinted white (L) | Tinted white |
| 7 | M | | Cape | | | |
| 7 | N | | Cape | | | |
| | O | | | | | |
| 8 | P | Tinted color | Light yellow | Tinted color | Tinted color | Tinted color |
| | Q | Tinted color | Light yellow | Tinted color | Tinted color | Tinted color |
| 9-10* | R | Tinted color | | Tinted color | Tinted color | Tinted color |
| 9-10* | S-X -Z | Tinted color | Yellow | Tinted color | Tinted color | Tinted color |

Left-margin labels:
- Small mounted stones appear colorless
- Mounted stones appear colorless
- Mounted stones appear increasingly tinted
- Mounted stones appear yellow

* AGS grade "9" corresponds to GIA, "R,S,T,U" inclusive.
  AGS grade "10" corresponds to GIA, "V,W" inclusive.
The use of the term "blue white" is discouraged today since it is usually misleading.

# What Is Fluorescence?

If the diamond you are considering is accompanied by a diamond grading report, it will indicate whether or not the diamond has some degree of fluorescence. This is a property that some stones possess which causes them to appear to be different colors in different lights. A diamond that fluoresces might look whiter than it really is in certain light. This is one reason why the color of any fine diamond should always be verified by a qualified gemologist.

If a diamond fluoresces, it normally will produce a bluish, yellowish, or whitish glow when viewed in *sunlight* or daylight-type fluorescent light (those long tubes you see in the ceiling of many stores and office buildings). To ensure that the true body color is being graded, a professional will always test for fluorescence with a special *ultraviolet* lamp prior to color-grading. Blue fluorescence is more common than yellow or white. Some white diamonds that produce a blue fluorescence may actually look "blue-white" in the right light. Normally, however, you will not really notice fluorescence with the naked eye.

It is also important to know whether or not a diamond fluoresces to prevent any unpleasant surprises. For example, if you buy a "fluorescent" diamond because it seems so "white" when you purchase it (resulting from exposure to fluorescent light in the jewelry store— which, except in the case of fluorescent stones, is the *proper* light for viewing diamond *color*), you might be disappointed by its yellower appearance in *evening light* where the stone won't fluoresce.

A white diamond can also fluoresce yellow, and look yellower than it really is. But remember, whatever color is produced by fluorescence, it occurs *only* in daylight or fluorescent light.

# Does Fluorescence Affect Value?

Generally, the presence or absence of fluorescence has little, if any, effect on value. However, if the stone has a strong yellow fluorescence it may sell for 10 to 15 percent less, since this will make the stone appear yellower in some lights than another stone with the same color grade.

The presence of blue fluorescence may be considered an added benefit—a little bonus—since it may make the stone appear whiter in some lights; and yet there may be no difference in cost. You must be careful, however, to look closely at stones with *very strong* blue fluorescence—some will have an "oily" or "murky" appearance. If the stone appears murky or oily in daylight or fluorescent light, it should sell for 15 to 20 percent less than comparable stones without the murky cast.

If a diamond fluoresces, its true body color can be misgraded. This can be costly to the buyer, but it can be easily avoided. Knowledgeable jewelers or appraisers will always test a diamond to see whether or not it fluoresces, and to what degree, in order to color-grade accurately.

# What is a "Premier"?

At this point we should mention a type of fluorescent diamond that is not encountered often, but which occurs frequently enough to warrant a brief discussion. It is called a *premier*. This does not mean the diamond is better than others. In fact, it should sell for much less than other white diamonds.

The true color of any premier diamond will be yellowish (cape), but the yellow color is masked by strong blue fluorescence. As with other diamonds that fluoresce blue, the premier will appear whiter than it really is in certain light. It may actually have a bluish tint, sometimes with a greenish cast. However, a premier will always have a murky or oily appearance in daylight or fluorescent light resulting from the coupling of the yellow with the blue. The murkiness detracts from its beauty and causes a reduction in value. The price of the premier varies depending on the degree of yellow present and the degree of murkiness.

Do not confuse a premier diamond with one that exhibits normal blue fluorescence. Many diamonds exhibit some degree of fluorescence. Many have a very fine white body color to begin with. But most important, they differ from the premier because they will not appear oily or murky in daylight-type light.

## Some Plain Talk About "Fancy" Colored Diamonds

Diamonds have been found to occur naturally in almost every color and shade—blue, red, green, yellow, lavender, pink, gunmetal blue, coffee brown, and black. The color can be intense or very pale. Some colors are rarer than others. The most common fancy colors are shades of yellow (a very intense, bright yellow is often called "canary"), orange, and brown. Such colors as pink, light green, and lavender occur much more rarely. Deep blue, red, and green diamonds are among the rarest—and most valuable—gems on earth. Black diamonds are relatively common. Most colored diamonds found in nature tend to be pastel.

Except for very pale yellow and very pale brown varieties—which are very common and not considered "fancies" but, more properly, off-white—colored diamonds often sell for more than fine colorless diamonds. An extremely rare red diamond with very poor clarity that weighed less than one carat brought the highest price ever paid for a single gem—almost $1 million per carat—at auction in 1987. A fine pink or blue diamond can bring hundreds of thousands of dollars per carat.

Fancy colored diamonds occur naturally, but fancy colors can also be produced artificially by exposing very inexpensive brownish or yellowish stones to certain types of radiation and heating techniques. Many unattractive, off-white stones are changed in this manner to beautiful "fancy" colors. Yellow, blue, and green diamonds are often the result of such treatment.

With the exception of some green diamonds, a stone's color can be tested by a qualified gemologist or gem-testing laboratory using spectroscopic examination, electro-conductivity, and ultraviolet response to determine whether color is natural or induced. Although the treated diamond may be comparable to the natural in beauty, if the color is induced, the price should be much less.

When buying any fancy colored diamond be sure to ask whether or not the color is natural, and be sure the bill of sale and any accompanying certification or appraisal specifies whether the color is natural or induced. Always verify natural color at a respected gem testing laboratory.

# Special Tips on the Subject of Color

## Keep It Clean If You Want the Color to Look Its Best

A dirty diamond will not look white (nor will it sparkle). An accumulation of dirt, especially greasy dirt, will give a diamond a yellowish cast, so if you want to see and enjoy its full beauty, keep your diamond clean.

This principle applies especially when you are looking at old jewelry for possible purchase. When considering old diamond pieces, pay particular attention to whether or not it is impacted with dirt accumulated by years of use. If it is, there is a possibility that the diamond will have a better color grade than it may appear to have at first glance. This is because the dirt may contain varying amounts of fatty deposits (from dishwashing, cosmetics, etc.), which yellow with age. When this type of dirt builds up, and is in contact with the diamond, it will also make the diamond appear yellower.

## White or Yellow Gold Setting?

The color of the metal in the setting (see chapter 19) can affect your perception of the color of your stone—sometimes adversely and sometimes beneficially. A very white diamond should be held in a white metal such as white gold, platinum, or palladium. If you prefer yellow gold, it's possible to have just that portion of the setting which holds the diamond itself fashioned in white metal. For example, a diamond ring can be made with a yellow gold "shank" to go around the finger, and white metal "head" to hold the diamond. An all-yellow setting may make a very white diamond appear less white because the yellow color of the setting itself is reflected into the diamond.

On the other hand, if the diamond you choose tends to be yellower than you'd like, mounting it in yellow gold, with yellow surrounding the stone, may make the stone appear whiter in contrast to the strong yellow of the gold.

The yellow gold environment may mask the degree of yellow in a yellow diamond, or it may give a colorless diamond an undesirable yellow tint. The setting can also affect future color grading should you ever need an updated insurance appraisal.

# 6

## Clarifying Clarity:
## How Flaws Affect Diamonds

Flaw classification—the *clarity* grade—is one of the most important criteria used to determine the value of a diamond. As with all things in nature, however, there is really no such thing as "flawless." Even though some very rare diamonds are classified "flawless," the term is somewhat misleading and you must be sure you understand what it really means.

When we talk about a diamond's clarity or flaw-grade, we are referring to the presence of tiny, usually microscopic, imperfections. As it forms in nature, *every* diamond develops imperfections. They might be microscopic cracks shaped like feathers, or microscopic diamond crystals, or even crystals of some other gemstone! Each diamond's internal picture—its internal character—is unique. No two are alike, so the clarity picture can be an important factor in identifying a specific diamond. To the buyer, however, the clarity grade is important because it indicates, on a relative basis, how "clean" the diamond is. The cleaner the stone, the rarer and costlier.

### How Is the Clarity Grade Determined?

Diamonds used in jewelry are usually very clean, and little, if anything, can be seen without magnification. This is starting to change as an increasing number of diamonds with visible cracks or other inclusions enter the market—stones in the $I_1$-$I_3$ range, and below— but for the most part, differences in clarity cannot normally be seen simply by looking at the stone with the naked eye. The clarity grade is based on what can be seen *when the diamond is examined using 10x magnification,* as provided by a loupe (see chapter 1). The "flawless" grade is given to a stone in which no imperfections can be seen internally ("inclusions") or externally ("blemishes") when it is examined with 10x, although at higher power inclusions will be visible in a flawless diamond. For clarity-grading purposes, if an inclusion can't be seen at 10X, it doesn't exist.

Clarity grading requires extensive training and practice, and proper grading can only be done by an experienced jeweler, dealer, or gemologist. If you want to examine a diamond with the loupe, remember that only in the lowest grades will an inexperienced person be able to see inclusions easily, and even with the loupe it will be difficult to see what a professional will see easily; few amateurs will see anything at all in diamonds with the highest clarity grades.

# Types of Diamond Imperfections

Among the two categories of flaws—internal flaws, or inclusions, and external flaws, or blemishes—are a variety of different types. The following lists will describe them and provide a working vocabulary of diamond imperfections.

## Internal Flaws or Inclusions

*Pinpoint.* This is a small, usually whitish (although it can be dark) dot that is difficult to see. A group of pinpoints is simply a cluster of pinpoint flaws, and cannot be classified as VVS. A cloud of pinpoints is hazy and is not easily seen.

*Dark spot.* This may be a small crystal inclusion or a thin, flat inclusion that reflects light like a mirror. It may also appear as a silvery, metallic reflector.

*Colorless crystal.* This is often a small crystal of diamond, although it may be another mineral. Sometimes it is very small, sometimes large enough to substantially lower the flaw grade to $SI_2$ or even $I_1$. A small group of colorless crystals lowers the grade from possible $VS_2$ to $I_3$.

*Cleavage.* A small cleavage is a crack that has a flat plane, which if struck, could cause the diamond to split.

*Feather.* This is another name for a crack. A feather is not dangerous if it is small and does not break out through a facet. Thermoshock or ultrasonic cleaners can make it larger.

*Bearding* or *girdle fringes.* These are usually the result of hastiness on the part of the cutter while rounding out the diamond. The girdle portion becomes overheated and develops cracks that resemble small whiskers going into the diamond from the girdle edge. Sometimes the bearding amounts to minimal "peach fuzz" and can be removed with slight repolishing. Sometimes the bearding must be removed by faceting the girdle. Bearding that is quite minimal can be classified as IF.

*Growth lines* or *graining*. These can be seen only when examining the diamond while slowly rotating it. They appear and disappear, usually instantaneously. They will appear in a group of two, three, or four pale brown lines. If they cannot be seen from the crown side of the diamond and are small, they will not affect the grade adversely.

*Knaat* or *twin lines*. These are sometimes classified as external flaws because they appear on the surface as very small ridges, often having some type of geometrical outline, or as a small, slightly raised dot with a tail resembling a comet. These are difficult to see.

## External Flaws or Blemishes

A *natural*. This usually occurs on the girdle and looks like a rough, unpolished area. It may resemble scratch lines or small triangles called *trigons*. A natural is a remnant of the original skin of the diamond, and is often left on the girdle when the cutter tries to cut the largest possible diameter from the rough. If a natural is no wider that the normal width of the girdle and does not disrupt the circumference of the stone, some do not consider it a flaw.

Often naturals are polished and resemble an extra facet, especially if they occur below the girdle edge.

*Nick*. This is a small chip, usually on the girdle, and can be caused by wear, especially if the girdle has been cut thin. Sometimes a nick or chip can be seen on the edge of the facets where they meet. If small, this bruised corner can be polished, creating an extra facet. This usually occurs on the crown.

A natural at the girdle

*Girdle roughness.* This blemish appears as crisscrossed lines, brighter and duller finishing, and minute chipping. This can be remedied by faceting or repolishing.

*Pits or cavities.* Pits or holes on the table facet, especially if they are deep, will quickly lower the grade of the stone. Removing pits involves recutting the whole top of the stone, and can also shrink the stone's diameter.

*Scratch.* A scratch is usually a minor defect that can be removed with simple repolishing. Remember, however, that in order to repolish the stone, it must be removed from its setting, and then reset after it has been polished.

# Five Commonly Used Clarity Grading Systems

The following five systems are commonly used for grading clarity.

1. **CIBJO** (International Confederation of Jewelry, Silverware, Diamonds, Pearls, and Stones). Participating member nations include Austria, Belgium, Canada, Denmark, Finland, France, Great Britain, Italy, Japan, the Netherlands, Norway, Spain, Sweden, Switzerland, and Germany, although not all members use this system.
2. **Scan D.N.** (Scandinavian Diamond Nomenclature)
3. **GIA** (Gemological Institute of America)
4. **AGS** (American Gem Society)
5. **HRD** (Hoge Raad voor Daimant, the Diamond High Council of Belgium)

The major grading system used in the United States, like the color-grading system, was developed by the Gemological Institute of America (GIA) as part of its diamond-grading system. The GIA system is only one of several in use, but it has gained wide acceptance in the United States and in many other countries around the world, including Great Britain and Japan.

Basically these systems grade the stone for its imperfections—both its internal inclusions and external blemishes. The clarity grade represents the total picture—the type, number, placement, and color—of the diamond's imperfections. These can be white, black, colorless, or even red or green in rare instances. The "flaw" grade is more commonly referred to as the "clarity" grade today. The terms, however, may be used interchangeably.

The following chart shows these five clarity-grading systems.

## COMMONLY USED FLAW (CLARITY) SYSTEMS

| CIBJO UNDER 0.47 CARAT | CIBJO 0.47 CARAT AND OVER | HRD | SCAN D.N. | GIA | AGS |
|---|---|---|---|---|---|
| Loupe clean | Loupe clean | Loupe clean | FL | FL | 0 |
| | | | IF (Internally Flawless) | IF | 1 |
| VVS | $VVS_1$ | $VVS_1$ | $VVS_1$ | $VVS_1$ | |
| | $VVS_2$ | $VVS_2$ | $VVS_2$ | $VVS_2$ | 2 |
| VS | $VS_1$ | $VS_1$ | $VS_1$ | $VS_1$ | 3 |
| | $VS_2$ | $VS_2$ | $VS_2$ | $VS_2$ | 4 |
| SI | $SI_1$ | SI | $SI_1$ | $SI_1$ | 5 |
| | $SI_2$ | | $SI_2$ | $SI_2$ | 6 |
| Piqué I | Piqué I | $P_1$ | 1st Piqué | $I_1$ (Imperfect) | 7 |
| | | | | | 8 |
| Piqué II | Piqué II | $P_2$ | 2nd Piqué | $I_2$ | 9 |
| Piqué III | Piqué III | $P_3$ | 3rd Piqué | $I_3$ | 10 |

VV = Very, Very
V = Very
S = Slight or Small
I = Inclusion or Included or Imperfect (Imperfection)

For example, VVS may be translated to mean Very, Very Slightly (Included); or Very, Very Small (Inclusion); or Very, Very Slightly (Imperfect). Some jewelers prefer to classify the stone as "very, very small inclusion" rather than "very, very slightly imperfect," because the former description may sound more acceptable to the customer. There is, in fact, no difference.

As you can see, there are eleven grades on the GIA scale, beginning with FL (flawless). A flawless, colorless, well-cut stone, particularly from one carat and up, is extremely rare and is priced proportionately much higher than any other grade. Some jewelers insist such stones don't exist today.

The grade of IF is given to a stone with no internal flaws and with only minor external blemishes—small nicks, pits, or girdle roughness, *not on the table*—that could be removed with polishing. These stones, in colorless, well-proportioned makes, are also rare and priced proportionately much higher than other grades.

VVS$_1$ and VVS$_2$ are grades given to stones with internal flaws that are very, very difficult for a qualified observer to see. These are also difficult grades to obtain, and are priced at a premium.

VS$_1$ and VS$_2$ are grades given to stones with very small inclusions difficult for a qualified observer to see. These stones are more readily available in good color and cut, and their flaws will not be visible except under magnification. These are excellent stones to purchase.

SI$_1$ and SI$_2$ grades are given to stones with flaws that a qualified observer will see fairly easily with 10x magnification, and, in some cases, may be able to see without magnification. They are less rare than other grades, so they sell at a lower price. They are still highly desirable and are being used increasingly in very fine jewelry, especially in sizes over two carats with good color and cut.

The imperfect grades are given to stones in which flaws may be seen by a qualified observer without magnification; they are readily available and are much less expensive. They are graded I$_1$, I$_2$ and I$_3$. (These grades are called *first piqué* (pronounced pee-kay), *second piqué,* and *third piqué* in some classification systems.) I$_1$, I$_2$, and some I$_3$ grades may still be desirable if they are brilliant and lively, and if there are no inclusions that might make them more susceptible than normal to breaking, and so should not be eliminated by a prospective purchaser who desires lovely diamond jewelry. As a general rule, however, imperfect grades may be difficult to resell should you ever try to do so.

## Exercise Care When Considering a Low Clarity-Grade

For those considering a diamond with an I$_3$ clarity grade, we must issue a word of warning: *some diamonds graded "I$_3$" today are actually industrial quality and not suited for jewelry use.* Some cutters are cutting material that is lower than what is considered acceptable for jewelry. Since there is no grade lower than I₃ at this time, these stones are lumped in with other "better" (jewelry quality) I₃ stones, and are given an I₃ grade as well. But I₃ grade diamonds are *not* all comparable in terms of their clarity, and some should sell for much less than others. Be sure to shop around and compare "I₃" diamonds to become familiar with what is acceptable for jewelry use.

## To What Extent Does Clarity Affect the Beauty of a Diamond?

The clarity grade can dramatically affect the value of a diamond because of differences in rarity, but it is very important to understand that clarity may have little or no effect on the *beauty* of a diamond if it falls within the first eight grades (FL–SI). Few people can discern any visible difference between stones until they reach the imperfect grades, and even then some have difficulty seeing anything in the stone without magnification. Juggling the clarity grade can give you tremendous flexibility in getting a whiter or larger diamond for your money, but it also means you must take care to know for sure what the specific clarity grade is.

## Clarity Enhancement

Today technological advances have made it possible to improve diamond clarity. Several clarity enhancement techniques are available, some more or less permanent, and others definitely not permanent. Unfortunately, clarity enhancement frequently is not disclosed, either to jewelers themselves or by jewelers to their customers. It is important to buy diamonds from knowledgeable, reputable jewelers who check for such treatments. In addition, prior to buying any diamond you must *ask* whether or not the stone has been clarity-enhanced. If the stone has been enhanced, ask what method was used, and be sure this is stated on the bill of sale. In addition, be sure to ask about special care requirements that might be necessitated by the process.

The two most widely used methods of clarity enhancement are lasering and fracture filling.

*Lasering.* Laser treatment is used today to make flaws less visible, and thus improve the stone aesthetically. Using laser technology, it is possible to "vaporize" black inclusions so they practically disappear. With the loupe, however, an experienced jeweler or gemologist can see the "path" cut into the diamond by the laser beam. This path looks like a fine, white thread starting at the surface of the stone and travelling into it. The effects of the laser treatment are permanent. If a lasered diamond is accompanied by a GIA diamond grading report, the report will state that the stone is lasered.

A lasered stone should cost less than another with the "same" clarity, so it may be an attractive choice for a piece of jewelry—as long as you *know* it's lasered and therefore pay a fair price for it.

*Fracture filling.* Fractures—cracks or breaks—that would normally be visible to the naked eye and detract from the beauty of a diamond can often be filled with a nearly colorless, glass-like substance. After filling, these breaks virtually disappear and will no longer be seen, except under magnification. Filling is *not* a permanent treatment, and special precautions are required when cleaning and repairing jewelry containing a filled diamond. With proper care, such stones may remain beautiful for many years. Careless handling, however, can cause the filler to leave the stone or change color, resulting in a much less attractive diamond. Some filling materials are much more stable than others, but at present it is usually not possible to know what filler has been used in a given stone. Should the filler be accidentally removed, your jeweler can have the treatment repeated to restore the stone's original appearance. GIA will *not* issue a grading report on a filled diamond.

Filled diamonds cost *much* less than other diamonds. They can be a very affordable alternative as long as you know what you are buying, understand the limitations, and pay the right price.

# How Does the Position of a Flaw Affect a Diamond's Grading and Value?

As a general rule, the position of any given inclusion will progressively downgrade and devalue a diamond as indicated below:

- *If seen only from the pavilion side,* or clearly only from the pavilion side, a flaw has the least adverse effect, since it is the least visible from the top.

- *If positioned near the girdle,* while perhaps more visible than described above, a flaw is still difficult to see, and hardly noticeable from the top. Such flaws can be easily covered with the prong of a setting.
- *Under any crown facet* (other than a star facet), a flaw is more easily visible, except when near the girdle.
- *Under a star facet,* a flaw will be much more easily visible.
- *Under the table* is the least desirable position, as it places the flaw where it is most noticeable, and may have the greatest effect on brilliance or fire, depending on the stone's size or color.

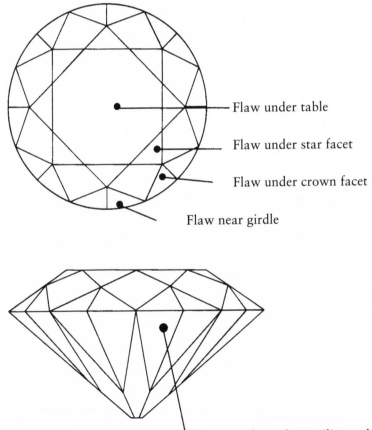

Flaw under table

Flaw under star facet

Flaw under crown facet

Flaw near girdle

Flaw seen from the pavilion only

Sometimes a small black or white flaw may be in such a position that it is reflected within the stone. It may be seen as a reflection to the opposite side of the stone, or, more unfortunately, it may reflect itself as many as *eight times* around the bottom or near the culet of the stone. A diamond with such a flaw might otherwise be classified as a $VS_1$ or $VS_2$, but because of the eightfold reflection resulting from its unfortunate position, the flaw grade will be lowered.

Remember, a diamond does not have to be flawless to be a very fine stone and to have a high value. Personally, we prefer a stone that might be slightly imperfect but has fine color and brilliance over a flawless stone with less sparkle and a less fine color. Color and brilliance are considered the most important factors in terms of a stone's *desirability*. And remember: Even a diamond graded $I_3$ can be beautiful and brilliant.

# 7

# Weight

## What Is a Carat?

Diamonds are sold by the *carat* (ct), not to be confused with *karat* (kt), which in the United States refers to gold quality. Since 1913 most countries have agreed that a carat weighs 200 milligrams, or ⅕ gram.

Before 1913 the carat weight varied depending upon the country of origin—the Indian carat didn't weigh the same as the English carat; the French carat was different from the Indian or the English. This is important if you have, or are thinking of buying, a very old piece that still has the original bill of sale indicating carat weight; the old carat weighed *more* than the new, post-1913 *metric carat*, which is 200 milligrams (⅕ gram). Therefore, an old three-carat stone will weigh more than three carats by the new standards. Today the term "carat" means the metric carat, the 200-milligram carat. There are five carats to one gram.

Jewelers often refer to the carat weight of diamonds in terms of points. This is particularly true of stones under one carat. There are 100 points to a carat, so if a jeweler says that a stone weighs 75 points, that means it weighs ⁷⁵⁄₁₀₀ of a carat, or ¾ carat. A 25-point stone is ¼ carat. A 10-point stone is ¹⁄₁₀ carat.

The carat is a unit of weight, not size. We wish to stress this point, since most people think that a one-carat stone is a particular size. Most people, therefore, would expect a one-carat diamond and a one-carat emerald, for example, to look the same size or to have the same apparent dimensions. This is not the case.

Comparing a one-carat diamond to a one-carat emerald and a one-carat ruby easily illustrates this point. First, emerald weighs less than diamond and ruby weighs more than diamond. This means that a one-carat emerald will look larger than a one-carat diamond, while the ruby will look smaller than a diamond of the same weight. Emerald, with a mineral composition that is lighter, will yield greater mass per carat; ruby, with its heavier composition, will yield less mass per carat.

Let's look at the principle another way. If you compare a one-inch cube of pine wood, a one-inch cube of aluminum, and a one-inch cube of iron, you would easily choose the cube of iron as heaviest, even though it has the same *volume* as the other materials. The iron is like the ruby, while the wood is like the emerald and the aluminum like the diamond. Equal *volumes* of different materials can have very different weights, depending on their density, also called mass or specific gravity.

Equal volumes of materials with the same density, however, should have approximately the same weight, so that in diamond, the carat weight has come to represent particular sizes. These sizes, as we've discussed, are based on diamonds cut to ideal proportions. Consequently, if properly cut, diamonds of the following weight should be approximately the size illustrated below. Remember, however, *that these sizes will not apply to other gems.*

# How Does Carat Weight Affect Value in Diamonds?

Diamond prices are usually quoted *per carat*. Diamonds of the finest quality are sold for the highest price per carat, and diamonds of progressively less fine quality are sold for a progressively lower price *per carat*. For example, the finest quality diamond might sell for $20,000 per carat. So, a stone in this quality weighing 1.12 carats would cost $22,400. On the other hand, a stone of the exact same weight, in a less fine quality, might sell for only $10,000 per carat, or $11,200.

Also, as a rule, the price increases per carat as we go from smaller to larger stones, since the larger stones are more limited in supply. For example, stones of the same quality weighing ½ carat will sell for more *per carat* than stones weighing ⅓ carat; stones weighing ¾ carat will sell for more *per carat* than stones of the same quality weighing ½ carat. For example, the per carat price of a particular quality ½ carat stone might be $5,000, while the per-carat price for a ⅓ carat stone of the same quality would be $3,000. The stones would cost $2,500 (½ x $5,000) and $1,000 (⅓ x $3,000) respectively

# Sizes & Weights of Various Diamond Cuts

| Weight (ct) | Emerald | Marquise | Pear | Brilliant |
|---|---|---|---|---|
| 5 | | | | |
| 4 | | | | |
| 3 | | | | |
| 2 ½ | | | | |
| 2 | | | | |
| 1 ½ | | | | |
| 1 ¼ | | | | |
| 1 | | | | |
| ¾ | | | | |
| ½ | | | | |

# Diameters & Corresponding Weights of Round, Brilliant-Cut Diamonds

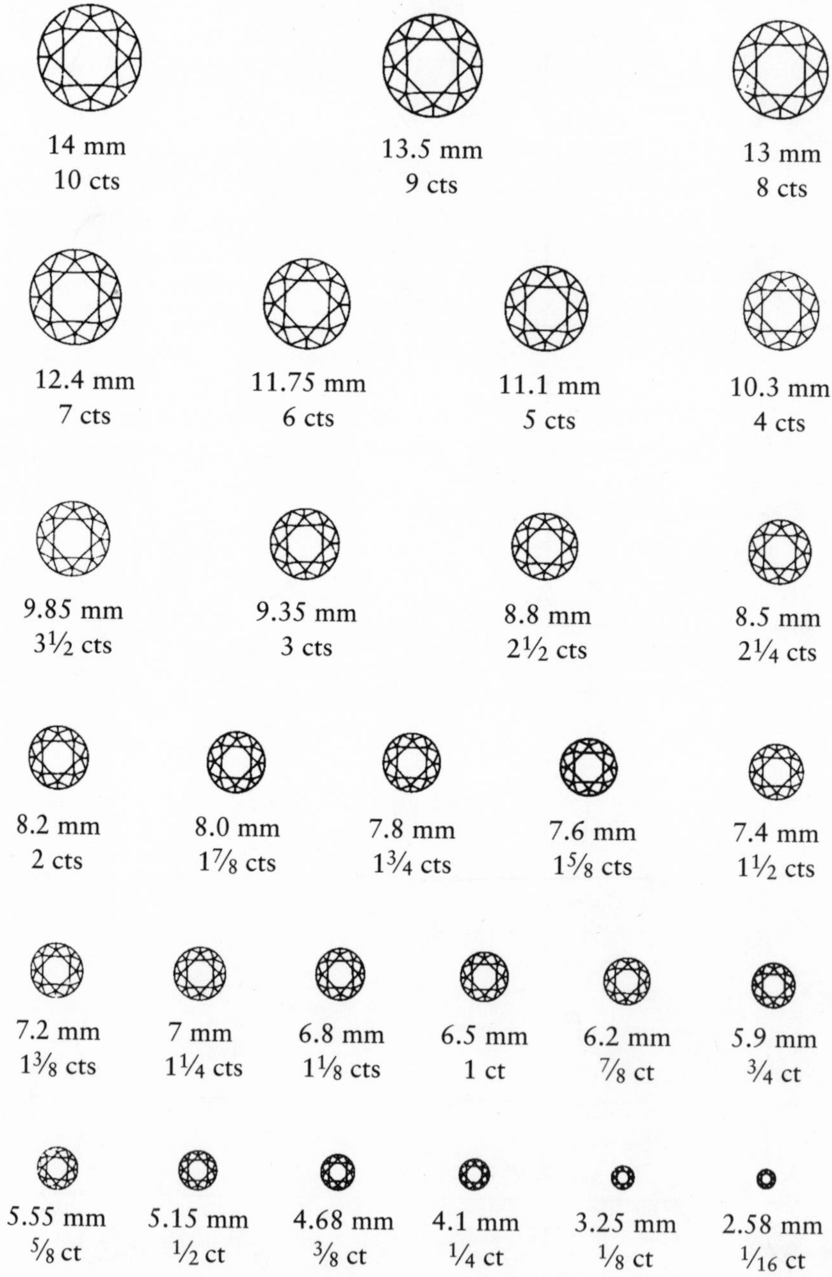

14 mm
10 cts

13.5 mm
9 cts

13 mm
8 cts

12.4 mm
7 cts

11.75 mm
6 cts

11.1 mm
5 cts

10.3 mm
4 cts

9.85 mm
3½ cts

9.35 mm
3 cts

8.8 mm
2½ cts

8.5 mm
2¼ cts

8.2 mm
2 cts

8.0 mm
1⅞ cts

7.8 mm
1¾ cts

7.6 mm
1⅝ cts

7.4 mm
1½ cts

7.2 mm
1⅜ cts

7 mm
1¼ cts

6.8 mm
1⅛ cts

6.5 mm
1 ct

6.2 mm
⅞ ct

5.9 mm
¾ ct

5.55 mm
⅝ ct

5.15 mm
½ ct

4.68 mm
⅜ ct

4.1 mm
¼ ct

3.25 mm
⅛ ct

2.58 mm
1/16 ct

Furthermore, stones of the same quality weighing exactly one carat will sell for *much* more than stones weighing 90 to 96 points. Thus, if you want a one-carat stone of a particular quality, but you can't afford it, you may find you can afford it in a 95-point stone—and a 95-point stone will give the impression of a full one-carat stone when set. You might be able to get your heart's desire after all.

As you will see, the price of a diamond does not increase proportionately; there are disproportionate jumps. And the larger and finer the stone (all else being equal in terms of overall quality), the more disproportionate the increase in cost per carat may be. A top-quality two-carat stone will not cost twice as much as a one-carat stone, it could easily be *four* times as much. A top-quality five-carat stone would not be five times the cost of a one-carat stone; it could easily be as much as ten times what a one-carat stone might cost.

## What Is Spread?

The term *spread* is often used in response to the question "How large is this diamond?" But it can be misleading. Spread refers to the size the stone *appears* to be, based on its diameter. For example, if the diameter of the stone measured the same as you see in the diamond sizes chart (see pages 57 and 58), which represents the diameter of a perfectly proportioned stone, the jeweler might say it "spreads" one carat. But this does not mean it *weighs* one carat. It means it *looks* the same size as a perfectly cut one-carat stone. It may weigh less or more, usually less.

Diamonds are generally weighed before they are set, so the jeweler can give you the exact carat weight, since you are paying a certain price per carat. Note, also, that the price per carat for a fine stone weighing 96 points is much less than for one weighing one carat or more. So it is unwise to accept any "approximate" weight, even though the difference seems so slight.

As you can see here, it is also important when buying a diamond to realize that since carat refers to weight, the manner in which a stone is cut can affect its apparent size. A one-carat stone that is cut shallow (see chapter 4) will appear larger in diameter than a stone that is cut thick (heavy). Conversely, a thick stone will appear smaller in diameter.

Furthermore, if the diamond has a thick girdle (see chapter 4), the stone will appear smaller in diameter. If this girdle is faceted, it tends to hide the ugly, frosted look of a thick girdle, but the fact remains that the girdle is thick, and the stone suffers because it will appear smaller in diameter than one would expect at a given carat weight. These stones are therefore somewhat cheaper per carat.

# 8

# Diamond Grading Reports

Today, few fine diamonds over one carat are sold without a diamond grading report (or certificate, as they are also called) from a respected laboratory. Reports issued by the GIA/Gem Trade Laboratory are the most widely used in the United States and in many countries around the world.

A grading report does more than certify the stone's genuineness— it *fully* describes the stone and evaluates each of the critical factors affecting quality, beauty, and value. Grading reports can be very useful for a variety of reasons. The information they contain can provide verification of the "facts" as represented by the seller and enable one to make a safer decision when purchasing a diamond. Another important function of reports is to verify the identity of a specific diamond at some future time—if, for example, it has been out of one's possession for any reason. For insurance purposes, the information provided on the report will help ensure replacement of a lost or stolen diamond with one that is truly "comparable quality."

Reports aren't necessary for every diamond, and many beautiful diamonds used in jewelry are sold without them. But when considering the purchase of a very fine diamond weighing one carat or more, we strongly recommend that the stone be accompanied by a report, even if it means having a stone removed from its setting (no reputable lab will issue a report on a mounted diamond), and then reset. If you are considering a stone that lacks a report, it is easy for your jeweler to obtain one. Or, now that GIA is issuing diamond grading reports to the public, you may submit a stone at GIA yourself (see Laboratory List in appendix).

## Don't Rely on the Report Alone

The availability and widespread use of diamond grading reports can, when properly understood, enable even those without professional skills to make valid comparisons between several stones, and thus make more informed buying decisions. Reports can be an important tool to help you understand differences affecting price. But we must caution you not to let them interfere with what you *like* or really want. Remember, some diamonds are very beautiful even though they don't adhere to established standards. In the final analysis, use your own eyes and ask yourself how you *like* the stone. We had a customer who was trying to decide between several stones. Her husband wanted to buy her the stone with the "best" report, but she preferred another stone which, according to what was on the reports, wasn't as "good." They decided against the "best" stone and bought the one that made her happiest. The important thing is that they knew exactly what they were buying, and paid an appropriate price for that specific combination of quality factors. In other words, they made an *informed* choice. The reports gave them assurance as to the facts, and greater confidence that they knew what they were really comparing.

## Improper Use of Reports Can Lead to Costly Mistakes

As important as diamond grading reports can be, they can also be misused and lead to erroneous conclusions and costly mistakes. The key to being able to rely on a diamond report—and having confidence in your decision—lies in knowing how to read it properly. For example, when trying to decide between two diamonds accompanied by diamond grading reports, buyers all too often make a decision by comparing just two factors evaluated on the reports—*color* and *clarity*—and think they have made a sound decision. This is rarely the case. No one can make a sound decision based on color and clarity alone. In fact, when significant price differences exist between two stones of the same color and clarity, you will find that often the cheaper stone is not the same quality as the more expensive stone, and often it is not the better value. Having the same color and clarity is only part of the total picture. Differences in price indicate differences in quality—differences you may not see or understand. With *round* diamonds, the information you need is on the report, but you need to understand what *all* the information means before you can make valid comparisons.

Properly used, diamond grading reports can give you a more *complete* picture, enable you to make sounder comparisons, and determine who is offering good value. Reading reports may seem complicated at first, but if you take the time to learn that skill, and seek the help of a knowledgeable jeweler to help you, you'll be amazed at how much more interesting—and unique—each diamond will become!

Before beginning, however, we must offer one important word of caution: Don't make a purchase relying solely on any report without making sure the report matches the stone, and that the stone is still in the same condition described. Always seek a professional gemologist, gemologist-appraiser, or gem-testing laboratory (see appendix) to confirm that the stone accompanying the report is, in fact, the stone described there, and that the stone is still in the same condition indicated on the report. We know of instances where a report has been accidentally sent with the wrong stone. And, in some cases, deliberate fraud is involved.

## How to Read a Diamond Grading Report

- *Check the Date Issued.* It is very important to check the date on the report. It's always possible that the stone has been damaged since the report was issued. This sometimes occurs with diamonds sold at auction. Since diamonds can become chipped or cracked with wear, one must always check them. For example, you might see a diamond accompanied by a report describing it as *D/* Flawless. If this stone were badly chipped *after the report was issued,* however, the clarity grade could easily drop to VVS, and in some cases, much lower. Needless to say, in such a case value would be dramatically reduced.
- *Who Issued the Report?* Check the name of the laboratory issuing the report. Is the report from a laboratory that is known and respected? If not, the information on the report may not be reliable. Several well-respected laboratories issue reports on diamonds. The best known in the United States include the Gemological Institute of America Gem Trade Laboratory (GIA/GTL), and the American Gemological Laboratories (AGL). Respected European labs issuing reports include the Belgian Diamond High Council (HRD), Gemological Laboratory Gubelin (Swiss), and Schweizerische Stiftung fur Edelstein-Forschung (SSEF—Swiss). See the appendix for additional information on these and other laboratories.

Whichever report you are reading (see page 73 for sample GIA report), all will provide similar information, including:

- *Identity of the stone.* This verifies that the stone is a diamond. Some diamond reports don't make a specific statement about identity because they are called *diamond* reports and are only issued for genuine diamonds. If the report is not called a "diamond grading report" then there must be a statement attesting that it is genuine diamond.
- *Weight.* The *exact* carat weight must be given.
- *Dimensions.* Any diamond, of any shape, should be measured and the dimensions recorded as a means of identification, especially for insurance/identification purposes. The dimensions given on a diamond report are very precise and provide information that is important for several reasons. First, the dimensions can help you determine that the diamond being examined is, in fact, the same diamond described in the report, since the likelihood of having two diamonds with exactly the same carat weight and millimeter dimensions is remote. Second, if the diamond has been damaged and recut since the report was issued, the millimeter dimensions may provide a clue that something has been altered, which might affect the carat weight as well. Any discrepency between the dimensions that you or your jeweler get by measuring the stone, and those provided on the report, should be a red flag to check the stone very carefully.

Finally, the dimensions on the report also tell you whether the stone is *round* or *out-of-round.* Out-of-round diamonds sell for less than those that are more perfectly round.

## Fine Diamonds Are "Well-Rounded"

The diamond's *roundness* will affect value, so it is determined very carefully from measurements of the stone's diameter, gauged at several points around the circumference. For a round diamond, the report will usually give two diameters, measured in millimeters and noted to the hundredth: for example, 6.51 rather than 6.5; or 6.07 rather than 6.0, and so on. These indicate the highest and the lowest diameter. Diamonds are very rarely perfectly round, which is why most diamond reports will show two measurements. Recognizing the rarity of truly round diamonds, some deviation is permitted, and the stone will not be considered "out-of-round" unless it deviates by more than the established norm—approximately 0.10 millimeter (one-tenth of a millimeter) in a one-carat stone.

To find out whether or not a diamond is round or out-of-round, simply subtract the smaller millimeter dimension from the higher dimension given on the report. In a one-carat stone, if the difference is 0.10 or less, the stone is considered "round." If the difference is greater, it is "out-of-round."

For diamonds over one carat, we have developed the following guide to help you determine if the deviation is acceptable. Slightly higher differences than those suggested below as "acceptable" will not significantly affect value, especially on larger stones (over two carats). Diamonds with much greater deviations than suggested below, however, should appear "out of round" when carefully examined, and should sell for less.

| Acceptable Tolerances For "Round" Diamonds* | | |
|---|---|---|
| Weight | Diameter (in millimeters) | Acceptable Deviation (in millimeters) |
| One carat | 6.50 | 0.10 |
| Two carat | 8.20 | 0.12 |
| Three carat | 9.35 | 0.14 |
| Four carat | 10.30 | 0.16 |
| Five carat | 11.10 | 0.17 |
| Ten carat | 14.00 | 0.21 |

* To calculate an acceptable deviation on a particular stone, average the high and low diameter dimensions given and multiply that number by 0.0154. For example, if the dimensions given are 8.20 and 8.31, the diameter averages 8.25. Multiply 8.25 by 0.0154 = 0.127. This is the acceptable deviation allowable for this stone (between 0.12 and 0.13). The actual deviation in this example would be 0.11 (8.31 minus 8.20), well within the tolerance, so this diamond would be considered "round." Some flexibility is permitted on diamonds over two carats.

Depending on the degree of out-of-roundness (how much it deviates from being perfectly round), price can be affected by at least 10 to 15 percent, or much more if the stone is very noticeably out-of-round. The greater the deviation, the lower the price should be.

## Dimensions for Fancy Shapes

While the dimensions for fancy shapes are not as important as they are for round diamonds, there are length-to-width ratios that are considered "normal" and deviations may result in price reductions of 15 percent or more. The following reflect acceptable ranges:

| | |
|---|---|
| Pear | 1.50:1 to 1.75:1 |
| Marquise | 1.75:1 to 2.25:1 |
| Emerald | 1.50:1 to 1.75:1 |
| Oval | 1.50:1 to 1.75:1 |

To better understand what this means, let's look at a marquise diamond as an example. If its report showed the length to be 15 millimeters and the width to be 10 millimeters, the length-to-width ratio would be 15 to 10, or 1.50:1. This would be acceptable. If, however, the dimensions were 30 millimeters long by 10 wide, the ratio would be 30 to 10, or 3:1. This would be unacceptable; the ratio is too great, and the result is a stone that looks much too long for its width. A marquise with an unacceptable length-to-width ratio should sell for at least 10 percent less than another marquise. *Note:* A long marquise is not necessarily bad, and some people prefer a longer shape, but it is important to understand that such stones should sell for less than those with "normal" lengths. Always keep in mind the length-to-width ratio of fancy cuts, and adjust the price for stones that are not in the "acceptable" range.

## Evaluating Proportioning from the Report

As we discussed earlier, good proportioning is as critical to a diamond as it is to the man or woman who wears it! The proportioning—especially the depth percentage and table percentage—is what determines how much brilliance and fire the stone will have.

The information provided on diamond reports pertaining to proportions is critically important for *round, brilliant-cut diamonds.* Unfortunately, it is only of minimal use with fancy shapes. For fancies, you must learn to rely on your own eye to tell whether or not the proportioning is acceptable: are there differences in brilliance across the stone? Or flatness? Or dark spots such as "bow-ties" resulting from poor proportioning (see chapter 4)?

Evaluating the proportioning of a diamond is as critical as evaluating the color and clarity grades. Diamonds that are cut close to "ideal" proportions, stones with "excellent" makes, can easily cost 15 to 25 percent more than the norm while diamonds with poor makes sell for less; very badly proportioned stones should be priced as much as 50 to 60 percent less. The information on a diamond report can help you evaluate the proportioning and know whether or not you should be paying more, or less, for a particular stone.

### "Depth Percentage" & "Table Percentage" Key to Beauty

To determine whether or not a round stone's proportioning—so critical to its beauty—is good, look at the section of the report that describes *depth percentage* and *table percentage.* The depth percentage represents the depth of the stone—the distance from the table to the culet—as a percentage of the width of the stone. The table percentage represents the width of the table as a percentage of the width of the entire stone. These numbers indicate how well a round stone has been cut in terms of its proportioning, and must adhere to very precise standards. Your eye may be able to see differences in sparkle and brilliance, but you may not be able to discern the subtleties of proportioning. The percentages on the report should fall within a fairly specific range in order for the stone to be judged acceptable, excellent, or poor.

We will not discuss how one calculates these percentages, but it is important for you to know what the ranges are, as outlined in the chart below.

Some reports also provide information about the *crown angle*. The crown angle tells you the angle at which the crown portion has been cut. This angle will affect the depth and table percentage. Normally, if the crown angle is between 34 and 36 degrees, the table and depth will be excellent; between 32 and 34, good; between 30 and 32 degrees, fair; and less than 30 degrees, poor. If the exact crown angle is not given, it is probably considered acceptable. If not, there is normally a statement indicating that the crown angle exceeds 36 degrees, or is less than 30 degrees.

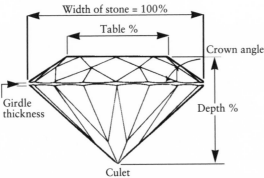

## Depth percentage

A round diamond cut with a depth percentage between 58 and 64 percent is normally a lovely, lively stone. You should note, however, that girdle thickness will affect depth percentage. A high depth percentage could result from a thick or very thick girdle, so when checking the depth percentage on the diamond report, check the "girdle" information as well.

Stones with a depth percentage over 64 percent or under 57 percent will normally be too deep or too shallow to exhibit maximum beauty and should sell for less. If the depth percentage is too high, the stone will look smaller than its weight indicates. If the depth percentage is exceptionally high, brilliance can be significantly reduced and a dark-ish center may also be produced. If the depth percentage is too *low*, brilliance will also be significantly affected. We've seen diamonds that were so shallow, that is, stones with such low depth percentages, that they had no brilliance and liveliness at all. When dirty, such stones look no better than a piece of glass.

We avoid stones with depth percentages over 64 percent or under 57 percent. If you are attracted to such stones remember that they should sell for much less per carat.

## Depth Percentage Guidelines

| Depth Percentage | Effect on Price |
|---|---|
| *Ideal*—approximately 58 to 60% | 20 to 30% more* |
| *Excellent*—60$^+$ to 62% | 10 to 20% more* |
| *Good*—62 to 64% | — — — |
| *Fair*—64 to 66% | 15 to 25% less |
| *Poor*—over 66% or less than 57% | 20 to 40% less |

*For *round* diamonds, combined with the right table percentage and fine overall cutting.

### Table percentage

Round stones cut with tables ranging from 53%–64% usually result in beautiful, lively stones. Diamonds with smaller tables usually exhibit more *fire* than those with larger tables, but stones with larger tables may have more *brilliance*. As you will see, table width affects the stone's personality, but deciding which personality is more desirable is a matter of personal taste.

## Table Percentage Guidelines

| Table Percentage | Effect on Price |
|---|---|
| *Ideal* —from 53 to 58% | 20 to 30% more* |
| *Excellent*—up to 60% | |
| (up to 62% in stones under ½ carat) | 10 to 20% more* |
| *Good*—to 64% | — — — |
| *Fair*—over 64 to 70% | 15 to 30% less |
| *Poor*—over 70% | 30 to 40% less |

*For *round* diamonds, combined with the right depth percentage and fine overall cutting.

## Finish

Under *finish* on the diamond report you will find an evaluation of the stone's *polish* and *symmetry*. Polish serves as an indicator of the care taken by the cutter. The quality of the stone's polish is a factor that cannot be ignored in evaluating the overall quality of a diamond, as well as its cost and value. Polish can be described on the report as *excellent, very good, good, fair,* or *poor.* The price per carat should be less on stones with "fair" or "poor" polish. Cost per carat is usually more for stones that have "very good" or "excellent" polish.

*Symmetry* describes several factors: (1) how the facet edges align with one another; (2) whether or not the facets from one side of the diamond match corresponding facets on the opposite side; and (3) whether or not facets in the top portion of the diamond are properly aligned with corresponding ones in the bottom portion. When the symmetry is described as "fair"—or worse—something is out of line.

When evaluating symmetry, the most important area to check is the alignment of the crown (top) to the pavilion (bottom). If it is not good, it will make a visual difference in the beauty of the stone, and correspondingly in its price. To check for proper alignment here, simply look at the stone from the side to see whether or not the facets just above the girdle align with the facets just beneath the girdle.

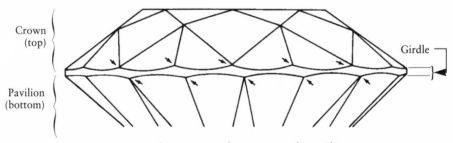

Misalignment of crown and pavilion

When the top and bottom facets don't line up, it indicates sloppy cutting and, more important, the overall beauty of the diamond is diminished. This will reduce price more than other symmetry faults.

## How Does the Girdle Affect Value?

The girdle is another important item described on diamond grading reports. The report will indicate whether or not the girdle is polished, or faceted, and how thick it is. Girdle thickness is very important for two reasons: (1) it affects value and (2) it affects the stone's *durability*.

Girdle thickness ranges from extremely thin to extremely thick. Diamonds with girdles that are excessively thin or thick normally sell for less than other diamonds. An extremely thin girdle increases the risk of chipping. Remember that despite their legendary hardness, diamonds are brittle, so a very thin edge poses a greater risk.

If a diamond has an extremely thick girdle, its cost should also be reduced somewhat because the stone will look smaller than another diamond of the same weight with a more normal girdle thickness. This is because extra weight is being consumed by the thickness of the girdle itself. (See chapter 4.)

There are some cases in which a very thick girdle is acceptable. Shapes that have one or more points, such as the pear-shape, heart, or marquise, can have thick to very thick girdles in the area of the points and still be in the acceptable range. Here the extra thickness in the girdle helps protect the points themselves from chipping.

Generally, a diamond with an extremely thin girdle should sell for less than one with an extremely thick girdle because of the stone's increased vulnerability to chipping. However, if the girdle is much too thick (as in some older diamonds), the price can also be significantly less because the stone can look significantly smaller than other stones of comparable weight.

## The Culet

The culet looks like a point at the bottom of the stone but it is normally another facet—a tiny, flat polished surface. This facet should be *small* or *very small*. A small or very small culet won't be noticeable from the top. Some diamonds today are actually pointed. This means that there really is no culet, that the stone has been cut straight down to a point instead. The larger the culet, the more visible it will be from the top. The more visible, the lower the cost of the stone. Stones described as having a large or "open" culet as in old-European or old-mine cut diamonds (see chapter 4) are less desirable because the appearance of the culet causes a reduction in sparkle or brilliance at the very center of the stone. These stones normally need to be recut, and their price should take the need for recutting into consideration. Normally the cost is determined by the estimated amount of weight loss resulting from the recutting and can be anywhere from 5 to 25 percent. For the same reasons, a chipped or broken culet will seriously detract from the stone's beauty and significantly reduce the cost.

## Color and Clarity Grades

The color and clarity grades found on a diamond report are the items most people are familiar with, and we have already discussed them in detail in chapters 5 and 6. They are important factors in terms of determining the value of a diamond, but as the preceding discussion has shown, they do not tell the whole story.

## A Word About Fluorescence

Fluorescence, if present, will also be indicated on a diamond grading report. It will be graded *weak, moderate, strong,* or *very strong.* Some reports indicate the color of the fluorescence as blue, yellow, white, and so on. If the fluorescence is moderate to very strong and the color is not indicated, you should ask the jeweler to tell you what color the stone fluoresces. A stone with strong yellow fluorescence should sell for less since it will appear yellower than it really is when worn in daylight or fluorescent lighting. The presence of blue fluorescence will not detract, and in some cases may be considered a bonus since it may make the stone appear whiter than it really is in daylight or fluorescent lighting. However, if the report shows a very strong blue fluoresence, there may be an oily or milky appearance to the diamond. If the stone appears milky or oily to you as you look at it, especially in daylight or fluorescent light, it should sell for less.

## Pay Attention to the Full Clarity Picture Provided

The placement, number, type, and color of internal and external flaws will be indicated on a diamond report, and may include a plotting—a diagram showing all the details. Be sure you carefully note *all* the details in addition to the cumulative grade. Remember, the *placement* of imperfections can affect value (see chapter 6).

A reliable diamond grading report *cannot* be issued on a *fracture-filled diamond,* so GIA and most other labs will not issue a report on stones that have been clarity enhanced by this method. The diamond will be returned with a notation that it is filled and cannot be graded. Reports *are* issued on stones that have been clarity enhanced by laser (see chapter 6). Remember, however, that no matter what the clarity grade, a lasered stone should cost less than another with the same grade.

## A Final Word about Reports

Diamond grading reports provide a very useful tool to aid in comparing diamonds and evaluating quality and value. But the key to their usefulness is proper understanding of how to read them, and how to look at the stone. Those who take the time to learn and understand what they are reading and, therefore, what they are really buying, will have a major advantage over those who do not.

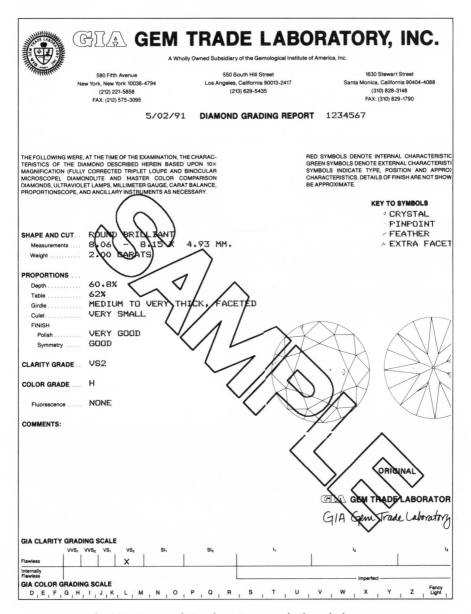

# GIA GEM TRADE LABORATORY, INC.

A Wholly Owned Subsidiary of the Gemological Institute of America, Inc.

| 580 Fifth Avenue | 550 South Hill Street | 1630 Stewart Street |
|---|---|---|
| New York, New York 10036-4794 | Los Angeles, California 90013-2417 | Santa Monica, California 90404-4088 |
| (212) 221-5858 | (213) 629-5435 | (310) 828-3148 |
| FAX: (212) 575-3095 | | FAX: (310) 829-1790 |

5/02/91    **DIAMOND GRADING REPORT**    1234567

THE FOLLOWING WERE, AT THE TIME OF THE EXAMINATION, THE CHARAC-
TERISTICS OF THE DIAMOND DESCRIBED HEREIN BASED UPON 10×
MAGNIFICATION (FULLY CORRECTED TRIPLET LOUPE AND BINOCULAR
MICROSCOPE), DIAMONDLITE AND MASTER COLOR COMPARISON
DIAMONDS, ULTRAVIOLET LAMPS, MILLIMETER GAUGE, CARAT BALANCE,
PROPORTIONSCOPE, AND ANCILLARY INSTRUMENTS AS NECESSARY.

RED SYMBOLS DENOTE INTERNAL CHARACTERISTIC
GREEN SYMBOLS DENOTE EXTERNAL CHARACTERISTI
SYMBOLS INDICATE TYPE, POSITION AND APPRO
CHARACTERISTICS. DETAILS OF FINISH ARE NOT SHOW
BE APPROXIMATE.

**KEY TO SYMBOLS**
⌀ CRYSTAL
· PINPOINT
⌁ FEATHER
∧ EXTRA FACET

**SHAPE AND CUT** .. ROUND BRILLIANT
Measurements .... 8.06 — 8.15 X 4.93 MM.
Weight .......... 2.00 CARATS

**PROPORTIONS** ...
Depth .......... 60.8%
Table .......... 62%
Girdle .......... MEDIUM TO VERY THICK, FACETED
Culet .......... VERY SMALL
FINISH
Polish ........ VERY GOOD
Symmetry ..... GOOD

**CLARITY GRADE** .. VS2

**COLOR GRADE** ... H

Fluorescence ..... NONE

**COMMENTS:**

ORIGINAL

GIA GEM TRADE LABORATOR

GIA Gem Trade Laboratory

**GIA CLARITY GRADING SCALE**

| | | VVS₁ | VVS₂ | VS₁ | VS₂ | SI₁ | SI₂ | I₁ | I₂ | I₃ |
|---|---|---|---|---|---|---|---|---|---|---|
| Flawless | | | | | X | | | | | |
| Internally Flawless | | | | | | | | Imperfect | | |

**GIA COLOR GRADING SCALE**

D  E  F  G  H  I  J  K  L  M  N  O  P  Q  R  S  T  U  V  W  X  Y  Z  Fancy Light

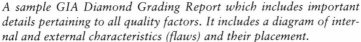

*A sample GIA Diamond Grading Report which includes important
details pertaining to all quality factors. It includes a diagram of internal and external characteristics (flaws) and their placement.*

# 9

## False Claims & Costly Bargains: How to Spot Fraud & Avoid Misrepresentation

As you have seen, many factors affect quality and value in diamonds. When the average person is looking at a stone already set, it is very difficult, if not impossible, to *see* differences that can dramatically affect cost. For this reason, we recommend buying any important diamond *unmounted,* and mounting it only after all the facts have been verified. But you don't have to be a "gemologist" or fear buying jewelry. If you follow a few simple steps, anyone can buy with confidence.

### Four Key Steps to Avoiding Fraud or Misrepresentation

- *The first step is to buy from someone both accessible and knowledgeable.* Sellers should have the skill to know for sure what they themselves are buying and selling. This is not to say that there aren't bargains to be found in flea markets, estate sales, and so on, but you run a higher risk when purchasing in such places because of possible misinformation, intentional or otherwise. You must weigh the risk versus the potential reward. In addition, before making a final purchasing decision, ask yourself whether or not you will be able to *find* the seller again if what you bought turns out to be other than represented. This is equally true when travelling and considering a jewelry purchase abroad.

  Keep in mind that unless the jeweler also does business in the country where you live, it may be cost prohibitive to try to rectify any misrepresentation if it occurs.

- *Second, ask the right questions.* Don't be afraid to ask direct, even pointed questions. The key to getting complete information about what you are buying is asking good questions so you can be sure you are aware of important factors affecting quality and value. (To help you ask the right questions, we provide a complete list in chapter 20.)
- *Third, get the facts in writing.* Be sure the seller is willing to put the answers to the questions you ask, and any representations made about the gem or jewelry you are considering, *in writing*. If not, we recommend against purchasing from this seller unless there is an unconditional return policy which allows merchandise to be returned within a reasonable period of time for a full refund (not a store credit). In this case, follow the next step to be safe.
- Finally, *verify the facts with a gemologist-appraiser.* It's especially important to *verify* whatever has been put in writing with a professional gemologist-appraiser (see chapter 23). Some unscrupulous dealers are willing to put anything in writing to make the sale, knowing that written assurances or claims about the stone are often sufficient to satisfy buyers' doubts. So this last step may be the most important to ensure you make a wise decision.

In general, you need not worry about fraud or misrepresentation, whether deliberate or unintentional, if you simply follow these four easy steps. They may require a little more time and nominal additional expense, but the end result will be greater knowledge—and assurance—about your jewelry choice and your jeweler. And, they may save you from a costly mistake.

# Types of Misrepresentation

## Beware of Bargains!

### Diamonds represented to be better than they are

Beware of bargains. Most are not. When a price seems too good to be true, it usually is, unless the seller doesn't know its true value (which reflects badly on the seller's expertise).

A large jewelry store in Philadelphia was recently found guilty of misrepresenting the quality of diamonds it was selling. Sales staff consistently represented their diamonds to be several color grades and/or flaw grades better than they actually were. As a result, their prices seemed much more attractive than those of other jewelers. Customers thought they were getting a much better buy from this firm than from others in the area, which may not have been the case; since customers didn't know the true quality of the stones they were buying, they couldn't make a fair comparison with what other jewelers were offering. Other jewelers in the area were, in fact, giving better value on stones comparable to what was actually being sold by this "bargain" firm.

Such firms can be found in every city. Many are even willing to put everything in writing, often including a full "appraisal." Such dishonest practices often go undetected because most people *assume* when a seller is willing to "put it in writing," he or she is properly representing the item. Most buyers never bother to have the facts verified.

## Scams involving "appraisals" prior to sale

Beware of jewelers not willing to put the facts in writing, but who offer to let you take the stone, prior to the sale, to an appraiser in the neighborhood. This may be a scam. It is often seen in wholesale districts like New York's famous 47th Street.

The first step in this scam is to build you up with all the reasons why you are going to get an exceptional buy—because the seller "bought it right" (whatever that means), or wants to "pass the savings on to you," or, isn't greedy ("I don't care who I sell to at wholesale, after all, a sale is a sale"), and so on. When you find something you are seriously interested in buying, the seller then explains, for a variety of seemingly valid reasons, why he or she will not put any information pertaining to the quality of the stone in writing, on the bill of sale. The salesperson offers to permit you to go—with one of the firm's "bonded guards"—to a local appraiser so that you can verify the facts and learn for yourself what a bargain you are getting. Many people are immediately hooked, and conclude erroneously that since they can get an appraisal if they choose, everything must be in order. So they *don't*. And they become the victims of intentional misrepresentation.

Those who do wish to get an appraisal usually face another problem. They don't know any appraiser, or certainly not any in the neighborhood. Many visitors to 47th Street, for example, are from out of town and don't know anyone local. Unscrupulous sellers often count on this because it gives them the opportunity to recommend several "reliable" appraisers. Or, rather than be so obvious, suggest you "choose" your own (some even make a fuss about not wanting to know who you choose). Many make a big mistake here because they don't realize that *all appraisers are not the same, nor are all appraisers equally competent or reliable* (see chapter 23). Unfortunately, the "reliable appraiser" in this situation often means the *seller* can rely on the *appraiser* to tell the prospective buyers what the seller wants them to hear.

One must always be careful of recommendations from the seller. While legitimate jewelers usually know better than anyone else who the best gemologist-appraisers are in their communities, and their recommendations should be respected, you must still be sure to check the credentials yourself to avoid such scams. Unfortunately, especially in the jewelry districts of major cities, far too many appraisers are not qualified, and some are in collusion with unscrupulous jewelers.

One of our clients had an experience that provides an excellent example of how this type of scam can work. She went to New York, to a 47th Street firm. She was offered a five-plus carat diamond ring at a price that was one-fourth the price most retailers had been quoting for what appeared to be comparable quality. She thought the ring looked very beautiful, and became very excited about being able to get such a bargain. But when she asked the seller if he would back up his description of the quality of the diamond in writing, he said it was against his store policy, but he would be happy for her to take the ring to a neighborhood appraiser before she purchased it.

This made her cautious, especially since she didn't know any local appraiser. Luckily, we were in New York at the time and were able to use a colleague's lab to examine the ring carefully (it was awkward for the seller to refuse). Not surprisingly, the quality was not as represented. The flaw grade had been misrepresented by *four* grades, and the color had been enhanced *seven grades* by "painting" (painted diamonds have a coating that doesn't come off with normal cleaning and may take months or years to wear off. We had to clean the stone chemically to determine it was painted, and reveal its true color)!

In this particular case, given the true value of the diamond, the price being asked for the ring was certainly not the "steal" it appeared to be. It wasn't a bad price, but other retailers were offering comparable stones at comparable prices, or less.

Such practices are overtly dishonest, of course, but all too often they leave honest jewelers in a bad light as a result. In such cases, the dishonest jeweler will appear to be offering the best price, while the honest jeweler—who may actually be offering the best value—falsely appears to be charging "too much."

In general, you need to guard against fraud or misrepresentation in one of the following four areas:
- Weight misrepresentation
- Color alteration and misgrading
- Flaw concealment and misgrading
- Certification—alteration and counterfeit certificates

# Weight

Giving "total weight" of all stones where more than one is involved, rather than the exact weight of the main stone, is another form of misrepresentation. This is in strict violation of Federal Trade Commission (FTC) rulings. In giving the weight, particularly on any display card, descriptive tag, or other type of advertising for a particular piece of jewelry, the weight of the main stone or stones should be clearly indicated as well as the total weight of all the stones.

Thus, if you purchase a "three-carat diamond" ring with one large center stone and two small side stones (as found in many engagement rings), the center stone's weight should be clearly stated; for example, "The weight of the center stone is 2.80 carats, with side stones that weigh .10 carats each, for a total weight of 3.00 carats." There is a tremendous price difference between a single stone weighing three carats and numerous stones having a total weight of three carats. A single three-carat stone of good quality could sell for $50,000, while three carats consisting of numerous stones (even with some weighing as much as a carat or more) of the same quality could sell anywhere from $5,000 to $20,000, depending on how many there are and the weight of each.

When inquiring about the weight of a diamond, don't ask the wrong question. Usually the jeweler will be asked how *large* the stone is, rather than how much it *weighs*. In any case, the answer should provide the exact carat weight. Beware when the response includes the word "spread" — "this stone *spreads* one carat." *A stone that spreads one carat does not weigh one carat.* It simply means it *looks* like a one-carat stone in its width.

# Color

## Enhancing color artificially

*Touching the culet, or side, of a slightly yellow stone with a coating of purple ink,* such as found in an indelible pencil, neutralizes the yellow, producing a whiter-looking stone. This can be easily detected by washing the stone in alcohol or water. If you have any questions about the color, tactfully request that the stone be washed (in front of you) for better examination. A reputable jeweler should have no objection to this request.

*Improving the color by utilizing a sputtering technique* (also called "painting" the diamond). This involves sputtering a very thin coating of a special substance over the stone or part of the stone, usually the back, where it will be harder to detect when mounted. The girdle area can also be "painted" with the substance and create the same effect. The substance, like indelible pencil, also neutralizes the yellow and thereby improves the color by as much as seven color grades, but unlike indelible ink, *the substance will not wash off.* It can be removed in two ways: by rubbing the stone briskly and firmly with a cleanser, or by boiling the stone carefully in sulfuric acid. If the stone is already mounted and is coated on the back, using cleanser is not feasible. The sulfuric acid method is the only way. But please note, using sulfuric acid can be extremely dangerous, and must be done only by an experienced person. We cannot overstate the hazards of conducting this test.

This technique is not frequently used, but stones treated in this manner do appear often enough to be worth mentioning.

*Coating the diamond with chemicals and baking it in a small lab-type oven.* This technique also tends to neutralize some of the yellow, thereby producing a better color grade. This coating will be removed eventually by repeated hot ultrasonic cleanings, which will gradually erode the coating. A more rapid removal can be accomplished by the more dangerous method of boiling in sulfuric acid.

*Radiation treatment.* Exposing off-color diamonds such as yellowish- or brownish-tinted stones (and also badly flawed stones in which the flaws would be less noticeable against a colored background) to certain types of radiation can result in the production of fancy colored stones. This treatment produces rich yellows, greens, and blues, and greatly enhances salability because these colors are very desirable. In and of itself, radiation is not fraud; in fact, it may make a "fancy" color diamond affordable to someone otherwise unable to afford one. But again, just be sure that the stone is properly represented and you know what you are buying, and that you are getting it at the right price—which should be much lower than that of the natural fancy.

Treated stones must be represented as "treated stones" and should be priced accordingly. Unfortunately, too often, in passing through many hands, the fact that they have been treated ("radiated" or "bombarded") is overlooked or forgotten—intentionally or accidentally. Whether the color is natural or treated can often be determined by spectroscopic examination, which can be provided by a gem testing laboratory (see appendix). Not all gemologists, however, are competent with spectroscopic procedures, and some fancy-color diamonds require examination with very sophisticated equipment not available to most labs. If your gemologist lacks the skill or equipment, stones can be submitted to a laboratory such as GIA's Gem Trade Laboratory for verification. Most *natural* fancy colored diamonds sold by jewelers in the United States are accompanied by a GIA report.

## Erroneous color grading

Mistakes in grading of color may be unintentional, (resulting from insufficient training or experience, or simply from carelessness) or they may be deliberate. You're safer considering the purchase of a stone that has had such important data as color described in a diamond grading report (or certificate) issued by one of several different laboratories offering this service (see chapter 8). Many jewelry firms now offer diamonds accompanied by grading reports, with reports issued by GIA the most widely used in the United States. Diamonds accompanied by reports usually sell for slightly more per carat, but provide an element of security for the average consumer, as well as credible documentation if you wish to sell this stone at some future time. If the stone you are considering is accompanied by such a report, be sure to verify that the information on the certificate is accurate by taking the stone to a competent gemologist or lab (see chapter 23).

# Clarity Enhancement and Flaw Concealment

## Clarity enhancement

Be especially alert to the possibility that clarity may be enhanced. The two most frequently used techniques are lasering inclusions and filling fractures. In both cases, dark inclusions or cracks which might normally be visible—in some cases, very visible—are concealed, or become much less noticeable (these techniques are discussed in chapter 6). Be sure to ask whether or not the stone has been lasered or filled. As long as you know, and pay the right price, a clarity-enhanced diamond may be an attractive choice.

## Flaw concealment

Where possible, flaws are concealed by their settings. The good stone setter will try to set a stone in such a manner that the setting will help to conceal any visible imperfections. For this reason flaws near or at the girdle will downgrade a stone less than those found in the center of a stone; since most settings cover all or part of the girdle, they are simply less visible here. Indeed, a setting can make a flaw "invisible."

There is nothing fraudulent in such uses of settings as long as the stone is properly represented. The only danger is that not only the customer but also the jeweler may not have seen the imperfection concealed by the setting.

*Can concealment affect value?* In most diamonds other than FL or IF, the presence of a minor flaw concealed under a prong will not affect the price significantly. However, given the difference in price between diamonds graded FL or IF and $VVS_1$, a minor blemish or inclusion hidden by the setting which might result in a $VVS_1$ stone being graded FL could have a significant effect on value, especially if the stone has exceptionally fine color. For this reason, FL or IF stones should be viewed *unmounted*.

# Certification of Diamonds

As discussed in chapter 8, today most fine diamonds weighing one carat or more are carefully evaluated prior to being set by a respected laboratory such as the GIA or the AGL, and are issued a diamond grading report. That report both certifies the diamond as genuine and describes it, providing such important information as color grade, flaw grade, weight, cutting and proportioning, and so on. If you are considering the purchase of a very fine diamond weighing one carat or more and it is *not* accompanied by such a report, we would strongly recommend that you or the seller have the stone evaluated by the GIA or another respected laboratory prior to purchase. You should do so even if it means having a stone that is already set removed from the setting and reset. Given the significant difference in cost that can result from a grading error in the rarer grades, we believe this procedure is worth the inconvenience and expense.

Unfortunately, the confidence of the public in stones accompanied by certificates has given rise to the practice of altering and counterfeiting them. While you can be relatively sure that "certificated" stones sold by reputable, established jewelry firms are what they claim to be, there are some suppliers and dealers who are seizing opportunities to prey on the unsuspecting.

## Altering certificates

Sometimes information is changed on an otherwise valid certificate; for example, the flaw or color grade may be altered. If you have any question regarding information on the certificate, a phone call to the lab giving them the certificate number and date will enable you to verify the information on the certificate.

## Counterfeit certificates

Producing a certificate from a nonexistent lab is an increasingly common problem. Stones accompanied by fancy "certificates" from impressive-sounding labs that don't exist are appearing more and more frequently. If the certificate is not from one of the recognized labs (see appendix), it should be carefully checked. Have reputable jewelers in the area heard of this lab? Has the Better Business Bureau had any complaints? If the lab seems legitimate, call to verify the information on the certificate, and, if all seems in order, you can probably rest comfortably. Otherwise, you may need to have the facts verified by another gemologist or recognized lab.

Some jewelers may not allow verification of an existing certificate by a little-known lab simply because they've been victims themselves or it isn't worth the inconvenience to them. In this case, you might ask the jeweler to get the stone certificated by one of the recognized labs. Many jewelers today are happy to provide this service. If not, then you must decide how badly you want the stone, how much you feel you can trust the jeweler, and what degree of monetary risk you can afford.

## Switching the stone described on a report

In some cases the report is bona fide but the stone has been switched. To protect both the consumer and the lab, some labs are taking advantage of ingenious techniques to ensure against switching. For example, a service called Gemprint utilizes laser technology to display a diamond's unique pattern of reflection and then records it photographically. The result is an electronic "fingerprint" of the diamond which can be used for identification purposes (see chapter 23). In addition, the GIA can now actually inscribe its report number, which is visible only under magnification, directly onto the diamond itself, along the girdle. By so doing, one can very easily be sure a specific stone matches a specific certificate simply by matching the numbers. There is an additional fee for this service.

In the absence of such a mark, one clue to a switched stone might be provided by comparing the carat weight and dimensions given on the report. If the measurements and weight match exactly, the probability is slim that the stone has been switched, provided the report hasn't been altered. But it's always a good idea to contact the lab to confirm the details of the report, and then double-check all the information. If the measurements don't match, the type and placement of inclusions or blemishes might enable you to determine if the stone in question is the one described on the report but has been altered; the dimensions might differ if, for example, the stone was nicked or chipped and subsequently re-cut or re-polished. In such a case, ask the jeweler to place the stone under the microscope to enable you to see what should be in the stone.

Unfortunately, if the stone has been mounted, it may be difficult to get precise measurements to compare. In this case, if there is any cause for suspicion, you may be taking a risk to buy the stone unless the seller allows you to have the stone removed from the setting and both the report and the stone verified by a qualified gemologist-appraiser. This arrangement requires an understanding in writing that the stone can be returned within a certain time limit if the customer learns it is not as represented.

Always make sure in this situation, for both your protection and the jeweler's, that the jeweler writes down on the bill of sale or memo *all* of the stone's dimensions as best as can be determined: diameter or length and width, depth, and weight. This is to help ensure that you aren't accused of switching the stone after leaving the premises in the event you must return it.

### Avoid "bargains"—and avoid costly mistakes

Take time to do your homework first, to learn what to look for and what questions to ask. Keep our recommended four-step procedure in mind, then shop carefully and compare stones being offered by several fine jewelers in your community. This will give you a chance to get a clearer sense of what something should legitimately sell for, decide whether or not something sounds "too good to be true," and, most important, make sounder decisions about which jeweler is asking a *fair* price.

And remember: No one gives away a valuable gem. There are very few "steals," and even fewer people qualified to truly know a "steal" when they see one.

## Is It a Diamond or a Diamond Imposter?

How can you tell if a stone is really a diamond? As we have said many times, unless you are an expert—or consult one—you cannot be sure about the identification of a stone. Nevertheless, there are a few simple tests you can perform that will show up most diamond imposters quite quickly. Here are a few things to look for.

*Is newsprint readable or observable through the stone?* If the stone is a round, modern-cut stone and is loose or mounted in such a way as to allow you to place it table-down over some small newsprint, check whether you can see or read any portion of the lettering. If so, it is not a diamond. Refraction of light within a genuine diamond is such you will not be able to see any of the letters in the newsprint.

*Is the stone glued into the setting?* Diamonds are seldom glued in. Rhinestones often are.

*Is the back open or closed?* If the stone is a properly set diamond, the back of the setting will usually be open, allowing you to readily see a portion of the pavilion. Some very small rose-cut or single-cut diamonds, as seen in some antique jewelry, may be mounted with a closed back. Otherwise, if a ring has a closed back, it is probably rhinestone, in which case the back is often closed in order to conceal the foil that has been applied to the back of the stone.

Recently a young woman called and asked if we would examine an antique diamond ring she'd inherited from her great-grandmother. She mentioned that as she was cleaning it, one of its two diamonds had fallen out of the setting, and inside the setting she saw what she described as pieces of "mirror." She added, "Isn't that strange?" Of course my suspicions were immediately aroused, and upon examination of the piece, they were completely confirmed.

When we saw the ring, we could immediately understand why she felt it was a valuable heirloom. It was beautiful, with a classic design. It held two "diamonds" appearing to be approximately one-carat each. The ring mounting was finely worked platinum filigree. But the design of the mounting, which had been common in her great-grandmother's day, made viewing the stones from the side of the ring almost impossible. The top of the stone and the beautiful platinum work were visible, but little more. Furthermore, the back was not completely enclosed; a small round hole would easily have led to the assumption that the stones were the real thing, since the setting wasn't completely closed, as were most imitations at that time. The "set" diamond appeared to be a well-proportioned "old-mine" cut with very good color. The loose stone, however, with some of the "shiny stuff" still clinging to it, lacked brilliance and fire.

This was one of the finest examples of fraud we had seen in a long time. The "stones" were well cut and proportioned; the mounting was beautifully worked in a precious metal; the stones were held by very small prongs, which was typical of good design at that time. But inside the mounting, backing the stones, was silver foil. They were not genuine diamonds, but foil-backed glass.

The use of silver foil is an effective method to "create" a diamond. It acts as a mirror to reflect light so that the stone appears so brilliant and lively that it can pass as a diamond. The foiling seen today consists of making the back facets into true mirrors and then giving the backs of these mirrors a protective coating of gilt paint. These are then set in jewelry so that their backs are hidden.

It's a sad story, but not an altogether uncommon one. We don't know how many more rings as cleverly done exist today, but approximately 5 percent of the antique jewelry we see is set with fake gems. Fine glass imitations (often referred to as "paste") have been with us since the Venetians of the Renaissance period perfected the art of glassmaking; fraud, unfortunately has been with us since time immemorial. Don't allow yourself to be deluded into believing that something you possess is "genuine" simply because it is "antique" or has "been in the family" for a long time.

*How many facets are visible on the top?* In cheaper glass imitations only 9 top facets are usually visible, as opposed to 33 visible top facets in a diamond or "good" simulation. Single-cut or Swiss-cut diamonds (see chapter 4) will also show only 9 facets on top, but they will be set in open-back mountings, whereas cheap glass imitations are usually set in closed-back mountings.

*Does the girdle of the stone appear to be "frosted?"* The girdles of most diamonds are unpolished, with a ground-glass-like appearance that suggests "frostiness." There are some diamond imitations that also have a frosted appearance, but of all of these, a diamond has the whitest frostiness—like clean, dry, ground glass. On the other hand, some diamonds do have polished or faceted girdles, and thus no frostiness will be present. You can develop an eye for this by asking a reliable jeweler to point out the differences between a polished girdle, an unpolished girdle, and a faceted girdle.

*Is the cut symmetrical?* Since diamond is so valuable and symmetry so important to its overall appearance and desirability, the symmetry of the faceting on a diamond will be very carefully executed, whereas in diamond simulations the symmetry of the facets may be sloppy. For example, the eight kite-shaped facets (sometimes called bezel facets) will often be missing one or more points on the side, or on the top or bottom, showing a small straight edge rather than a point. This sloppy faceting can be an important indication that the stone in question is not a diamond, since it indicates that the cutter did not take proper care. It should be noted that some poorer-grade or old-cut diamonds may also show sloppiness.

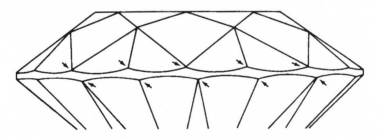

Misalignment of crown and pavilion

*Are the crown and the pavilion of the stone properly aligned?* While occasionally a diamond may show partial misalignment, imitations are frequently and often badly misaligned.

*Are the facet edges or faces scratched, chipped, or worn?* Diamond imitations include some stones that are very soft and/or brittle, such as zircon, GGG (a man-made simulation), Fabulite (a man-made diamond simulation also known as Wellington Diamond), and glass. Due to their lack of hardness and, in the case of zircon, possible brittleness, these imitations will show wear easily, and one can often detect scratches or chips on the facet edges or faces. The edges are somewhat more vulnerable and scratches or chips may be more easily seen there, so check the edges first. Then check the flat faces for scratches. Check both the areas that would be most exposed and areas around the prongs, where a setter might accidentally have scratched the stone while setting it.

Zircon, a stone found in nature that is often confused with cubic zirconia (CZ), a man-made imitation, is relatively hard but very brittle, so it will almost always show chipping at the edges of the facets if the stone has been worn in jewelry for a year or more. Glass and Fabulite will also show scratches after minimal exposure to handling and wear. Fabulite further differs from diamond in its fire; it will show even *more* fire than diamond, but with a strong bluishness to it.

In addition, with a very good eye or the aid of a magnifier, you can examine the lines or edges where the facets come together in these imitation materials. In diamond, these facet edges are very sharp because of the stone's spectacular hardness. In most simulations, however, since the stone is so much softer, the final polishing technique rounds off these edges, and that sharpness is absent.

Some diamond look-alikes, however, are more durable and resistant to noticeable wear. These include colorless synthetic spinel, colorless synthetic sapphire, colorless quartz, YAG (man-made), and CZ. While these may scratch or chip over time with regular wear and daily abuse, scratches or chips are not as numerous, and will be less noticeable.

*Does the stone, loose or mounted, exhibit fluorescence under ultraviolet light?* We do not feel this is something readily accomplished by an amateur, nor comprehensible to the average person because of numerous variables and scientific complexities. If, after the above tests, you still have doubt, take the stone to a qualified gemologist with lab facilities and ask him to identify the stone. If it is a diamond, have him note the nature of the stone's fluorescence, as it can prove a valuable tool for identification if ever needed.

# An Important Word About Cubic Zirconia

Cubic zirconia (CZ) is the best diamond simulation made to date, and even some jewelers have mistaken these stones for diamonds. Shortly after its appearance, several well-known Washington, D.C., jewelers found themselves stuck with CZ instead of the one-carat diamonds they thought they'd purchased. The crooks were very clever. A well-dressed couple would arrive at the diamond counter and ask to see various one-carat round, brilliant-cut loose diamonds. Because of their fine appearance and educated manner, the jewelers relaxed their guard. The couple would then leave, not making a purchase decision just then, but promising to return. When the jewelers went to replace their merchandise, something didn't seem quite right. Upon close examination, the jewelers discovered that the "nice couple" had pocketed the genuine diamonds and substituted CZ.

CZ is almost as brilliant as diamond, has even greater fire (which masks its lesser brilliance), and is relatively hard, giving it good durability and wearability. CZ is also being produced today in fancy colors—red, green, and yellow—and can provide a nice diamond "alternative" as a means to offset or dress up colored stones in jewelry if diamonds are unaffordable.

But make sure you *know* what you are buying. For example, if you are shown a lovely amethyst or sapphire ring dressed up with "diamonds" make sure to ask whether the colorless stones are diamonds. And if you are having your own piece of jewelry custom made, you might want to consider using CZ. You can ask your jeweler to order them for you. CZ makes attractive jewelry that can be worn every day without worry.

# How Can You Tell If You Have a CZ?

Some of the tests already discussed may help you detect a CZ. The following, however, may eliminate any remaining doubt.

*If it is a loose stone, have it weighed.* If you are familiar with diamond sizes (see pages 57 and 58) or have a spread gauge (which can be purchased for under $10), you can estimate the diamond carat weight by its spread. A loose stone can be weighed on a scale, which most jewelers have handy, and you can determine how much it should weigh if it is truly a diamond. If the weight is much greater than the diamond weight should be, based on its spread, then it is not a diamond. A CZ is approximately 75 percent heavier than a diamond of the same spread. For example, a CZ that looks like a 1-carat diamond size-wise will weigh 1¾ carats; a CZ that looks like a ¼ carat diamond in terms of size will weigh approximately $^{40}/_{100}$ carat.

**Look at the girdle.** If the girdle is frosted, a subdued whiteness resembling slightly wet or oiled frosted glass will indicate CZ. Unfortunately, looking at girdles to differentiate between the appearance of frosted CZ and frosted diamond girdles requires considerable experience.

**Test the stone with a carbide scriber.** CZ can be scratched with a finepoint carbide scriber, also available at most jewelry supply houses for under $15. If the scriber is forcibly pushed perpendicularly to any of the facets (the table being the easiest) and then drawn across this flat surface, you will scratch it. You cannot scratch a diamond except with another diamond. But be sensible and considerate. Don't heedlessly scratch merchandise that doesn't belong to you—particularly if the jeweler or seller doesn't represent the stone as a diamond.

**Examine the stone, loose or mounted, for fluorescence.** Both CZ and diamond fluoresce, but the colors and intensities will be different.

**Use an electronic diamond tester.** There are pocket-size diamond testers for under $175 which will tell you whether or not you have a diamond. If you follow the instructions, they are easy to use and fairly reliable. Most won't tell you what you have if it's *not* diamond, but only confirm whether or not it *is* diamond.

If after these tests you have some questions, take the stone to a qualified gemologist with lab facilities for positive identification.

## Comparison of Diamond & Diamond Look-alikes

| Name of Stone | Hardness (MOHS' Scale 1—10) 1 = Soft, 10 = Hardest | Read-through* | Degree of Dispersion (Fire, Flashes of Color Observed) | Wearability |
|---|---|---|---|---|
| Diamond | 10 (Hardest natural substance in existence) | None, if properly cut | High; lots of fire and liveliness | Excellent |
| Strontium titanate (also known as "Fabulite" or "Wellington Diamond") | 5—6 (Soft) | None, if properly cut | Extremely high; too high (much more than diamond); shows lots of blue flashes | Poor—scratches and wears badly |
| Cubic zirconia (CZ) | 8.5 (Hard) | Slight | Very high; lots of life | Very good |
| Gadolinium gallium garnet (GGG; produced very briefly) | 6.5 (Somewhat soft) | Moderate | High; almost identical to diamond | Fair—scratches easily; wears badly; sunlight causes brownish discoloration |
| Yttrium aluminum garnet (YAG; used extensively) | 8.5 (Hard) | Strong | Very low; almost no visible display of fire | Good |
| Synthetic rutile (shows yellowish color) | 6.5 (Soft) | None | Extremely high; lots of life—but strong yellowish flashes | Poor; scratches easily and shows excessive wear |
| Zircon | 7.5 (Moderately hard) | Moderate | Good; lively | Fair—hard but brittle, so chips easily and shows wear equivalent to much softer stones |
| Synthetic sapphire | 9 (Very hard) | Very strong | Very low; little life or display of color flashes | Very good |
| Synthetic spinel | 8 (Hard) | Very strong | Low; little "life" | Very good |
| Glass | 5—6.5 (Soft) | Very strong | Variable—low to good depending on quality of glass, and cut | Poor; susceptible to scratches, chipping, and excessive wear |

*This technique—the ability and ease with which one can read print while looking through the stone—is reliable only when looking at round, brilliant-cut stones (although it is *sometimes* useful for ovals and some fancy cuts).

# 10

---

# Comparing Diamond Prices

All too often people look for easy answers to complex problems. Many would like to have a simple list of diamond grades and corresponding prices, by size. Unfortunately, market conditions are constantly changing, and, more important, significant differences in price often result from subtle differences in quality not readily discernable to any but the professional (see chapter 8 on reading diamond reports). Therefore, it is not possible to provide a simple answer to this complex question.

But that does not mean we cannot provide you with some general guidelines that will help you understand the *relative* effects of each of the four primary factors used to determine the value of diamonds. The following charts are not intended as hard price lists of what you should be paying in a jewelry store; they should be used, instead, as a guideline, a foundation upon which you can place more current information that reflects the variations in a constantly fluctuating market. Keep in mind that these prices are for unmounted stones. Fine settings and custom designed one-of-a-kind pieces can add substantially to the price.

*Extreme differences* between the prices given on the following pages and a price you might be quoted for a diamond should be examined carefully; if the price is *much lower,* be sure to seek a gemologist or gemologist-appraiser to check the quality and verify that the stone is as represented. If the price is *much higher,* do some comparison shopping in your community to be sure the seller is offering good value.

Note that the prices given here are for round, brilliant-cut diamonds with "good" proportioning; stones with "excellent" proportioning will sell for more, while stones with poor proportioning can sell for much less. Diamonds having "fancy" shapes, i.e., shapes other than round, normally sell for anywhere from 5 to 15 percent less. However, if a particular shape is in great demand, the price can be higher than for round stones.

Finally, before relying too heavily on the prices listed in this chapter, be sure to read chapter 8, which tells you how to use the information on diamond grading reports. This knowledge will give you additional input on adjusting diamond prices according to the more subtle factors that affect quality and value. Finally, if you are contemplating the purchase of a particular stone, be sure to have the facts verified by a qualified gemologist-appraiser.

# RETAIL PRICE GUIDES

Notice both the tremendous price fluctuation among stones of the same size due to differences in the flaw grades and color grades, and the disproportionate jumps in cost *per carat*, depending upon size.

PRICE PER CARAT
PRICE PER STONE  U.S. Dollars – 1993

**COLOR GRADE**                                    **1/2 CARAT (.50+)**

FLAW (CLARITY) GRADE

|  | D | E | F | G | H | I | J | K |
|---|---|---|---|---|---|---|---|---|
| IF | 13,400 | 10,800 | 9,800 | 8,600 | 7,400 | 6,000 | 4,800 | 3,800 |
|  | 6,700 | 5,400 | 4,900 | 4,300 | 3,200 | 3,000 | 2,400 | 1,900 |
| VVS$_1$ | 10,800 | 10,200 | 8,400 | 7,800 | 6,800 | 5,200 | 4,600 | 3,600 |
|  | 5,400 | 5,100 | 4,200 | 3,900 | 3,400 | 2,600 | 2,300 | 1,800 |
| VVS$_2$ | 10,000 | 8,200 | 7,800 | 6,800 | 6,000 | 5,000 | 4,400 | 3,400 |
|  | 5,000 | 4,100 | 3,400 | 3,400 | 3,000 | 2,500 | 2,200 | 1,700 |
| VS$_1$ | 8,600 | 7,600 | 6,400 | 5,800 | 5,400 | 4,600 | 4,200 | 3,200 |
|  | 4,300 | 3,800 | 3,200 | 2,900 | 2,700 | 2,300 | 2,100 | 1,600 |
| VS$_2$ | 7,000 | 6,200 | 5,600 | 5,200 | 5,000 | 4,400 | 3,800 | 3,000 |
|  | 3,500 | 3,100 | 2,800 | 2,600 | 2,500 | 2,200 | 1,900 | 1,500 |
| SI$_1$ | 5,600 | 5,200 | 5,000 | 4,600 | 4,400 | 4,000 | 3,400 | 2,800 |
|  | 2,800 | 2,600 | 2,500 | 2,300 | 2,200 | 2,000 | 1,700 | 1,400 |
| SI$_2$ | 4,600 | 4,400 | 4,200 | 4,000 | 3,800 | 3,400 | 3,000 | 2,600 |
|  | 2,300 | 2,200 | 2,100 | 2,000 | 1,900 | 1,700 | 1,500 | 1,300 |
| I$_1$ | 3,600 | 3,400 | 3,200 | 3,000 | 2,800 | 2,400 | 2,200 | 2,100 |
|  | 1,800 | 1,700 | 1,600 | 1,500 | 1,400 | 1,200 | 1,100 | 1,100 |

# RETAIL PRICE GUIDES

Notice both the tremendous price fluctuation among stones of the same size due to differences in the flaw grades and color grades, and the disproportionate jumps in cost *per carat*, depending upon size.

| PRICE PER CARAT |
| PRICE PER STONE | U.S. Dollars – 1993 |

**COLOR GRADE**                                      3/4 CARAT (.70+)

FLAW (CLARITY) GRADE

| | D | E | F | G | H | I | J | K |
|---|---|---|---|---|---|---|---|---|
| IF | 14,600 | 11,600 | 11,000 | 10,200 | 9,000 | 7,200 | 5,800 | 4,600 |
| | 10,950 | 8,700 | 8,250 | 7,650 | 6,750 | 5,400 | 4,350 | 3,450 |
| VVS₁ | 11,600 | 11,000 | 10,000 | 8,800 | 7,800 | 6,600 | 5,400 | 4,400 |
| | 8,700 | 8,250 | 7,500 | 6,600 | 5,850 | 4,950 | 4,050 | 3,300 |
| VVS₂ | 11,000 | 10,000 | 9,000 | 7,600 | 7,000 | 5,800 | 5,000 | 4,200 |
| | 8,250 | 7,500 | 6,750 | 5,700 | 5,250 | 4,350 | 3,750 | 3,150 |
| VS₁ | 9,800 | 8,800 | 7,800 | 7,000 | 6,200 | 5,400 | 4,800 | 4,000 |
| | 7,350 | 6,600 | 5,850 | 5,250 | 4,650 | 4,050 | 3,600 | 3,000 |
| VS₂ | 8,200 | 7,400 | 7,000 | 6,400 | 5,600 | 5,200 | 4,600 | 3,800 |
| | 6,150 | 5,550 | 5,250 | 4,800 | 4,200 | 3,900 | 3,450 | 2,850 |
| SI₁ | 7,000 | 6,600 | 6,200 | 5,600 | 5,200 | 4,600 | 4,200 | 3,600 |
| | 5,250 | 4,950 | 4,650 | 4,200 | 3,900 | 3,450 | 3,150 | 2,700 |
| SI₂ | 6,200 | 5,800 | 5,400 | 5,000 | 4,400 | 4,000 | 3,800 | 3,200 |
| | 4,650 | 4,350 | 4,050 | 3,750 | 3,300 | 3,000 | 2,850 | 2,400 |
| I₁ | 4,000 | 3,800 | 3,600 | 3,400 | 3,200 | 3,000 | 2,800 | 2,600 |
| | 3,000 | 2,850 | 2,700 | 2,550 | 2,400 | 2,250 | 2,100 | 1,950 |

**COLOR GRADE**                                      Light 1–CARAT (.96+)

FLAW (CLARITY) GRADE

| | D | E | F | G | H | I | J | K |
|---|---|---|---|---|---|---|---|---|
| IF | 18,000 | 13,400 | 12,400 | 11,400 | 9,600 | 8,200 | 6,800 | 5,400 |
| | 17,280 | 12,864 | 11,904 | 10,944 | 9,216 | 7,872 | 6,528 | 5,184 |
| VVS₁ | 13,600 | 12,400 | 12,000 | 10,200 | 8,600 | 7,200 | 6,400 | 5,200 |
| | 13,056 | 11,904 | 11,520 | 9,792 | 8,256 | 6,912 | 6,144 | 4,992 |
| VVS₂ | 12,400 | 11,800 | 10,800 | 9,000 | 7,800 | 6,800 | 6,000 | 5,000 |
| | 11,904 | 11,328 | 10,368 | 8,640 | 7,488 | 6,528 | 5,760 | 4,800 |
| VS₁ | 11,200 | 10,000 | 9,200 | 7,800 | 7,000 | 6,200 | 5,600 | 4,800 |
| | 10,752 | 9,600 | 8,832 | 7,488 | 6,720 | 5,952 | 5,376 | 4,608 |
| VS₂ | 9,600 | 8,800 | 8,200 | 7,600 | 6,600 | 5,800 | 5,400 | 4,600 |
| | 9,216 | 8,448 | 7,872 | 7,296 | 6,336 | 5,568 | 5,184 | 4,416 |
| SI₁ | 8,400 | 7,600 | 7,200 | 6,800 | 5,800 | 5,400 | 5,200 | 4,200 |
| | 8,064 | 7,296 | 6,912 | 6,528 | 5,568 | 5,184 | 4,992 | 4,032 |
| SI₂ | 7,000 | 6,600 | 6,400 | 6,000 | 5,500 | 5,100 | 4,600 | 4,000 |
| | 6,720 | 6,336 | 6,144 | 5,760 | 5,280 | 4,896 | 4,416 | 3,840 |
| I₁ | 5,200 | 4,400 | 4,200 | 4,000 | 3,800 | 3,600 | 3,400 | 3,200 |
| | 4,992 | 4,224 | 4,032 | 3,840 | 3,648 | 3,456 | 3,264 | 3,072 |

Prices compiled from *The Guide*, Gemworld International, Inc., and adjusted to retail based on keystone.

# RETAIL PRICE GUIDES

Notice both the tremendous price fluctuation among stones of the same size due to differences in the flaw grades and color grades, and the disproportionate jumps in cost *per carat*, depending upon size.

PRICE PER CARAT
PRICE PER STONE  U.S. Dollars – 1993

**COLOR GRADE**        **1 CARAT (1.00+)**

FLAW (CLARITY) GRADE

| | D | E | F | G | H | I | J | K |
|---|---|---|---|---|---|---|---|---|
| **IF** | 29,000 | 19,000 | 16,400 | 14,000 | 11,400 | 9,400 | 8,000 | 7,000 |
| | 29,000 | 19,000 | 16,400 | 14,000 | 11,400 | 9,400 | 8,000 | 7,000 |
| **VVS$_1$** | 19,000 | 16,400 | 14,000 | 12,000 | 10,200 | 8,400 | 7,400 | 6,600 |
| | 19,000 | 16,400 | 14,000 | 12,000 | 10,200 | 8,400 | 7,400 | 6,600 |
| **VVS$_2$** | 16,400 | 14,000 | 12,000 | 10,200 | 9,200 | 7,800 | 7,200 | 6,400 |
| | 16,400 | 14,000 | 12,000 | 10,200 | 9,200 | 7,800 | 7,200 | 6,400 |
| **VS$_1$** | 13,600 | 10,600 | 10,400 | 9,200 | 8,200 | 7,400 | 7,000 | 6,000 |
| | 13,600 | 10,600 | 10,400 | 9,200 | 8,200 | 7,400 | 7,000 | 6,000 |
| **VS$_2$** | 11,600 | 10,200 | 9,000 | 8,200 | 7,800 | 7,200 | 6,800 | 5,800 |
| | 11,600 | 10,200 | 9,000 | 8,200 | 7,800 | 7,200 | 6,800 | 5,800 |
| **SI$_1$** | 8,800 | 8,200 | 7,800 | 7,400 | 7,200 | 6,800 | 6,400 | 5,400 |
| | 8,800 | 8,200 | 7,800 | 7,400 | 7,200 | 6,800 | 6,400 | 5,400 |
| **SI$_2$** | 7,200 | 6,800 | 6,600 | 6,400 | 6,200 | 6,000 | 5,600 | 5,200 |
| | 7,200 | 6,800 | 6,600 | 6,400 | 6,200 | 6,000 | 5,600 | 5,200 |
| **I$_1$** | 5,200 | 5,000 | 4,800 | 4,600 | 4,400 | 4,200 | 4,000 | 3,800 |
| | 5,200 | 5,000 | 4,800 | 4,600 | 4,400 | 4,200 | 4,000 | 3,800 |

**COLOR GRADE**        **2 CARAT (2.00+)**

FLAW (CLARITY) GRADE

| | D | E | F | G | H | I | J | K |
|---|---|---|---|---|---|---|---|---|
| **IF** | 44,000 | 34,000 | 29,000 | 22,600 | 19,800 | 15,400 | 12,000 | 10,200 |
| | 88,000 | 68,000 | 58,000 | 45,200 | 39,600 | 30,800 | 24,000 | 20,400 |
| **VVS$_1$** | 34,000 | 29,000 | 23,000 | 19,600 | 16,600 | 14,000 | 11,200 | 9,800 |
| | 68,000 | 58,000 | 46,000 | 39,200 | 33,200 | 28,000 | 22,400 | 19,600 |
| **VVS$_2$** | 29,000 | 23,000 | 19,600 | 16,600 | 15,000 | 13,400 | 11,000 | 9,400 |
| | 58,000 | 46,000 | 39,200 | 33,200 | 30,000 | 26,800 | 22,000 | 18,800 |
| **VS$_1$** | 22,600 | 19,600 | 16,000 | 15,000 | 13,600 | 11,800 | 10,000 | 8,400 |
| | 45,200 | 39,200 | 32,000 | 30,000 | 27,200 | 23,600 | 20,000 | 16,800 |
| **VS$_2$** | 19,600 | 16,400 | 15,000 | 13,800 | 11,400 | 10,800 | 9,000 | 8,000 |
| | 39,200 | 32,800 | 30,000 | 27,600 | 22,800 | 21,600 | 18,000 | 16,000 |
| **SI$_1$** | 14,400 | 13,200 | 12,400 | 11,800 | 10,800 | 9,600 | 8,200 | 7,400 |
| | 28,800 | 26,400 | 24,800 | 23,600 | 21,600 | 19,200 | 16,400 | 14,800 |
| **SI$_2$** | 10,600 | 9,800 | 9,000 | 8,600 | 8,000 | 7,600 | 7,000 | 6,600 |
| | 21,200 | 19,600 | 18,000 | 17,200 | 16,000 | 15,200 | 14,000 | 13,200 |
| **I$_1$** | 7,800 | 7,400 | 7,000 | 6,600 | 6,200 | 6,000 | 5,800 | 5,000 |
| | 15,600 | 14,800 | 14,000 | 13,200 | 12,400 | 12,000 | 11,600 | 10,000 |

Prices compiled from *The Guide*, Gemworld International, Inc.

# RETAIL PRICE GUIDES

Notice both the tremendous price fluctuation among stones of the same size due to differences in the flaw grades and color grades, and the disproportionate jumps in cost *per carat*, depending upon size.

PRICE PER CARAT / PRICE PER STONE     U.S. Dollars – 1993

COLOR GRADE                                               3 CARAT (3.00+)

FLAW (CLARITY) GRADE

| | | D | E | F | G | H | I | J | K |
|---|---|---|---|---|---|---|---|---|---|
| IF | | 70,000 | 51,000 | 43,000 | 32,000 | 27,000 | 21,000 | 17,200 | 14,800 |
| | | 210,000 | 153,000 | 129,000 | 96,000 | 81,000 | 63,000 | 51,600 | 44,400 |
| VVS$_1$ | | 51,000 | 43,000 | 32,000 | 27,600 | 24,000 | 18,800 | 16,000 | 14,000 |
| | | 153,000 | 129,000 | 96,000 | 82,800 | 72,000 | 56,400 | 48,000 | 42,000 |
| VVS$_2$ | | 43,000 | 32,000 | 27,600 | 24,000 | 21,600 | 17,800 | 15,200 | 13,000 |
| | | 129,000 | 96,000 | 82,800 | 72,000 | 64,800 | 53,400 | 45,600 | 39,000 |
| VS$_1$ | | 32,000 | 27,000 | 24,200 | 22,200 | 19,000 | 17,000 | 14,400 | 12,200 |
| | | 96,000 | 81,000 | 69,600 | 66,600 | 57,000 | 51,000 | 43,200 | 36,600 |
| VS$_2$ | | 27,400 | 24,200 | 22,200 | 19,000 | 16,400 | 15,200 | 13,200 | 11,000 |
| | | 82,200 | 69,600 | 66,600 | 57,000 | 49,200 | 45,600 | 39,600 | 33,000 |
| SI$_1$ | | 23,200 | 21,000 | 19,800 | 17,400 | 14,800 | 13,600 | 11,600 | 10,400 |
| | | 69,600 | 63,000 | 59,400 | 52,200 | 44,400 | 40,800 | 34,800 | 31,200 |
| SI$_2$ | | 17,200 | 16,000 | 14,400 | 14,000 | 12,600 | 11,600 | 10,800 | 9,400 |
| | | 51,600 | 48,000 | 43,200 | 42,000 | 37,800 | 34,800 | 32,400 | 28,200 |
| I$_1$ | | 13,200 | 12,000 | 11,000 | 10,400 | 9,600 | 8,600 | 8,200 | 7,200 |
| | | 39,600 | 36,000 | 33,000 | 31,200 | 28,800 | 25,800 | 24,600 | 21,600 |

Prices compiled from *The Guide*, Gemworld International, Inc.

# 3

# Colored Gemstones

# 11

## The Mystery & Magic of Colored Gems

The fascination with colored gemstones dates back to the very beginning of civilization. For our ancestors, the blue of sapphire produced visions of the heavens; the red of ruby was a reminder of the very essence of life. By Roman times, rings containing colored gems were prized symbols of power—and the most powerful wore rings on every joint of every finger!

Since ancient times, colored stones have been thought to possess innate magical powers and the ability to endow the wearer with certain attributes. According to legend, emeralds are good for the eyes; yellow stones cure jaundice; red stones stop the flow of blood. At one time it was believed that a ruby worn by a man indicated command, nobility, lordship, and vengeance; worn by a woman, however, it indicated pride, obstinacy, and haughtiness. A blue sapphire worn by a man indicated wisdom, and high and magnanimous thoughts; on a woman, jealousy in love, politeness, and vigilance. The emerald signified for a man joyousness, transitory hope, and the decline of friendship; for woman, unfounded ambition, childish delight, and change.

Colored gems, because of the magical powers associated with them, achieved extensive use as talismans and amulets; as predictors of the future; as therapeutic aids; and as essential elements to many religious practices—pagan, Hebrew, and Christian.

### Zodiac Stones

The following list of the zodiacal gems and their special powers has been passed on from an early Hindu legend.

Aquarius (Jan. 21-Feb. 21)    *Garnet*—believed to guarantee true friendship when worn by an Aquarian

Pisces (Feb. 22-Mar. 21)    *Amethyst*—believed to protect a Pisces wearer from extremes of passion

Aries (Mar. 22-Apr. 20)    *Bloodstone*—believed to endow an Aries wearer with wisdom

Taurus (Apr. 21-May 21)    *Sapphire*—believed to protect from and cure mental disorders if worn by a Taurus

Gemini (May 22-June 21)    *Agate*—long life, health, and wealth were guaranteed to a Gemini if an agate ring was worn

Cancer (June 22-July 22)    *Emerald*—eternal joy was guaranteed to a Cancer-born if an emerald was taken with him on his way

Leo (July 23-Aug. 22)    *Onyx*—would protect a Leo wearer from loneliness and unhappiness

Virgo (Aug. 23-Sept. 22)    *Carnelian*—believed to guarantee success in anything a Virgo tried if worn on his or her hand

Libra (Sept. 23-Oct. 23)    *Chrysolite* (peridot)—would free a Libra wearer from any evil spell

Scorpio (Oct. 24-Nov. 21)    *Beryl*—should be worn by every Scorpio to guarantee protection from "tears of sad repentance"

Sagittarius (Nov. 22-Dec. 21) *Topaz*—protects Sagittarians, but only if they always show the stone

Capricorn (Dec. 22-Jan. 21)    *Ruby*—a Capricorn who has ever worn a ruby will never know trouble

An old Spanish list, probably representing an Arab tradition, ascribes the following stones to the various signs of the zodiac:

| | |
|---|---|
| *Aquarius*—Amethyst | *Leo*—Topaz |
| *Pisces*—(indistinguishable) | *Virgo*—Magnet (lodestone) |
| *Aries*—Crystal (quartz) | *Libra*—Jasper |
| *Taurus*—Ruby and diamond | *Scorpio*—Garnet |
| *Gemini*—Sapphire | *Sagittarius*—Emerald |
| *Cancer*—Agate and beryl | *Capricorn*—Chalcedony |

It was believed that certain planets influenced stones, and that stones could therefore transmit the powers attributed to those planets. A further extension of this belief can be seen in the practice of engraving certain planetary constellations on stones. For example, a stone engraved with the two bears, Ursa Major and Ursa Minor, would make the wearer wise, versatile, and powerful. And so it went. And from such thought came the belief in birthstones.

# The Evolution of Birthstones

The origin of the belief that a special stone was dedicated to each month and that the stone of the month possessed a special virtue or "cure" that it could transmit to those born in that month, goes back to at least the first century. There is speculation that the twelve stones in the great breastplate of the Jewish high priest may have had some bearing on this concept. In the eighth and ninth centuries, the interpreters of the Bible's book of Revelation began to ascribe to each of those stones attributes of the twelve apostles. The Hindus, on the other hand, had their own interpretation.

But whatever the reason, one fact is clear. As G. F. Kunz points out in *The Curious Lore of Precious Stones,* "There is no doubt that the owner of a ring or ornament set with a birthstone is impressed with the idea of possessing something more intimately associated with his or her personality than any other stone, however beautiful or costly. The idea that birthstones possess a certain indefinable, but none the less real significance has long been present, and still holds a spell over the minds of all who are gifted with a touch of imagination and romance."

## Present-Day Birthstones

The following is the list of birthstones adopted in 1912 by the American National Association of Jewelers:

| Month | Birthstone | Alternate Stone |
|---|---|---|
| January | Garnet | |
| February | Amethyst | |
| March | Bloodstone | Aquamarine |
| April | Diamond | |
| May | Emerald | |
| June | Pearl | Moonstone |
| July | Ruby | |
| August | Sardonyx | Peridot (carnelian) |
| September | Sapphire | |
| October | Opal | Tourmaline |
| November | Topaz | |
| December | Turquoise | Lapis lazuli |

Besides the lists of birthstones and zodiacal or talismanic stones, there are lists of stones for days of the week, hours of the day, for states of the union, for each of the seasons, even anniversaries!

## Anniversary Stones

| | | | | | |
|---|---|---|---|---|---|
| 1 | Gold Jewelry | 9 | Lapis Lazuli | 25 | Silver Jubilee |
| 2 | Garnet | 10 | Diamond Jewelry | 30 | Pearl Jubilee |
| 3 | Pearl | 11 | Turquoise | 35 | Emerald |
| 4 | Blue Topaz | 12 | Jade | 40 | Ruby |
| 5 | Sapphire | 13 | Citrine | 45 | Sapphire |
| 6 | Amethyst | 14 | Opal | 50 | Golden Jubilee |
| 7 | Onyx | 15 | Ruby | 55 | Alexandrite |
| 8 | Tourmaline | 20 | Emerald | 60 | Diamond Jubilee |

# The Importance of Color and Its Mystical Symbolism in Gems

The wide spectrum of color available in the gemstone realm was not lost on our forebears. Not only did strong associations with specific stones evolve, but also associations of color with personal attributes. Over time, a fairly detailed symbolism came to join color with character. Those attributes, as they have come down to us, include:

Yellow    Worn by a man, denotes secrecy (appropriate for a silent lover); worn by a woman, it indicates generosity.

White (colorless)    Signifies friendship, integrity, and religious commitment for men; purity, affability, and contemplation for women.

Red    On a man, indicates command, nobility, lordship, and vengeance; on a woman, pride, haughtiness, and obstinacy.

Blue    On a man, indicates wisdom and high magnanimous thoughts; on a woman, jealousy in love, politeness, vigilance.

Green    For men, signifies joyousness, transitory hope, decline of friendship; for women, unfounded ambition, childish delight, and change.

Black    For men, means gravity, good sense, constancy, and strength; for young women, fickleness and foolishness, but for married women, constant love and perseverance.

Violet    For men, signifies sober judgment, industry, and gravity; for women, high thoughts and spiritual love.

# What Colored Stones Are Available Today?

## New stones add exciting choices

Today, gems are worn primarily for their intrinsic beauty and are chosen mainly for aesthetic reasons, not for mythical attributes. While we may own a birthstone that we wear on occasion, our choice of stones is usually dictated by personal color preferences, economics, and fashion. The world of colored gems today offers us an almost endless choice. New gems have been discovered and are being made available through the major jewelry companies. If you like red, there are rubies, garnets, red tourmalines, red spinels, and even red diamonds and red "emeralds" (the more correct name for red emerald, gemologically, is red beryl—see chapter 16 on emeralds). If you prefer blue, there are sapphires, iolite, blue spinel, blue topaz, blue tourmaline, tanzanite, and blue diamonds. For those who prefer green, there are emeralds, tsavorite (green garnet), green zircons, green tourmalines, green sapphires, peridots, and even green diamonds. And for those who love unusual shades of blue and green, dazzling neon shades in sparkling, transparent stones, there are the remarkable, rare, newly discovered "Paraiba" or "Hetorita" tourmaline from Brazil—considered by many to be the most exciting gemological discovery, in terms of color, in this century.

The following chapters will look at colored stones in more detail, and will suggest a variety of stones available today in every hue. With colored gems available for almost everyone, in almost any color, at almost any price, you have a wide range of affordable options.

# 12

---

# Determining Value in Colored Gems

Color is the most important determinant of value in colored gems. It is also, too often, the principal determinant in erroneous identification because, unfortunately, most people don't realize how many gems look alike in color. And even professionals in the trade can be misled or caught off-guard. Too often recognition and identification are based on color alone because so few jewelers and customers are aware of the large number of similarly colored stones that are available.

Until recently, the gemstone industry has promoted very few colored stones, concentrating instead on the more precious and profitable gems. But the growing popularity of colored stones has expanded the market so that consumers now find they have a choice. If you want an emerald-green stone but can't afford a fine emerald, you might choose a green garnet (tsavorite), a green or "chrome" tourmaline, or perhaps green "tanzanite" (tanzanite is the blue variety of *zoisite;* now there is a green variety, which is sometimes called green tanzanite). And there are at least four gem materials from which to choose, no matter what color you prefer. New gems are being discovered each year, and known gems are being discovered in new colors. Increasingly, fine jewelers and designers are creating exciting pieces using the full color spectrum. It's a wonderful time to be part of the jewelry world, and to start exploring the possibilities at local jewelers!

## The Four Cs of Colored Gems

We've already discussed the four Cs to consider in choosing a diamond (see chapter 3), but colored gems have four Cs of their own: color, color, color, and color! This statement may sound like an exaggeration, but not so much as you might think. Generally speaking, the finer and rarer the color, the less impact cutting, clarity, and carat weight have on the value of the gem. On the other hand, the more common the color, the more impact these other factors have.

When we discuss color, we are not talking simply about hue. Color science, and the evaluation of color, is a very complex area. But if you understand the various elements that must be factored into the evaluation of color, you can begin to look at colored gems in a totally different light.

Color is affected by many variables that make it difficult to evaluate precisely. Perhaps the most significant factor is light; the type of light and its intensity can affect color dramatically. In addition, color can be very subjective in terms of what is considered pleasing and desirable. Nonetheless, there has been extensive research and development in the field of color science, and experts are working to develop a viable color-grading system. Gemologists at the GIA have produced a machine called *Color Master,* a type of visual colorimeter, around which they have developed a color-grading system that is gaining increasing acceptance. American Gemological Laboratories has continued to develop its *ColorScan* system, and several other systems are gaining acceptance, one of the most promising newcomers being Howard Rubin's *GemDialogue.* Most gem pricing guides use at least one of these systems to describe the quality of the stones they are pricing, but problems still exist with color communication, and no solution seems imminent. A great degree of subjectivity reigns where colored gems are concerned, and no system has yet replaced the ages-old eye-and-brain combination, coupled with years of experience in the colored-stone field.

## The Key Elements in Describing Color

The color we see in gems is always some *combination* of the pure spectral colors—which range from pure red to pure violet—coupled with varying degrees of brown, white, black, and gray. It is these latter colors, in combination with the spectral colors, that affect the *tone* of the color seen and that make the classification of color so difficult. For example, if white is present with red, you will have a lighter tone or shade of red; if black is present, a darker tone or shade. Depending upon the degree of gray, white, black or brown an almost infinite number of color combinations can result.

As a general rule, the closer a stone's color is to the pure spectral hue, the better the color is considered to be; the closer it comes to a pure hue, the rarer and more valuable. For example, if we are considering a green stone, the purer the green, the better the color. In other words, the closer it comes to being a pure spectral green, having no undertone (tint) of any other color such as blue or yellow, the better

## *Rare and Distinctive —*
## *Fancy Natural Color*
# *Diamonds*

Diamonds occur naturally in more colors and more shades of color than any other gemstone — virtually every color in the rainbow.

# Red and Pink Gemstones to Warm Any Heart

Red gems occur in a wide range of hues and tones to please every taste and budget.

Rubellite (Red Tourmaline)

Morganite

Kunzite

Rhodolite Garnet

Tourmaline

Topaz

Topaz

Ruby

Red Beryl (Red "Emerald")

Sapphire

Morganite

Spinel

**Rare red beryl,** also referred to as red "emerald"—
*Left:* The crystal as it occurs in nature
*Right:* A brilliantly cut and polished gem waiting to be set

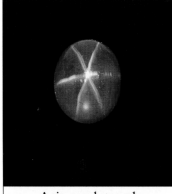

**A six-rayed star ruby**

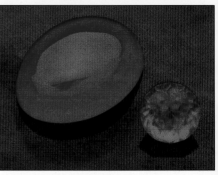

*Right:*
**Rhodochrosite,** an oval cabochon and a rare round faceted stone

# Blue Gemstones Offer Heavenly Choices

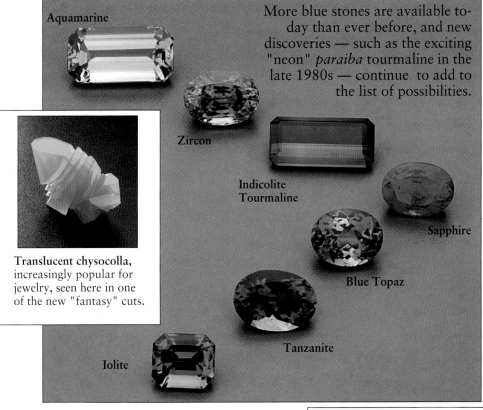

Aquamarine

More blue stones are available today than ever before, and new discoveries — such as the exciting "neon" *paraiba* tourmaline in the late 1980s — continue to add to the list of possibilities.

Zircon

Indicolite Tourmaline

Sapphire

Blue Topaz

Tanzanite

Iolite

**Translucent chysocolla,** increasingly popular for jewelry, seen here in one of the new "fantasy" cuts.

"Neon" tourmalines from Paraiba, Brazil

Exceptionally fine **star sapphire** showing rich blue and strong star can be very costly today.

**Moonstones,** exhibiting their magical "adularescence" — a bright, billowing, milky sheen moving within the stone.

# Yellow and Orange Gems to Brighten the Day

Andalucite

Yellow and orange gemstones come in a wide range of warm, sunny hues and tones.

*Left:* **Sunstone,** one of today's hot newcomers. It occurs in orangy hues as well as red, including salmon and peachy colors.

Chrysoberyl (Cat's Eye)

Topaz

Garnet

Scapolite

Zircon

Sapphire

Chrysoberyl

Garnet

Sapphire

Tourmaline

Sapphire

(Orange) Fancy Sapphire

Yellow Golden Beryl

Precious topaz, also known as "imperial" topaz

Notice the similarity in color between some citrine and topaz. Citrine is often mistaken and misrepresented as topaz. Citrine is a lovely gem, but it is less brilliant, less rare and less costly than topaz.

Citrine, the yellow member of the quartz family, comes in shades from pale yellow to rich amber.

# *Green and Blue-Green Gems Offer Rich and Uncommon Alternatives*

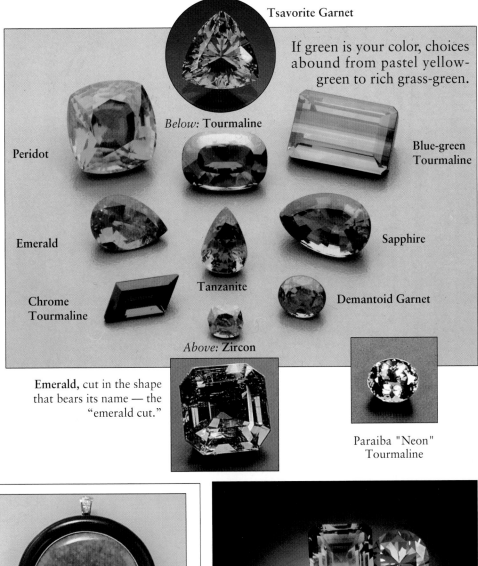

Tsavorite Garnet

If green is your color, choices abound from pastel yellow-green to rich grass-green.

*Below:* Tourmaline

Peridot

Blue-green Tourmaline

Emerald

Sapphire

Chrome Tourmaline

Tanzanite

Demantoid Garnet

*Above:* Zircon

**Emerald,** cut in the shape that bears its name — the "emerald cut."

Paraiba "Neon" Tourmaline

Fine Art Deco period brooch with very fine green jadeite centerpiece.

Laboratory-grown synthetics offer convincing and affordable alternatives to fine, rare natural gems. Above, a laboratory-grown ruby, emerald and sapphire.

# Opals - A Firey World of Color

In addition to the widely available white opal, very affordable "fire" opals and rare, costly black opals create excitement.

*Above:* **Australian Andamooka** crystal opal and Andamooka matrix opal beads

*Right:* **Mexican "Fire" opals**

*Below left:* **Fine black opal**
*Below center:* **Boulder opal**
*Below right:* **Fine black opal**

# Ornamental Stones and Decorative Art

Numerous colorful opaque and translucent materials are available for a variety of jewelry and ornamental uses from beads to belt buckles, sculpture to intarsia (intricate inlay technique).

Coral

Malachite

Blue Lace Agate

Snowflake Obsidian

Agate

Black Onyx

Lapis

Jasper

Unakite

Tiger's Eye

**An exquisite box** showing intricate intarsia work using malachite, azurite, lapis, sugilite, turquoise, and opal for inlay. (Nicolai Medvedev)

*Above:* **Sterling belt buckles** using *(top)* rhodochrosite and small lapis triangles, and *(bottom)* lapis with small round green chrysoprase accents
*Right:* Rich, sensual **sculpture** in very fine lapis (Michael Dyber)

# Popular Diamond Shapes

Trilliant

Pear

Radiant

Round

Heart

Classic Oval

Emerald-cut

Dream-cut "Oval"

Classic Marquise

New shapes such as the "dream" and "royal"cuts (Chapter 4) will look larger than traditional shapes of same weight.

Royal-cut "Marquise" *(called Duchess™)*

*Left:* "Quadrillion" princess-cut
*Right:* Ring using "quadrillions" to set off the round center stone

*Left:* Side view of 144-facet round diamond, showing extra facets (note above and below girdle) that account for its increased brilliance
*Right:* Classic 58-facet round, brilliant cut diamond

the color. There is no such thing in nature, however, as a perfectly *pure* color; color is always modified by an undertone of another hue. But these undertones can create very beautiful, unusual, distinctive colors that are often very desirable.

In describing color we will often refer to these factors:

- *Hue*—the precise spectral color (red, orange, yellow, green, blue, violet, indigo)
- *Intensity* (or saturation)—the brightness or vividness (or dullness or drabness) of the color
- *Tone*—how much black, white, gray or brown is present (how light or dark the stone is)
- *Distribution*—the even (or uneven) distribution of the color

Both intensity and tone of color can be significantly affected by the proportioning of the cut. In other words, a good lapidary (stone cutter) working with a fine stone will be able to bring out its inherent, potential beauty to the fullest, increasing the gem's desirability. A poor cutter may take the same rough material and create a stone that is not really pleasing, because the cut can significantly reduce the vividness and alter the depth of color, usually producing a stone that is much too dark to be attractive, or one in which the color seems washed out or watery.

In general, stones that are either very light (pale) or very dark sell for less per carat. There seems to be a common belief that the darker the stone, the better. This is true only to a point. A rich, deep color is desirable, but not a depth of color that approaches black. The average consumer must shop around and train the eye to distinguish between a nice depth of color and a stone that is too dark.

As a general rule, it is even more important to shop around when considering colored stones than it is when buying diamonds. You must develop an eye for all of the variables of color—hue, intensity, tone, and distribution. Some stones simply exhibit a more intense, vivid color than other stones (all else being equal), but only by extensive visual comparison can you develop your eye to perceive differences and make reliable judgments.

For example, let's discuss the variations among rubies for a moment. The finest red rubies are Burmese. While they are not a pure red, these are the closest to pure. The tone may vary, however, from very light to very dark. As with most stones, the very light stones and the very dark sell for less per carat. Burmese rubies are the most highly prized, and the most expensive, because of the desirability of their color and their scarcity. They also exhibit a beautiful red in all light, while rubies from most other locations may exhibit a lovely red only in incandescent light (such as you find in candlelight, lamplight, chandeliers, and most evening light) and become pinkish or purplish when seen in fluorescent or daytime light.

Thai rubies can vary tremendously in hue and tone, going from a light to a dark red with varying degrees of a bluish undertone, giving them a purplish cast and making them look like the much cheaper reddish purple gemstone, the garnet. While some Thai rubies can have very fine color rivalling the Burmese (these are very expensive), most Thai stones are much less expensive than the Burmese, primarily because the color can't compare.

African rubies from Tanzania usually have a tint or undertone of brown or orange, which makes them also much cheaper than the Burmese reds, but depending upon the precise shade, often more valuable than the Thai ruby, depending on the latter's color. Rubies from newly discovered deposits in Kenya, Cambodia, Vietnam, and parts of China are very close in hue and tone to Burmese, and may also retain their color in all light. These stones can command very high prices if other quality factors are fine.

Ceylon rubies are also encountered with relative frequency. However, these are usually so pale that in the United States they would be called "pink sapphire" rather than ruby since the tone is consistently so light. The saturation of color is too weak to be technically described as ruby, since ruby should be red, not pink. You should be aware that in the United States, the color must be deep enough to be considered red to be called "ruby" while in other parts of the world, the name "ruby" may be applied if the stone falls anywhere in the pink-to-red range. (It should be noted that sapphire and ruby are the same stone, physically and chemically. The red variety is called ruby, while the equally popular blue is called sapphire. Both belong to the "corundum" family).

Next, let's look at the spectrum of emerald colors. Some of the finest emeralds today come from Colombia and are the color of fresh, young green grass—an almost pure spectral green with a faint tint of either yellow or blue. The color found in the finest of these emeralds is unique to Colombia. Emeralds from other countries can also be very fine, with exceptional color, but few can match the color of the finest Colombian. Unfortunately, very fine Colombian emeralds with exceptional color are extremely rare now, and thus very costly.

African emeralds can also exhibit a lovely shade of green, but with a bluer undertone, and a slightly dark tone, probably due to traces of iron, which may make the stone less desirable, and thus less valuable than a fine emerald from Colombia. However, the African stones usually have fewer inclusions (flaws) than the Colombian, and cut a more vivid stone. Therefore, some of the African stones, depending on depth of color, compare very favorably to the Colombian, aesthetically, while costing less per carat.

## Light and Environment Affect the Color You See

The color of a stone can be drastically affected by the kind of light and the environment in which the examination is being conducted; that is, variables as disparate as the color of wallpaper or the tint of a shirt can alter a stone's appearance. If examined under a fluorescent light, a ruby may not show its fullest red, because most fluorescent lights are weak in red rays; this causes the red in the ruby to be diminished and to appear more as a purple red. The same ruby examined in sunlight or incandescent light (an ordinary electric light bulb), neither of which is weak in red rays, will appear a truer, fuller red. Because the color of a ruby is dependent upon the "color temperature" or type of light used, it will always look best in *warm* light. A ruby looks even redder if examined against a piece of orange-yellow paper. For this reason, loose rubies are often shown in little envelopes, called "parcel papers," that have a yellow-orange inner paper liner to show the red color to the fullest.

Blue sapphire, another intensely colored gem, comes in numerous tones of blue—from light to very dark, some so dark that they look black in incandescent (warm) light. Most sapphires, however, look bluest in fluorescent light, or daylight. Many contain some degree of green. The more green, the lower the price. Some even exhibit a color change—we've seen blue sapphires that were a magnificent blue in daylight turn to an amethyst-purple in incandescent light. Some, like the stones from the Umba Valley in Tanzania, turn slightly lavender over time. The lighter blues are generally referred to as Ceylon-colored sapphire; the finest and most expensive blue sapphires generally come from Burma (now called Myanmar) and Kashmir and exhibit a rich, true blue in all kinds of light. Those from Kashmir exhibit a more subdued, soft, velvety look by comparison to Burmese or Ceylon-type sapphires.

An environment that is beneficial to your stone can also be created by the setting in which the stone is mounted. For example, an emerald-cut emerald mounted in a normal four-prong setting will not appear to have as deep a color as it will if mounted in a special box-type setting that completely encloses the stone so that light is prevented from entering its sides. The "shadowing" effect created by this type of enclosure deepens the color of the stone. This technique, and other types of special mounting, can be used to improve the color of any colored gemstone where it is desirable to intensify the color.

Another example is found with a fine expensive imperial jade. A fine jade cabochon (a smooth, rounded cut which has no facets) is often mounted with a solid rim around the girdle (bezel set), with the back of the ring constructed much deeper than the actual bottom of the stone, and the back side of the ring nearly completely closed except for a small opening at the bottom center. This is done either to hide a stone's defect or to improve its body color.

Opal, too, is often set in ways that enhance color. The environment in this case is a closed, flat backing which has been blackened to intensify the play of color (fire) seen in the stone.

## A Word about Color Distribution or Zoning

Even though zoning doesn't really describe color, and is sometimes evaluated as part of the "clarity" grade, we think it should be discussed as part of color evaluation.

In some stones the color isn't always evenly distributed but exists in *zones;* in some stones, the pattern created by alternating zones of color and color*less*ness resembles stripes. Zoning is frequently observed in amethyst, ruby, and sapphire. These zones are most easily seen if you look through the *side* of the stone and move it slowly, while tilting and rotating it.

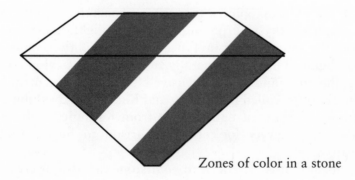

Zones of color in a stone

Sometimes a stone in the rough is colorless, or nearly so, but has a spot or layer of color. If the cutter cuts the stone so that the culet is in the color spot, the whole stone will appear that color. If there is a layer and the cutter cuts the stone so that the layer lies in a plane nearly parallel to the table, the whole stone will look completely colored. Evenness of color and complete saturation of color are very important in determining the value of colored gems. Even though you may not notice the zones themselves when looking at the stone from the top, a heavily zoned stone will lack the color vibrance of another stone without such zoning. Normally, if the zoning isn't noticeable from the top, value is not dramatically reduced, but a stone with even color will face-up better and will cost more. And, depending upon the hue and tone, possibly much more.

## A Word about "Color-Change" Stones

Some stones exhibit a very strange phenomenon when viewed in different types of light—they change color completely. These stones are called "color-change" gems. There are color-change spinels, color-change sapphires, color-change garnets, and so on. In these gem families, however, the color-change phenomenon is rare. The gem alexandrite, on the other hand, *always* exhibits a color-change, and its value is based largely upon the degree of change. There are even color-change synthetics, such as the inexpensive synthetic color-change sapphire that is often misrepresented and sold as genuine alexandrite. Alexandrite is a bluish-green gem in daylight or under daylight-type fluorescent light, and a deep red or purple red under incandescent light.

## Clarity

As with diamonds, *clarity* refers to the absence of internal flaws (inclusions) or external blemishes. Flawlessness in colored stones is perhaps even rarer than in diamonds. However, while clarity is important, and the cleaner the stone the better, flawlessness in colored stones does not usually carry the premium that it does with diamonds. Light, pastel-colored stones will require better clarity because the flaws are more readily visible in these stones; in darker-toned stones the flaws may not be as important a variable because they are masked by the depth of color.

The *type* and *placement* of flaws is a more important consideration in colored stones than the presence of flaws in and of themselves. For example, a large crack (*feather*) that is very close to the
surface of a stone—especially on the top—might be dangerous
because it weakens the stone's durability. It may also break the light
continuity, and may show an iridescent effect as well. Iridescence
usually means that a fracture or feather breaks through the surface
somewhere on the stone. Such a flaw would detract from the stone's
beauty and certainly reduce its value. But if the fracture is small and
positioned in an unobtrusive part of the stone, it will have minimal
effect on durability, beauty, or value. Some flaws actually help a
gemologist or jeweler to identify a stone, since certain types of flaws
are characteristic of specific gems and specific localities. In some
cases the presence of a particular flaw may provide positive identification of the exact variety or origin and actually cause an *increase* in
the per-carat value. For more information on the types of inclusions
found in colored gems, we recommend our book *Gem Identification
Made Easy.* We should note, however, that a very fine colored gem
that really is flawless will probably bring a disproportionately *much
higher* price per carat because it is so rare.  Because they are so rare,
flawless rubies, sapphires, emeralds, and so on should always be
viewed with suspicion; have their genuineness verified by a gem-testing lab. The newer synthetic gems are often flawless, and easy to confuse with genuine, natural gems.

If the flaws weaken the stone's durability, affect color, are easily
noticeable, or are too numerous, they will significantly reduce price.
Otherwise, they may not adversely affect price, and in some cases, if
they provide positive identification and proof of origin, they may
actually increase the cost rather than reduce it, as with Burmese
rubies and Colombian emeralds.

Again, it is important to shop around and become familiar with
the stone you wish to purchase and to train your eye to discern what
is "normal" so you can decide what is acceptable or objectionable.

# Terms used to Describe Optical Effects in Faceted and Nonfaceted Gems

Physical characteristics of colored stones are often described in
terms of the way light travels through them, their unique visual
effects, and the way they are cut. Here are a few terms you need to

know:

*Transparent.* Light travels through the stone easily, with minimal distortion, enabling one to see through it easily.

*Translucent.* The stone transmits light but diffuses it, creating an effect like frosted glass. If you tried to read through such a stone, the print will be darkened and obscured.

*Opaque.* Transmits no light. You cannot see through it even at a thin edge.

## Special Optical Effects

*Adularescence.* A billowy, movable, colored cloud effect seen in some stones, such as moonstone; an internal, movable sheen.

*Asterism.* Used to describe the display of a star effect (four- or six-rayed) seen when a stone is cut in a nonfaceted style (star ruby, garnet, and sapphire.)

*Chatoyancy.* The effect produced in some stones (when cut in a cabochon style) of a thin, bright line across the stone that usually moves as the stone is moved from side to side; sometimes called a cat's-eye effect.

*Iridescence.* A rainbow color effect produced by a thin film of air or liquid within the stone. Most iridescence seen in stones is the result of a crack breaking their surface. This detracts from the value, even if it looks pretty.

*Luster.* Usually refers to the surface of a stone and the degree to which it reflects light. Seen as the shine on the stone. Diamond, for example, has much greater luster than amethyst. Pearls are also evaluated for their luster, but pearls have a softer, silkier-looking reflection than other gems. The luster in pearls is often called "orient."

*Play of color.* Used frequently to describe the fire seen in opal.

## Cut

Colored gems can be *faceted* or cut in the *cabochon,* or unfaceted, style. Generally speaking, the preference in the United States until recently was for faceted gems, so the finest material was usually faceted. However, this was not always the case in other eras and other countries; in Roman times, for example, it was considered vulgar to wear a faceted stone. Preference also varies with different cultures and religions and the world's finest gems are cut in both styles. Don't draw any conclusions about quality based solely on style of cut.

*Cabochon.* A facetless style of cutting that produces smooth rather than faceted surfaces. These cuts can be almost any shape. Some are round with high domes; others look like squarish domes (the popular "sugarloaf" cabochon); others are "buff-topped," showing a somewhat flattened top.

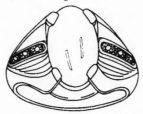

Note the oval's smooth dome-shaped top.

Cabochon cut

Many people around the world prefer the quieter, often more mysterious personality of the cabochon. Some connoisseurs believe cabochons produce a richer color. Whatever the case, today we are seeing much more interest and appreciation for cabochons around the world, and more beautiful cabochons than have been seen in the market in many years.

*Faceted.* A style of cutting that consists of giving to the stone many small faces at varying angles to one another, as in various diamond cuts. The placement, angle, and shape of the faces, or facets, is carefully planned and executed to show the stone's inherent beauty—fire, color, brilliance—to fullest advantage. Today there are many "new" faceted styles, including "fantasy" cuts which combine rounded surfaces with sculpted backs.

# The Importance of Cut

As stated earlier, cutting and proportioning in colored stones are important for two main reasons:

1. They affect the *depth* of color seen in the stone.
2. They affect the *liveliness* projected by the stone.

Color and cutting are the most important criteria in determining the beauty of a colored stone, after which carat weight must be factored in; the higher carat weight will usually increase the price per carat, generally in a nonlinear proportion. If a colored stone was a good quality material to begin with, a good cut will enhance its natural beauty to the fullest and allow it to exhibit its finest color and liveliness. If the same material is cut poorly, its natural beauty will be lessened, causing it to look dark, too light, or even "dead."

Therefore, when you examine a colored stone that looks lively to your eye and has good color—not too dark and not too pale—you can assume the cut is reasonably good. If the stone's color is poor, or if it lacks liveliness, you must examine it for proper cut. If it has been cut properly, you can assume the basic material was poor. If the cut is poor, however, the material may be very good and can perhaps be recut into a beautiful gem. In this case you may want to confer with a knowledgeable cutter to see if it is worthwhile to recut, considering cutting costs and loss in weight. if you don't know any cutters, a reputable jeweler, gemologist-appraiser, or local lapidary club may be able to recommend one.

### Evaluating the cut of a colored gem

When examining the stone for proper cut, a few considerations should guide you:

*Is the shade pleasing, and does the stone have life and brilliance?* If the answer is yes to both questions, then the basic material is probably good, and you must make a decision based on your own personal preferences and budget.

*Is the color too light or too dark?* If so, and if the cut looks good, the basic uncut material was probably too light or too dark to begin with. Consider purchase only if you find the stone pleasing, and only if the price is right, i.e., significantly lower than stones of better color.

*Is the stone's brilliance even, or are there dead spots or flat areas?* Often the brilliance in a colored gemstone is not uniform. If the color is exceptional, subdued brilliance may not have a dramatic effect on its allure, desirability, or value. However, the less fine the color, the more important brilliance becomes.

# Weight

As with diamonds, weight in colored stones is measured in carats. All gems are weighed in carats, except pearls and coral. These materials are sold by the grain, momme, and millimeter. A grain is $\frac{1}{4}$ carat; a momme is 18.75 carats.

Normally, the greater the weight, the greater the value per carat, unless the stones reach unusually large sizes, for example, in excess of 50 carats. At that point, size may become prohibitive for use in some types of jewelry (rings or earrings), selling such large stones can be difficult, and price per carat may drop. There are genuine cut topazes weighing from 2,500 to 12,000 carats, which could be used as paperweights.

As with diamonds, do not confuse *weight* with *size*. Some stones weigh more than others; the density (specific gravity) of the basic material is heavier. Ruby is heavier than emerald, so a one-carat ruby will have a different size than an identically shaped and proportioned emerald; the ruby will be smaller in size since it is heavier. Emerald weighs less than diamond, so a one-carat emerald cut in the same shape and with the same proportioning as a diamond will look larger than the diamond, because it is lighter, and more mass is required to attain the same weight.

Some stones are readily available in large sizes; tourmaline, for example, often occurs in stones over 10 carats. For other stones, sizes over 5 carats may be very rare and therefore considered large, and will also command a proportionately higher price. Examples include precious topaz, alexandrite, demantoid and tsavorite garnets, ruby, and red beryl. With gems that are rare in large sizes, a 10-carat stone can command any price—a king's ransom. A 30-carat blue diamond was sold in 1982 for $9 million. Today, $9 million would be considered a bargain for that stone!

Scarcity of certain sizes among the different colored stones affects the definition of "large" in the colored-gem market. A fine 5-carat alexandrite or ruby is a very large stone; an 18-carat tourmaline is a "nice size."

As with diamonds, stones under 1 carat sell for less per carat than stones over 1 carat. but here it becomes more complicated. The definition of "large" or "rare" sizes differs tremendously, as does price, depending upon the type of stone. For example, an 8-carat tourmaline is an average-size stone, fairly common, and will be priced accordingly. A 5-carat tsavorite is extremely rare, and will command a price proportionately much greater than a 1-carat stone. Precious topaz used to be readily available in 20-carat sizes and larger, but today even 10-carat stones of very fine color are practically nonexistent and their price has jumped tremendously.

The chart of colored gemstones in chapter 15 indicates the availability of stones in large sizes, and shows where scarcity may exist, and at what size.

# Colored Gemstone Certificates

Systems for grading colored gemstones are relatively new and standards are not yet established worldwide. As a result, certificates or grading reports for colored gemstones are not yet used extensively. While diamond grading reports are widely relied upon to describe and confirm diamond quality using precise, universally accepted standards, reports for colored stones have a much more limited value. Nonetheless, reports for colored gems are becoming much more important. Today's synthetics and other newly discovered gemstone materials are creating a need for reports that verify both *identity* (the type of gem) and *genuineness* (whether it is synthetic or not). For any expensive colored gemstone today, especially gems of unusual size or exceptional quality and rarity, we recommend obtaining a report from a recognized laboratory (see appendix). The most widely recognized reports for colored gemstones include those issued in the United States by American Gemological Laboratories, Inc. (AGL), and the GIA Gem Trade Laboratory; in Switzerland, leading firms are Laboratory Gubelin and Schweizerische Stiftung fur Edelstein-Forschung (SSEF).

At the least, colored gemstone reports should identify the gemstone and verify whether it is natural or synthetic. You can also request a *grading report* which will provide, in addition to identity, a full description of the stone and a rating of the color, clarity, brilliance, and other important characteristics. These provide essential information pertaining to the stone's quality. This information is always useful for insurance purposes and can also be helpful if you are comparing several stones with an eye toward purchase.

Where sufficient gemological data can be compiled from careful examination and with proper testing, some reports will also disclose whether or not the stone's color is *natural* or *enhanced* and, if enhanced, by what method. (Reports issued by Laboratory Gubelin, one of the most respected gem testing laboratories in the world, as a matter of policy will not disclose treatments. They believe that since most colored gemstones have been routinely treated in some manner for centuries, it is unimportant and that comparative quality, beauty, and rarity are the important considerations.) Also, depending upon the information the gemologist can obtain from the gemstone during examination, some laboratories will indicate country of origin, if requested. Laboratory Gubelin and AGL *will* indicate origin where possible; GIA will not indicate country of origin.

Fees for colored gemstone reports vary depending upon the type of gem, the type of report requested, and the time, skill and gemological equipment necessary to perform conclusive tests. An estimate can usually be provided by telephoning the laboratory.

When considering a colored gemstone that is accompanied by a report, keep in mind the different types of reports available. Also keep in mind that the information provided on the report is only as reliable as the gemologist performing the evaluation, so be sure the report is issued by a respected laboratory; if in doubt, check with one of the labs listed on page 251 to see if they are familiar with the laboratory in question. Next, ask yourself what the report is really telling you—is it confirming identity and genuineness only? If so, remember that *quality* differences determine value—a genuine one-carat ruby, sapphire, or emerald can sell for $10 or $10,000 or more, depending upon the quality of the particular stone. *Being genuine doesn't mean a stone is valuable.* Only by taking time to look at many stones, ask questions, and make comparisons can you develop an understanding of the differences that affect quality rating, beauty, and value.

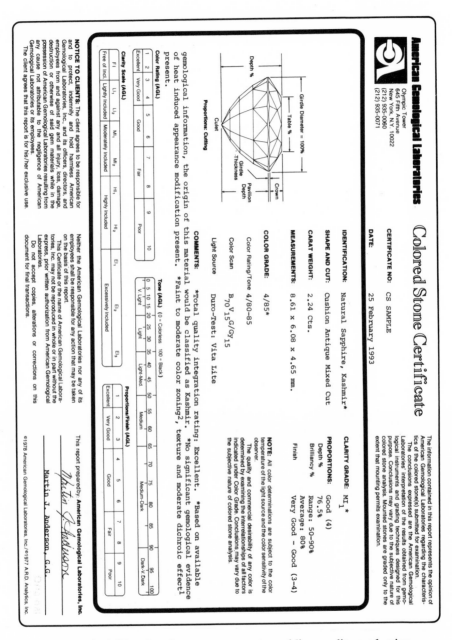

A sample AGL colored gemstone report providing quality evaluation and country of origin.

# 13

## Colored Gemstone Synthesis & Treatment

In addition to the wide variety of natural gemstone alternatives from which to choose today, numerous synthetic and treated materials are available. They make attractive jewelry, but you must understand what you have, and pay the appropriate price for it.

### All Synthetics Are Not the Same

Scientific advances and new technology has resulted in a whole world of *synthetic* gemstone materials, but it's important to understand that a synthetic is *not* an imitation. Technically, the term "synthetic" indicates that the material is made by man *using the same chemical ingredients found in natural products;* in other words, using Mother Nature's recipe. This means that a synthetic gemstone will have essentially the same physical, chemical, and optical properties observed in natural gemstones. From a practical standpoint, this also means that they will respond to various gem-identification tests the same way as natural stones. This can make them difficult to distinguish from the natural gem.

An *imitation* is also made by man, but not by using "nature's recipe," so it is very different physically and chemically from the gem it is imitating, and very easy to separate from the natural gem with standard gem identification techniques. For example, a glass "gem" is an imitation. Red glass could imitate ruby. But it resembles ruby only *in color;* a quick examination with a simple jeweler's loupe would reveal telltale signs that it is glass, and any gemological test would clearly corroborate this conclusion.

Today there are numersous synthetic gems, but they are not all produced the same way. Some are produced inexpensively and, although they are made with nature's recipe, they don't really look like the natural gem. They are made quickly ("flame fusion"), by a process very different from nature's. These are often confused with imitations because of their unnatural appearance and low cost. This type of synthetic is widely available today, and has been made for almost 100 years.

In recent years, technological advances have enabled scientists to create environments which come much closer to duplicating what is found in nature. As a result, crystals can actually be "grown" in laboratories, creating a product that very closely resembles the natural gem. These are called "flux-grown," "created," or "laboratory-grown" synthetics.

Laboratory-grown synthetics are expensive to produce and cost much more than other synthetics; in fact, the cost can be so high that consumers sometime mistakenly conclude they are natural gemstones. Next to the natural, there is nothing that can compare to a fine lab-grown synthetic, and even though the stone may be expensive, it is only a fraction of the cost of a rare, natural gem with a comparable appearance. Synthetics can make excellent alternatives for buyers unable to afford a natural gem in the quality they desire. Be sure, however, not to confuse terms such as "created" or "grown" with *naturally* created or grown. All synthetic products are made by man. Also, remember that inexpensive synthetics are abundant, so be sure you have a lab-grown synthetic and not an inexpensive type if you are paying a premium for it. As you shop around and compare various synthetic products, you will find that there are significant visual differences among them. Develop an eye for the type you want.

# Gemstone Treatment Is Routine in Today's Jewelry Scene

For hundreds of years mankind has been enhancing natural colored gems. In most cases the trade finds the practice acceptable because the prevailing attitude is that these treatments simply continue the process that Mother Nature started; all gems are exposed to heat, and many to radiation, as they are forming in nature. Today certain gems are routinely heated or exposed to some type of radiation to change or enhance their color, and pricing is based on the assumption that enhancement has occurred. On the other hand, if the color of a gem is very fine, and if it can be documented that the color is *natural*, the stone will command a *much higher price*. Such gems are very rare today and are sought by collectors and connoisseurs. Some of the best sources for fine, natural-color gems are major estate pieces that sometimes reenter the market when well-known international auction houses such as Sotheby's and Christie's hold their "Magnificent" or "Important" jewelry sales.

Whether from an auction house or another source, fine rare gems with natural color normally will be accompanied by a gem testing report verifying that fact. Without a report, or any representations to the contrary, assume that the color of any gemstone sold today has been enhanced in some manner. When buying any expensive rare gem represented to have natural color, be sure it is accompanied by a report from a respected gem-testing lab that verifies this fact, or make the purchase contingent upon getting a report.

## Heating

Subjecting certain gems to sophisticated heating procedures is a practice that is hundreds of years old and is accepted within the jewelry industry as long as the change induced is *permanent*. Most sapphires and rubies are heated. The treatment may lighten, darken, or completely change the color. A skilled gemologist or gem-testing laboratory can often determine whether or not the color of these gems has been altered by heating by examining the stone's *inclusions* under the microscope. Sapphire and ruby, for example, can withstand high temperatures, but often the heat causes small crystal inclusions present inside the stone to melt or explode. These altered inclusions then provide the evidence of heating.

It may be easy to determine that a stone *has* been heated, but it is often impossible to know for certain that it has *not* been, that is, that its color is natural. Making this determination can require a high degree of skill and sophisticated equipment, often only available at a major laboratory such as GIA; even then, it may not be possible to ascertain definitively. Gemologists must carefully examine the internal characteristics of the particular stone. Sometimes they see an unaltered inclusion that would lead to a conclusion that the color is natural; other times they see an altered inclusion that indicates treatment; and sometimes the inclusions, or changes and abnormalities in them, that one seeks to make a positive determination simply are not present. When there is nothing inside the gem to indicate whether it has or has not been heated, we cannot be sure.

## Radiation

Radiation techniques are relatively new. Frequently used on a wide range of gemstones, radiation is sometimes combined with heating. The effect is permanent on some stones, and accepted in the trade; it is not acceptable on other stones because the color fades or changes back to its original over a relatively short time. There are still some questions regarding radiation levels and the long-term effects on health. The Nuclear Regulatory Agency has been working to establish standards, and the GIA Gem Trade Laboratory now has a facility with the capability to test gemstones for "acceptable" and "unacceptable" radiation levels.

## Diffusion treatment

Diffusion is a newcomer to the world of treated gemstones and is already surrounded by controversy. Diffusion (sometimes called "deep diffusion" or "surface diffusion") is a process which alters the color of a gem by exposing the surface to certain chemicals (the same used by nature) and heating it over a prolonged period of time. At present the procedure has only been used successfully to produce *blue sapphire,* although diffused ruby may become available in the near future. The material being treated, however, is usually *colorless* or very, very pale sapphire, and *the beautiful color produced by the treatment is confined to the surface of the gem only.* If you sliced a diffused sapphire in half, you would see an essentially colorless stone, with a very narrow rim of blue along its perimeter. This could create a problem if the stone is ever badly chipped or nicked and needs to be recut or polished; the surface color might be removed in the recutting, leaving a colorless sapphire in its place. The treatment could be repeated, should this happen, to restore the original color. When repeated on a previously diffused stone, the process requires less time, and the restored color is virtually identical to the original.

It is possible that the process will be improved to produce a treatment in which color penetrates the entire stone. At this time, however, "deep" diffusion simply means the color penetrates a little deeper than in the earliest diffused stones. The color is still confined to the surface.

Fortunately, the presence of diffused sapphire in the jewelry market should not cause alarm because it is really easy for gemologists to detect in most stones. Unfortunately, however, many surface-diffused blue sapphires have been found mixed in with parcels of non-diffused sapphires and some may inadvertently have been set in jewelry and sold. So it is important to buy any fine blue sapphire only from a knowledgeable, reputable jeweler. We also recommend double-checking for diffusion to avoid any unintentional misrepresentation. Ask your jeweler if he or she has the means to check for you; in most cases it is a simple, quick test with an "immersion cell." If this is not possible, be sure to make the sale contingent upon the stone's not being diffused and take it to a gemologist for verification. You or your jeweler can also submit it to the GIA Gem Trade Lab. If you should find the stone is diffused, you should have no problem exchanging it, getting a reduced price, or obtaining a refund.

Diffused sapphire offers a beautiful "blue" at a very affordable price (about one-sixth the normal cost of blue sapphire). Just be sure you know whether or not the stone is diffused. If it is, pay the right price for it, and exercise some care in wearing and handling.

## Affordable Beauty

Treated gemstones can be a way for consumers to own lovely pieces at affordable prices. The most important consideration, here as in all purchases of gemstones, is to know exactly what you are buying. While some fraudulent practices involving treated stones certainly exist (see chapter 14), the selling of treated gemstones is perfectly legitimate so long as all the facts are disclosed, the type of treatment used for enhancement is acceptable in the trade, and all important representations are stated on the bill of sale. With these safeguards you can be reasonably secure about the purchase you are contemplating and can enjoy the fine color and beauty of a treated stone for many years come.

# 14

# Fraud & Misrepresentation in Colored Gems

We would like to begin by emphasizing here, as we did in the chapter on diamonds, that the percentage of misrepresentation and fraud among total jewelry transactions is quite low, and that most jewelers are reputable professionals in whom you can place your trust. In the colored gem market, there is a greater occurrence of misrepresentation than in the diamond market, however, primarily because of the scientifically complex nature of colored stones. So it is even more important to be aware of the deceptive practices you might encounter when buying a colored gem, both to protect yourself from the more obvious scams, and to better understand the importance of dealing with a reliable jeweler. We also stress the importance, to an even greater degree, of seeking verification from a qualified gemologist—one with extensive experience with colored gems—when buying any expensive colored gem. Take precautions that your gemstone is what it is represented to be.

## Misrepresenting Synthetic as Natural

Today it is very important to verify the genuineness of any fine, valuable gemstone because the new generation of synthetic products is so similar to the natural that the two can be easily confused. As we discussed in chapter 13, many very fine synthetics are available, and they can make attractive jewelry choices when properly represented. Still, you should protect yourself from intentional and sometimes *unintentional* misrepresentation.

Synthetics have been on the market for many years. Good synthetic sapphires, rubies, and spinels have been manufactured commercially since the early 1900s, and very good synthetic emeralds since the 1940s. While these early synthetics were attractive and popular because of their very low price, they didn't really look like natural stones. Most looked "too good to be true," so that they were readily distinguished from the real thing by a competent jeweler.

Today, this is often not the case. While older techniques for producing synthetics are still used and their products still easy to recognize, new, sophisticated methods result in products that no longer possess the signature characteristics with which gem dealers and jewelers have long been familiar. To further complicate matters of identification, synthetics now often contain characteristics very similar to their natural counterparts. As a result, some are being sold as natural, intentionally and unintentionally. A gemologist with extensive experience, or a gem testing laboratory such as GIA or AGL, however, can differentiate between them and verify genuineness.

A true experience dramatically illustrates why making the extra effort required to verify genuineness is so important. We know a jeweler with an excellent reputation for honesty, reliability, and professional expertise. He had been in the business for many years and had extensive gemological training. Nonetheless, he bought a new-type synthetic ruby as a natural stone, then sold it to a customer for just under $10,000.

His customer, who had purchased the stone at a reasonable price, proceeded to resell it to a third party for a quick profit. The third party took it to a very competent gemologist with a reputation for having the skill and equipment necessary to identify new synthetic materials. The truth about the stone quickly came to light. The second and third parties in this case lost nothing (one of the benefits of buying from a reputable jeweler). The jeweler, however, suffered both a heavy financial loss and considerable damage to his reputation.

You may ask how he made such a mistake. It was easy. He was knowledgeable, like many other jewelers, and thought he knew how to distinguish a natural from a synthetic stone. But he had not kept current on technological advances and new synthetic products entering the marketplace. So he made the purchase of this lovely stone over-the-counter from a private party who had procured it in the Orient. Many of these new synthetics are produced in the United States and then find their way to the Orient—the source of many natural stones—where they are more easily sold as the "real thing." The jeweler had no recourse, because he had no way of locating the seller, who had simply walked in off the street.

As this story shows, it is essential to have a highly qualified gemologist verify authenticity, particularly for fine rubies, emeralds, and sapphires. Thousands of dollars may be at stake, for jewelers may innocently buy one of these stones believing it to be natural, and pass their error on to the customer. Don't delude yourself into believing that if a piece is purchased from a well-respected firm it is always what it is represented to be; even the best-known firms have made mistakes in this area. It may be inconvenient to obtain an expert analysis, and it may require an additional expense, but we believe it is better to be safe now than sorry later.

With sophisticated modern equipment and a greater knowledge of crystals, man can now "create" or "grow" almost any gemstone. As a general rule, remember that any gem—amethyst, alexandrite, ruby, emerald, sapphire, opal—even turquoise—could be synthetic; that many synthetics are themselves expensive; and that most have become more difficult to distinguish from their natural counterparts, resulting in inadvertent misrepresentation. So make sure you take time to verify a stone's true identity.

## Simulated stones

As already discussed (see chapter 13), simulated or imitation stones should not be confused with synthetics, which possess essentially the same physical, chemical, and optical properties of the natural gem. A simulated stone is usually a very inexpensive man-made imitation which resembles the natural stone in *color,* but little else. Many imitations are glass, but they can also be plastic. Imitations, or "simulants," as they are also called, are very easily differentiated from the genuine by careful visual examination and simple gemological testing. There are glass simulations of all the colored stones, and glass and plastic simulated pearls, turquoise, and amber are also common.

Imitations are frequently found in estate jewelry, sometimes mixed with natural gems in the same piece.

## Look-alike substitution

Another form of deception involves misrepresenting a more common, less expensive stone for a rarer, more expensive gem of similar color. Today, as more and more natural gemstones in a wide variety of colors enter the market, both deliberate and accidental misrepresentation can occur.

# Color Alteration

As we discussed in chapter 13, color enhancement of gemstones is ages old, and many of the techniques used today have been used for generations. Many are routine, and do not in themselves constitute fraud. Some treatments, however, should not be applied to certain gems, normally because the results are not permanent and color may revert to the original. Such treatments are not accepted by the trade.

Because color enhancement is so common, it's important for the consumer to understand exactly which procedures are acceptable in the industry and which represent deceptive or fraudulent practices aimed at passing off inferior stones as much more expensive ones.

Here we will discuss various treatments, and explain which are routine, and which may constitute fraud or misrepresentation.

## Heat treated stones

Subjecting stones to sophisticated heating procedures is the most commonly used method of changing or enhancing a gem's color and is used routinely on a variety of gems to lighten, darken, or completely change color. Heat treatment is not a fraudulent practice when used on certain gems, on which the results are permanent. This procedure is an accepted practice routinely applied to the following:

*Sapphire*—to lighten or intensify color; to improve uniformity

*Amber*—to deepen color and add "sun spangles"

*Aquamarine*—to deepen color and remove any greenish undertone to produce a "bluer" blue

*Tanzanite*—to produce a more desirable blue shade

*Tourmaline*—to lighten the darker shades, usually of the green variety

*Amethyst*—to lighten color; to change color of pale material to "yellow" stones sold as citrine and topaz

*Citrine*—often produced by heating other varieties of quartz

*Topaz*—in combination with radiation, to produce shades of blue; to produce pink

*Zircon*—to produce red, blue, or colorless stones

*Kunzite*—to improve color

*Morganite*—to change color from orange to pinkish

The color obtained by these heating procedures is usually permanent.

## Radiated stones

Radiation techniques are now in common use, produced by any of several methods, each of which has a specific application. Sometimes radiation is used in combination with heat treatment. As long as the technique produces stable results, color enhancement by radiation techniques is not considered fraudulent.

Radiation techniques are routinely used for the following stones:

*Aquamarine*—used in conjunction with heat to improve blue

*Diamond*—to change the color from an off-white color to a fancy color—green, yellow, etc.

*Topaz*—to change from colorless or nearly colorless to blue; to intensify yellow and orange shades

*Tourmaline*—to intensify pink, red, purple shades.

*Pearl*—to produce blue and shades of gray ("black" pearls)

*Yellow beryl*—often produced by radiation

Some very deep blue topazes have been found to be radioactive and may be harmful to the wearer. Most blue topaz sold in the United States since 1992 has been tested for radiation level by the GIA or other centers established for that purpose. Exercise caution when purchasing deep blue topaz outside the United States, in countries where radiation testing is not required.

As far as we know now, the color changes resulting from radiation treatment on the above stones are usually permanent. Some stones subjected to radiation, however, obtain a beautiful color that is temporary. Some irradiated "blue" and "yellow" sapphire will fade quickly. Irradiation of sapphire is not accepted in the trade. We have seen nice "yellow" sapphires treated by radiation quickly lose their color when exposed to the flame of a cigarette lighter. If you are considering a "yellow," it may be worthwhile to try this simple flame test if the jeweler will permit. If not, be sure to have it "fade" tested by a qualified gemologist or gem lab.

The color of fancy-colored diamonds can usually be verified as "natural" or "irradiated." However, for most other gems on which radiation is used, testing procedures for determining whether or not color is natural have not been developed as of this date.

### Diffusion treated stones

Diffusion treatment involves introducing chemicals (titanium and iron, the same coloring agents present in natural blue sapphire) into the surface of colorless or nearly colorless sapphire, and heating the stone over a prolonged period. This treatment produces a lovely blue color, but on the surface of the stone only; the center remains colorless.

Diffused sapphires are being substituted for non-diffused sapphires by unscrupulous merchants and purchased by dealers and jewelers unknowingly in parcels of stones that are subsequently mounted in jewelry. They are also appearing in antique and estate jewelry. When buying any fine sapphire today, it is important to purchase from a knowledgeable, reputable jeweler, and be especially wary of bargains! Note: Diffusion treated *ruby* may soon be available and warrant the same caution.

### Dyed stones

Gemstones have been dyed since earliest times. Numerous examples of dyed chalcedony (an inexpensive variety of quartz) can be found in antique jewelry, imitating other gems. Gems that are frequently dyed include jade, opal, coral, lapis, and to a lesser degree poor-quality star rubies, star sapphires, and emeralds.

Dyed material may be very stable, but it can also be very temporary. We've seen dyed lapis in which the "blue" came off with a cotton ball moistened in fingernail polish remover. Dyed gems may be genuine stones which have been dyed to enhance their color (as in dyeing pale green jadeite to a deeper green), or they may be a different gem altogether.

Dyed gems should always cost less than gems with natural color. Fine lapis and jadeite should always be checked for dyeing. Here are some other gemstones that often are dyed:

*Chalcedony*—dyed to produce "black onyx," which rarely occurs naturally, and "banded agate" with white bands alternating with strong colored bands; dyed reddish brown to sell as carnelian (which also occurs naturally); dyed green to imitate fine jadeite or chrysoprase (which also occurs naturally)

*Jade* (jadeite)—color frequently improved by dyeing to a beautiful emerald or young grass green color, to look like "imperial" jade. While jade occurs naturally in almost every color, it may also be dyed other colors.

*Coral and lapis*—dyed to deepen the color, or create more uniform color

*Swiss lapis*—jasper dyed blue and sold as "lapis" or "Swiss lapis"

## Blackening techniques

These are used to alter color, not by dyeing but by introducing a chemical reaction (sugar-acid chemical reaction) that introduces black carbon, which blackens the color. The following stones are commonly exposed to this treatment:

*Opal*—to blacken so as to resemble the more valuable, precious black opal

*Black onyx*—chalcedony is blackened by this technique to create the black onyx used today in most jewelry

## Waxing

This is a process consisting of rubbing the stone with a tinted wax-like substance to hide surface cracks and blemishes and to slightly improve the color. This is used often on cheaper Indian star rubies, and sometimes on star sapphires.

## Oiling

This technique is commonly used on emeralds. The emerald is soaked in oil (which may or may not be tinted green). Its purpose is to fill fine cracks, which are fairly common in emerald. These cracks look whitish and therefore weaken the green body color of the emerald. The oil fills the cracks, making them "disappear," and thereby improves the color by eliminating the white.

This is an accepted procedure and will normally last for many years. However, if the stone is put in a hot ultrasonic cleaner (which is dangerous to any emerald and *never* recommended), or soaked in an organic solvent such as gasoline, xylene, or substances containing these, such as paint remover, the oil may be slowly dissolved out of the cracks and the whitish blemishes will then reappear, weakening the color. If this should happen, the stone can be reoiled. Using green-tinted oil, however, is not an accepted trade practice.

## Painting

This technique is often used with cabochon (nonfaceted) transparent ("jelly") or semi-transparent opals to create a stone that looks like precious black opal. This is done by putting the stone in a closed-back setting that has a high rim (bezel). A black cement or paint is spread on the inside of the setting so that when the opal is placed inside, the light entering it gets trapped and reflected back, giving the opal the appearance of a fine black opal. (See also the section below, describing composite stones and opal doublets.)

## Foil-backed stones

This technique is not frequently encountered in modern jewelry, but anyone interested in antique jewelry should be aware of it. It is seen with both nonfaceted and faceted stones, set usually in a closed-back mounting. This technique involves lining the inside of the setting with silver or gold *foil* to add brilliance and sparkle (as with foil-backed glass imitating diamond), or with colored foil to change or enhance color by projecting color into the stone. Always be apprehensive when considering a piece of jewelry that has a closed back. While relatively common in antique jewelry, foil backing is also seen in modern jewelry.

We recently examined a heavy, yellow-gold cross set with five fine, flawless emeralds which appeared to have exceptionally fine green body color. The stones were set "in the gold" so that the backs of the stone couldn't be seen. Our suspicions were aroused, since the emeralds were all flawless and the color was so uniformly fine. Upon closer examination it became clear that the green body color was projected into the stones by a fine emerald-green foil back. The stones were probably not even emerald, but near-colorless aquamarines. Since both aquamarine and emerald belong to the same mineral family (beryl—emerald is the name given to the rare green variety of beryl, while we call the more common blue variety aquamarine), an inexperienced jeweler or gemologist using standard, basic procedures to identify the stones could have erroneously identified them as fine emeralds.

## Smoking

This is a technique used only on opals. It is used to give off-white to tan-colored opals from Mexico a more desirable, moderately dark coffee-brown color that greatly enhances the opal fire. It consists of taking a cut and polished opal, wrapping it tightly in brown paper, and putting it in a covered container over moderate heat until the paper is completely charred. When cooled and removed, the opal now has a much more intense brown body color and fire. But if this smoke-produced color coating were to be badly scratched, the underlying color would show through and the stone would have to be resmoked.

This treatment can be easily detected by wetting the stone (preferably with saliva). While wet, some of the fire disappears, and then reappears after the surface has dried.

### Fracture filling

As with diamonds, fractures which break the surface of a colored gem can be filled with a liquid glass or glass-like substance. The filler makes the crack less visible and improves the stone's overall appearance. A coloring agent can also be added to the filler to simultaneously improve the stone's overall color. Selling a filled gem without disclosure is not an accepted trade practice. To do so knowingly constitutes fraud, but it's being done, nonetheless, with increasing frequency.

## Composite Stones

Composite stones are exactly what the term implies—stones composed of more than one part. Composites come in two basic types. Doublets are composite stones consisting of two parts, sometimes held together by a colored bonding agent. Triplets are composite stones consisting of three parts, usually glued together to a colored middle part.

Colorless synthetic spinel ——

Colored layer ——

Colorless synthetic spinel ——

Soudé type

Line of fusion

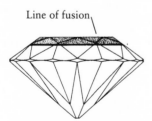

Garnet-topped doublet

When some composite stones are immersed in *liquid* (such as alcohol or methylene iodide) one can often see two or three distinct parts. With soudé emeralds, the top and bottom may seem to disappear, leaving only a green plane visible across the girdle area. (Note: Immersion will not reveal garnet-topped doublets.)

## Doublets

Doublets are especially important to know about because, while widely used in antique jewelry before the development of synthetics, today they are making a comeback and reappearing throughout the jewelry market.

In antique pieces, the most commonly encountered doublet, often referred to as a *false doublet,* consisted of a red garnet top fused to an appropriately colored glass bottom. With the right combination, any colored gem could be simulated by this method. Garnets were used for the top portion of these false doublets because they possessed nice luster and excellent durability and were readily available in great quantity, which made them very inexpensive.

Another form of the doublet is made from two parts of a colorless material, fused together with an appropriately colored bonding agent. An "emerald" (sometimes sold as "soudé" emerald) can be made, for example, using a colorless synthetic spinel top and bottom, held together in the middle (at the girdle) by green glue. Red glue or blue glue could be used to simulate ruby or sapphire.

*True doublets* are created by using two *genuine* stone parts, fusing them together with an appropriately colored glue to create a "larger" gem of better color than the original components. For example, we sometimes see emerald doublets composed of two parts of genuine *pale green* emerald, fused with deep green glue to create a large, deep green "gem" emerald.

A clever version of a true doublet which we sometimes still encounter is a "sapphire" doublet composed of two pieces of genuine sapphire, but pale yellow sapphire fused together with blue glue. This creates an especially convincing "fine blue sapphire." The same techniques are used to make ruby doublets, although they don't look as convincing. And the same basic procedures can produce emerald doublets, using beryl instead of sapphire.

Opal doublets also occur, usually consisting of a thin top layer of genuine opal cemented to a base that can be either a poorer grade of opal or some other substance altogether. The most commonly encountered opal doublets are those made to look like the precious black opal. This doublet is usually composed of a translucent or transparent top that is cemented by black cement to a bottom portion of cheaper opal or other material that acts as a support. Please note that the tops of these "black opal" doublets are usually not genuine black opal, though they certainly look like it.

Opal doublets are also made by cementing a thin piece of fine opal to a larger piece of less fine opal to create a larger overall appearance. The doublets can be identified by observing the *join* of the two pieces at the girdle; you can see the dark line of the cement between the two pieces.

Because so many doublets are flooding the market, those who love sapphire, ruby, and emerald must be particularly careful and buy only from reputable jewelers. We know a woman who paid $16,000 recently for a pair of "genuine" emerald earrings from a jeweler on New York's 47th Street. They contained four "soudé" emerald doublets and were worth only a couple hundred dollars, and that for the gold and diamonds in the settings. Luckily, this woman had all the right information on the bill of sale, discovered the error in time, and was able to return the pieces and get her money back from the jeweler.

It is alarming to see the large number of ruby and sapphire doublets consisting of genuine tops—usually nearly colorless or a very inexpensive greenish-brown color—and synthetic sapphire and ruby bottoms that are being sold as genuine. Avoid "bargains" from any merchant unless you can check them out and be especially wary of street peddlars when travelling in Asia and South America. We've seen an incredible number of doublets in jewelry and "unmounted" stones brought back by unsuspecting travelers, especially those journeying to exotic spots known for gems.

Many of the doublets now appearing in jewelry sold by reputable firms were originally slipped in with genuine stones shipped to buyers around the world. Since doublets are difficult to spot and will even pass four gemological tests providing positive identification, it is easy to pass one on to a customer unknowingly, especially when set in sleek, modern "bezel" settings.

## Jewelry manufacturers offer true doublets as affordable alternative to natural gems

On the other hand, we are also seeing, for the first time, the legitimate marketing by manufacturers of doublets as an affordable and desirable alternative to natural stones. One company is mass-producing an emerald doublet that, like those described earlier, consists of two parts of colorless beryl (the mineral we call emerald when green, aquamarine when blue) fused together with green glue to produce a composite being sold as the "Lannyte Emerald Doublet."

There is nothing wrong with buying a doublet as long as you know what you are buying, and pay a fair price. Just be careful not to buy a doublet unknowingly. Be sure to verify all the facts.

## Triplets

Triplets are frequently encountered in the opal market and have substantially replaced the doublet there. The triplet is exactly like the opal doublet except that it has a cabochon-shaped colorless quartz cap (the third part) that covers the entire doublet, giving the delicate doublet greater protection from breakage and providing greater luminescence (brightness) to the stone.

With careful examination a competent jeweler or gemologist should be able to easily differentiate a doublet or triplet from a natural. We should note, however, that detection of an opal doublet may be very difficult if it is set in a mounting with a rim (bezel set) covering the seam where the two pieces are cemented together. It might be necessary to remove the stone from its setting for positive identification. Because of opal's fragile nature, removal must be performed only by a very competent bench jeweler (a jeweler who actually makes or repairs jewelry), and he may agree to do so only at your risk, not wanting to assume responsibility for any breakage. In the case of a black opal worth several thousand dollars, it is well worth the additional cost and inconvenience to be sure it is not a doublet worth only a few hundred dollars. Always be apprehensive when buying a "flat-topped opal" that is bezel-set.

# Misleading Names

Another form of misrepresentation occurs when colored stones are called by names that lead the buyer to believe they are something they are not. This practice is frequently encountered, especially outside the United States. When any stone is described with a qualifier, as in "Rio Topaz" or "Zambian emerald," be sure to ask whether the stone is a genuine, natural stone. Ask why there is a qualifier.

Let's examine two examples: "Japanese amethyst" and "Ceylon Sapphire." In the case of Japanese amethyst, the stone is not genuine, but synthetic and the name, therefore, is clearly misleading. However, in the case of the Ceylon sapphire, "Ceylon" refers to the location from which that gem was mined, and most Ceylon sapphires are always a particular tone of blue (a lighter shade, and very lively). Furthermore, because of their particular color, Ceylon sapphires sell for more per carat than certain other varieties, such as Australian or Thai. Therefore, in this case," Ceylon" is very important to the stone's complete description.

Let's look at one more example, Ceylon-*colored* sapphire. In this case, the qualifier is the word "colored." In most cases the presence of this word implies some type of color alteration or treatment. A Ceylon-colored sapphire is not a Ceylon sapphire but a sapphire that has been treated to obtain the Ceylon color.

There is nothing actually wrong with selling "Japanese amethyst" or "Ceylon-colored sapphire," or other similarly named stones, as long as they are properly represented and priced. Then the decision becomes yours—either you like it or you don't; it meets your emotional need for an amethyst or Ceylon sapphire or it doesn't; and the price is right or it isn't. The following lists provide some examples of names to be aware of—"descriptive" names that are important to the stone's complete description; and misnomers, misleading names that are meant to do exactly that, mislead:

| DESCRIPTIVE NAMES | MISNOMERS (and What They Really Are) |
|---|---|
| **DIAMOND** | |
| *Canary diamond* (refers to fancy *intense* yellow color) | *Alaska diamond* (hematite) |
| *Fancy diamond* (refers to colored diamond) | *Arkansas diamond* (quartz) (although genuine diamond is found in Arkansas) |
| | *Bohemian diamond* (quartz) |
| | *Cape May diamond* (quartz) |
| | *Ceylon diamond* (zircon) |
| | *Herkimer diamond* (quartz) |
| | *Kenya diamond* (rutile) |
| | *Matura diamond* (zircon) |
| | *Mogok diamond* (topaz) |
| | *Pennsylvania diamond* (pyrite) |
| | *Radium diamond* (smoky quartz) |
| | *Rainbow diamond* (rutile) |
| | *Rangoon diamond* (zircon) |
| | *Rhine diamond* (quartz; original rhinestone) |

| DESCRIPTIVE NAMES | MISNOMERS (and What They Really Are) |
|---|---|

## EMERALD

*Brazilian emerald* (refers to emerald mined in Brazil)

*Colombian emerald* (refers to emerald mined in Colombia. The best Colombian emerald is considered the finest. It is rare and very expensive.)

*Zambian emerald* (refers to emerald mined in Zambia)

*African emerald* (refers to emerald mined in Africa)

*Esmeralda emerald* (green tourmaline)
*Evening emerald* (peridot)
*Mascot emerald* (doublet)
*Oriental emerald* (green sapphire)
*Soudé emerald* (doublet)

## JADE

*Ax stone* (nephrite jade)
*California jade* (both jadeite and nephrite jade)
*Greenstone* (nephrite jade, New Zealand)
*Imperial jade* (fine, gem-quality jadeite jade)
*Jade* (both nephrite jade and also jadeite jade)
*Kidney stone* (nephrite)
*Maori* (nephrite jade from New Zealand)
*Spinach jade* (nephrite jade)

*African jade* (green massive garnet)
*Australian jade* (chrysoprase quartz)
*Colorado jade* (amazonite feldspar)
*Fukien jade* (soapstone)
*Honan jade* (soapstone)
*Indian jade* (aventurine quartz)
*Korea jade* (serpentine [bowenite])
*Manchurian jade* (soapstone)
*Mexican jade* (dyed green calcite)
*New jade* (serpentine [bowenite])
*Oregon jade* (dark green jasper [quartz])
*Soochow jade* (serpentine or soapstone)
*Swiss jade* (dyed green jasper [quartz])
*Virginia jade* (amazonite, variety feldspar)

## OPAL

*Andamooka opal* (a type of opal from Andamooka Australia)

*Black opal* (a rare type of genuine opal with a dark body color)

*Boulder opal* (a type of genuine opal in which brown host rock may be seen)

*Gilson opal* (imitation or synthetic)
*Slocum opal* (imitation) Japanese opal (plastic imitation)

| DESCRIPTIVE NAMES | MISNOMERS (and What They Really Are) |
|---|---|

**OPAL cont.**

*Fire opal* (opal with strong reddish or orangish color, mostly from Mexico)

*Harlequin opal* (very rare genuine opal that exhibits a "harlequin" pattern)

*Jelly opal* (a transparent type of opal that has a jelly-like appearance)

---

**PEARLS**

*Biwa pearl* (a freshwater cultured pearl grown in Lake Biwa, Japan)

*Cultured pearl* (Pearl with a mother-of-pearl nucleus implanted by man.)

*Oriental pearl* (genuine, natural pearl)

*Atlas pearls* (imitation-satinspar type gypsum beads)

*Girasol pearls* (imitation)

*Laguna pearls* (imitation)

*Majorica pearls* (imitation)

*Red Sea pearls* (coral beads)

*Tecla pearls* (pink conch pearl)

---

**RUBY**

*African ruby* (ruby from Africa)

*Burma ruby* (ruby from Burma—most desirable red color; most expensive)

*Ceylon ruby* (ruby from Sri Lanka [Ceylon])

*Thai ruby* (ruby from Thailand)

*Almandine ruby* (garnet)

*Australian ruby* (garnet)

*Balas ruby* (spinel)

*Bohemian ruby* (garnet)

*Cape ruby* (garnet)

*Ruby spinel* (spinel)

*Siberian ruby* (tourmaline)

---

**SAPPHIRE**

*Australian sapphire* (sapphire from Australia)

*Burmese sapphire* (sapphire from Burma; fine and expensive

*Ceylon sapphire* (fine sapphire from Ceylon; very fine lighter blue than Burmese)

*Kashmir sapphire* (sapphire from Kashmir; fine and expensive)

*Montana sapphire* (sapphire from Montana)

*Oriental sapphire* (an older term that means "genuine")

*Thai sapphire* (sapphire from Thailand)

*Brazilian sapphire* (blue tourmaline. Brazil also has sapphire but they are called simply "sapphire.")

*Lux sapphire* (iolite)

*Water sapphire* (iolite)

| DESCRIPTIVE NAMES | MISNOMERS (and What They Really Are) |
|---|---|

**TOPAZ**

| | |
|---|---|
| *Precious* (Imperial) topaz (usually fine appricot brown) | *Madeira topaz* (citrine quartz) |
| | *Occidental topaz* (citrine quartz)* |
| | *Palmeira topaz* (citrine quartz) |
| | *Rio topaz* (citrine quartz) |
| | *Saffranite topaz* (citrine quartz) |
| | *Scottish topaz* (citrine quartz) |
| | *Smokey topaz* (smokey quartz) |
| | *Spanish topaz* (citrine quartz |

*Much of the citrine quartz as seen on the market today is produced by heating the purple variety (amethyst). This heating alters the color from purple to shades of yellow, yellow- brown, or golden yellow.

# Other Names You Might See

## Names

## What They Really Are

| Names | What They Really Are |
|---|---|
| Aquagem | light blue synthetic spinel |
| Black amber | jet |
| California moonstone | chalcedony quartz |
| California turquoise | variscite |
| Esmeralda | green tourmaline |
| German lapis | dyed blue jasper (quartz) |
| Goldstone | man-made glass with copper crystals |
| Hematine | imitation hematite |
| Hematite garnet | iron (YIG) equivalent to YAG |
| Imperial yu stone (*yu* is the Chinese word for jade) | fine green aventurine quartz |
| Japanese amethyst | synthetic amethyst |
| Oriental chrysoberyl | yellow green sapphire |
| Oriental topaz | yellow sapphire |
| Rose zircon | synthetic pink spinel |
| Saffronite | yellow citrine quartz |
| South Sea cat's-eye | operculum, door of a univalve shellfish |
| Swiss lapis | dyed blue jasper (quartz) |

# 15

## Buying Colored Gems

When you go to buy colored gemstones today, you will find yourself immersed in color—every hue, every shade of the spectrum. There has never been a more exciting time to search for a colored gem because there have never been so many alternatives. Whatever color you prefer, and whatever your budget, there is a sparkling natural gem awaiting your discovery.

You will see "new" gems only recently discovered—emerald-green garnets (tsavorite), blue and green tanzanite (technically, the green variety should be called green zoisite, since *blue* zoisite is what we know as tanzanite), "neon" tourmalines from Brazil (Paraiba, also called Hetorita) in blue and green shades never seen before. Sapphires abound in virtually every color, as do tourmaline. Even diamond can now be seen in a wide variety of natural "fancy" colors (some at very "fancy" prices).

The new colors are exciting, but so are the new cuts; there are unusual shapes in both faceted and cabochon (or nonfaceted) cuts, "fancy" and "fantasy" cuts, "sculpted" cuts.

In the following pages we will present some of the most popular gemstone alternatives, by color, and a guide to how they compare in terms of price, availability, and wearability. Then the gems will be discussed individually.

## Guides to Popular Gems

The following charts show what stones are available in various colors, as well as their wearability, price, and availability. Chapter 16 describes the stones—beginning with "precious" and followed alphabetically by the other popular gem families—and provides important information particular to each. It should be noted that the terms *precious* and *semiprecious* are discouraged today since they can be

145

misleading; rubies, sapphires, and emeralds are only "precious" in rare qualities, and there are many "semiprecious" gemstones today that are rarer and more valuable than so-called "precious" gems.

Prices quoted are for faceted gemstones. Cabochon-cut stones often cost less. Prices shown are for "good" to "extra fine" quality. Gems used in mass-produced jewelry sold in many jewelry stores are often "commercial" quality and may cost significantly less than prices indicated here. Also, note that it is rare to find gems sold by jewelry retailers that exceed the prices shown for "extra fine" quality. Rare gems in exceptionally fine quality and rare stones of unusual size can sell for much more than the prices indicated here. If the price of a gem you are considering is higher than what we indicate, we strongly recommend taking extra steps to confirm its exceptional quality prior to purchase; in some cases we would recommend having the seller obtain a quality grading report from the American Gemological Laboratory.

This guide's purpose is twofold: to help you understand how prices for different gems in a given color *compare with one another*; and to demonstrate how significant the price *range* might be for a given type of stone, so that you will have a clearer understanding of the importance of quality differences.

# How to Use the Following Guides

The guides can be especially useful—and help you avoid mistakes—if you follow these steps:

- *Decide what color you want in a gem and then make a list of the gems available in that color.* If you want an emerald-green gem, for example, and can't afford emerald itself, you would use the guide to see what other similarly colored emerald-green gems are available—tsavorite garnet, chrome tourmaline, or green tourmaline, green sapphire, for example.
- *Compare their prices* to get a sense of the relative cost of each. In comparing prices for these green gems, you would immediately see that tsavorite garnet is the most expensive (but still much more affordable than emerald), chrome tourmaline is next in cost, then green tourmaline, and finally, the most affordable, green sapphire.
- *Note availability* to determine how easy or difficult it might be to locate the particular gem you think you want. In this exam-

ple, you would see that of the choices, green sapphire is not as readily available as several other choices, and might be difficult to find.

- *Note the range in price* for the stones that interest you. *The larger the price range in a given stone, the more critical any differences in quality become.* A wide price variance would indicate that you must be especially careful to spend time comparing and learning about the stone, developing an eye to spot subtle quality differences.
- *Read about each gem individually.* Now turn to chapter 16 and read about each of the gems you're considering individually. You may find there is something about the stone, its history, mythology, or wearability, that makes it an even more interesting choice for you. Here you will also learn if there is anything special you need to know, to look for or look *out* for, as you shop.

Now, you're ready to embark on a sparkling search. But always remember: *being genuine doesn't mean a stone is a "gem" or that it is "valuable."* There are genuine rubies, sapphires, and emeralds that can be bought for a couple of dollars per carat, and some you couldn't pay us to take! A gem must be beautiful and rare, attributes that are related to *quality.* The finer the quality, the more beautiful, and the more rare. The quality of the individual stone is what determines whether or not it is a "gem," and it is the *quality* that determines its value. The range in price for any colored gemstone is directly related to quality differences—and it can be enormous. Be sure you have read chapter 12 carefully, and understand the factors that determine quality before making any decision.

After reading these chapters you will know what to ask the jeweler to show you. But don't forget to do a lot of window-shopping, looking, and asking questions, until you really have developed a feel for that particular stone and its market.

# Gem Alternatives By Color

| Color Family | Popular Name of Stone | Gem Family |
|---|---|---|
| Red—*from red to shades of pink* | *Ruby*—red bluish red to orange red | Corundum |
| | *Garnet*—several red color varieties | Garnet |
| | *Pyrope*—brownish red to red | Garnet |
| | *Almandine*—violet to pure red | Garnet |
| | *Spessartite*—orange red to reddish brown to brownish red | Garnet |
| | *Rhodolite*—red to violet | Garnet |
| | *Spinel*—red to brownish red and pink | Spinel |
| | *Pink sapphire*—pinkish red | Corundum |
| | *Zircon*—brownish red to deep, dark red | Zircon |
| | *Sunstone*—rich red to orange red | Feldspar |
| | *Scapolite*—light red | Scapolite |
| | *Rubellite*—red to violet red and pink | Tourmaline |
| | *Red beryl*—red | Beryl |
| | *Morganite*—pink to orange pink | Beryl |
| | *Kunzite*—violet pink to pink violet | Spodumene |
| | *Rose quartz*—pure pink | Quartz |
| | *Andalusite*—pink to reddish brown | Andalusite |
| | *Diamond*—all shades of pink and red | Diamond |
| Orange | *Padparadscha sapphire*—pinkish orange | Corundum |
| | *Scapolite*—orange | Scapolite |
| | *Sunstone*—rich red to orange red | Feldspar |
| | *Topaz*—brownish orange, yellow orange, pinkish orange | Topaz |
| | *Spinel*—brown to orange | Spinel |
| | *Zircon*—orange to golden brown | Zircon |
| | *Hessonite*—orange brown | Garnet |
| | *Malaya*—pink orange to brownish red | Garnet |
| | *Tourmaline*—orangy brown, yellow orange | Tourmaline |
| | *Diamond*—various shades including yellow-orange to brownish orange | Diamond |
| Yellow | *Scapolite*—yellow | Scapolite |
| | *Sapphire*—yellow | Corundum |
| | *Beryl*—golden yellow | Beryl |
| | *Sphene*—green yellow to golden yellow to brown | Sphene |
| | *Chrysoberyl*—yellow, yellow green, yellow brown | Chrysoberyl |
| | *Citrine*—yellow to yellow brown | Quartz |
| | *Grossularite*—yellow to yellowish green to yellowish brown | Garnet |
| | *Zircon*—yellow to yellow brown | Zircon |
| | *Diamond*—all shades | Diamond |

| Color Family | Popular Name of Stone | Gem Family |
|---|---|---|
| Green | *Emerald*—yellowish green to bluish green | Beryl |
| | *Tsavorite*—yellowish green to bluish green | Garnet |
| | *Sphene*—grass green to yellow green | Sphene |
| | *Tourmaline*—all shades of green | Tourmaline |
| | *Peridot*—yellow green to green | Peridot |
| | *Zircon*—green to yellow green to gray green | Zircon |
| | *Alexandrite*—daylight: bluish to blue green; artificial light: violet red | Chrysoberyl |
| | *Sapphire*—yellow green to blue green to gray green | Corundum |
| | *Scapolite*—greenish gray | Scapolite |
| | *Demantoid*—yellow green to emerald green | Garnet |
| | *Tanzanite*—grey-green to blue-green | Zoisite |
| | *Diamond*—blue-green to yellow green to gray-green | Diamond |
| Blue | *Benitoite*—blue to violet blue to gray-blue | Benitoite |
| | *Sapphire*—cornflower blue to greenish blue to inky blue | Corundum |
| | *Tanzanite*—violet blue | Zoisite |
| | *Spinel*—gray blue, greenish blue, true pastel blue | Spinel |
| | *Aquamarine*—pastel to deep blue to blue green | Beryl |
| | *Indicolite*—inky blue, greenish blue | Tourmaline |
| | *Paraiba*—intense blue to violet blue to green-blue | Tourmaline |
| | *Topaz*—pastel to dark blue to blue green | Topaz |
| | *Zircon*—pastel blue | Zircon |
| | *Water sapphire*—violet blue | Iolite |
| Violet | *Scapolite*—violet blue to greenish to bluish gray, lilac to violet | Scapolite |
| | *Amethyst*—lilac to violet to reddish purple to brownish purple | Quartz |
| | *Sapphire*—purple to violet | Corundum |
| | *Rhodolite*—red violet | Garnet |
| | *Spinel*—Grayish violet to pure purple | Spinel |
| | *Paraiba*—violet to blue violet | Tourmaline |
| | *Kunzite*—pinkish violet to red violet | Spodumene |

# Guide to Popular Gems and Their Prices*

| FAMILY | POPULAR NAME | COLOR(S) | APPROX. RETAIL COST PER CARAT JANUARY 1993 | BRILLIANCE | WEAR-ABILITY | AVAIL-ABILITY |
|---|---|---|---|---|---|---|
| Andalusite | "Poor man's alexandrite" | Changes color from grayish green to reddish brown, emerald green to bright yellow | 1 to under 5 cts: $50-$300<br>5 to under 10 cts: $100-$400 | Good | Good | Large: scarce<br>Smaller: fair |
| Beryl[1] | Aquamarine | Pastel blue to medium deep blue | 1 to under 5 cts: $50-$850<br>5 to under 15 cts:$170-$1,250 | Good | Good | Good |
| | Golden beryl (Heliodor) | Yellow; brownish yellow | 1 to under 5 cts: $50-$125<br>5 to under 10 cts: $75-$200<br>10 to under 20 cts: $100-$500 | Good | Good | Good |
| | Emerald[2] | Yellow green to blue green | 1/2 to 1 ct: $1,000-$10,000<br>1 to under 2 cts:$2,000-$18,000 | Fair to good | Fair to good | Very fine Colombian, rare; Others, good<br>Fine: rare Medium: good |
| | Morganite | Pink to orange pink | 1 to under 5 cts: $75-$200<br>5 to under 10 cts: $200-$800 | Good | Good | |
| Chrysoberyl | Alexandrite | Changes from greenish in daylight to reddish in incandescent light | 1/2 to under 1 ct: $2,000-$13,000<br>1 to under 2 cts: $3,000-$18,000 | Good | Excellent | Large: scarce Small: fair |
| | Chrysoberyl | Yellow to yellow brown to yellow green | 1 to under 5 cts: $50-$150<br>5 to under 10 cts: $75-$300 | Good | Excellent | Fair |
| | Precious cat's-eye | Greenish to brownish–yellow with "eye" effect | 1 to under 3 cts: $600-$3,600<br>3 to under 5 cts: $1,200-$5,000 | Negligible | Excellent | Fair to good |
| Corundum | Ruby[2] | Red to bluish or purplish–red to yellow red | 1/2 to under 1 ct: $1,100-$10,000<br>1 to under 2 cts: $2,200-$20,000 | Fair to good | Excellent | Burmese: rare<br>Thai: good<br>Kenya: fair<br>Ceylon: good<br>Cambodia: fair<br>Vietnam: fair |

150

| | | Color | Price | | | |
|---|---|---|---|---|---|---|
| (Corundum cont.) | Blue sapphire[2] | Bright blue to inky blue | 1/2 to under 1 ct: $250-$3,000<br>1 to under 2 cts: $500-$10,000 | Good | Excellent | Kashmir: scarce<br>Burmese: scarce<br>Thai: good<br>Australian: good |
| | Colorless sapphire | White (colorless) | under 1 ct: $25-$50<br>1-1.5 cts: $50-$100 | Good | Very good | Good in sizes under 1 ct |
| | Green sapphire | Clear green to brownish or bluish green | 1 to under 3 cts: $50-$200<br>3 to under 5 cts: $100-$225 | Good | Excellent | Large: scarce<br>Others: fair |
| | Pink sapphire | Light to very dark pink (almost red) | 1 to under 2 cts: $600-$4,500<br>2 to under 3 cts: $800-$6,000 | Good | Excellent | Fair |
| | Yellow sapphire | Yellow (most are heat treated; natural yellow usually less brilliant). | 1 to under 5 cts: $125-$850<br>5 to under 10 cts:$500-$2,000<br>10 to under 20 cts: $700-$2,500 | | Excellent | Good |
| Garnet | Almandine (common garnet) | Violet to pure red | 1 to under 3 cts: $10-$50<br>3 to under 5 cts: $25-$75<br>5 to under 20 cts: $50-$100 | Fair to good | Good | Good |
| | Demantoid | Yellow green to emerald green | 1 to under 2 cts: $800-$8000<br>2 to under 3 cts: $2,000-$12,000 | Very good | Good | Poor |
| | Grossularite | Yellowish to yellowish green to yellowish brown | 1 to under 5 cts: $50-$150<br>5 to under 10 cts: $125-$350 | Fair to good | Good | Good |
| | Malaya | Pink orange to brownish red | 1 to under 5 cts: $85-$400<br>5 to under 10 cts: $250-$500 | Good | Good | Good |
| | Pyrope (common garnet) | Yellowish red to dark red | 1 to under 5 cts: $10-$75<br>5 to under 20 cts: $25-$100 | Fair to good | Good | Good |
| | Rhodolite | Red violet | 1 to under 5 cts: $25-$225<br>5 to under 20 cts: $75-$450 | Good | Good | Good |
| | Spessarite | Brownish orange to reddish brown to brownish red | 1 to under 5 cts: $50-$600<br>5 to under 20 cts: $75-$800 | Good | Good | Fair |
| | Tsavorite | Yellowish green to bluish green | 1 to under 2 cts: $600-$2,500<br>2 to under 3 cts: $1,000-$3,600 | Good | Good | Over 5 cts: scarce; other sizes: fair to good |

(Price Charts continued on next page)

*Prices compiled from *The Guide*, Gemworld International, Inc., and adjusted to retail based on keystone.

| FAMILY | POPULAR NAME | COLOR(S) | APPROX. RETAIL COST* PER CARAT JANUARY 1993 | BRILLIANCE | WEAR-ABILITY | AVAIL-ABILITY |
|---|---|---|---|---|---|---|
| Iolite | Water sapphire | Violet blue to gray blue | 1 to 5 cts: $25-$125<br>5 to 10 cts: $60-$350 | Good | Fair | Good |
| Pearls[3] (cultured) | Round[4] | Silver, silver white, pink white, white, cream | *16" to 18" strands*<br>6-6.5 mm: $500-$1750<br>7-7.5 mm: $650-$3,200<br>8-8.5 mm: $1,600-$9,000<br>9-9.5 mm: $4,500-$20,000 | Not applicable | Good | Gem quality over 8 mm: rare<br>Others: good |
| | South Sea (round) | Silver, silver white, pink white, white, cream | *(Prices are per pearl)[5]*<br>11-12 mm: $1,600-$6,600<br>12-13 mm: $2,200-$7,500<br>14-15 mm: $5,000-$12,000<br>16+ mm: $10,000-$24,000 | Not applicable | Good | Gem quality: very rare<br>Fine quality over 16 mm: rare<br>Others: fair-good |
| | Baroque | White to creamy white | *16" to 18" strands*<br>7.5-8 mm: $400-$1,200<br>8.5-9 mm: $500-$1,600 | Not applicable | Good | Good |
| | Freshwater | All colors | *16" to 18" strands*<br>3-4 mm: $8-$15<br>4-5 mm: $15-$30<br>6-7 mm: $25-$75 | Not applicable | Good | Good |
| | Black/Gray (round Tahitian) | Deep gray to black—*Not dyed* | *(Prices are per pearl)[5]*<br>8.5-9 mm: $500-$1,200<br>10-10.5 mm: $1,100-$2,500<br>11.5-12 mm: $3,500-$6,000 | Not applicable | Good | Small sizes: fair<br>Larger sizes: rare |
| Peridot | Peridot | Yellow green to deep green to rich chartreuse | 1 to under 5 cts: $30-$175<br>to under 10 cts: $85-$300<br>10 to under 20 cts: $100-$650 | Fair to good | Fair–will scratch easily | Large: scarce<br>Smaller: plentiful |

| Gem | Variety | Color | Price | | | |
|---|---|---|---|---|---|---|
| Quartz | Amethyst | Purple, reddish purple to brownish purple | 1 to under 5 cts: $10-$75<br>5 to under 10 cts: $10-$85<br>10 to under 20 cts: $15-$100 | Fair to good | Good | Very good |
| | Citrine | Yellow to yellow brown | 1 to under 5 cts: $10-$50 5<br>5 to under 25 cts: $25-$75 | Good | Good | Good |
| | Rose quartz<br>Smokey | Pure pink<br>Brown shades | (Prices are per stone)<br>Most sizes: $2-$15<br>Most sizes: $2-$15 | Good<br>Good | Good<br>Good | Good<br>Very good |
| Spinel | Red spinel | Red to brownish red | 1 to under 3 cts: $200-$2,800<br>3 to under 5 cts: $400-$3,900 | Very good | Very good | Ruby red: scarce<br>Others: good |
| | Pink spinel | Lively or bright pink to brownish pink | 1 to under 3 cts: $100-$1,500<br>3 to under 5 cts: $150-$1,800 | Very good | Very good | Fair |
| | Blue spinel | Medium gray blue to deep blue to violet | 1 to under 3 cts: $60-$1,000<br>3 to under 5 cts: $100-$1,200 | Good | Very good | Good |
| Spodumene | Kunzite | Lilac, violet, pink | 1 to under 5 cts: $10-$120<br>5 to under 20 cts: $35-$175 | Good | Poor for rings | Good |
| Topaz | Blue Topaz | Blue | 1 to under 5 cts: $6-$35<br>5 to under 20 cts: $10-$40 | Good | Fair | Good |
| | Pink Topaz | Pink (red also available, but very rare and much more expensive) | 1 to under 3 cts: $125-$850<br>3 to under 5 cts: $175-$950 | Good | Fair | Fair to good |
| | Imperial | Golden with pinkish/reddish overtone | 1 to under 3 cts: $100-$800<br>3 to under 5 cts: $150-$900 | Good | Fair | Fair to good except in very large sizes |
| | Yellow Topaz | Yellow/golden (no pink/red overtone) | 1 to under 5 cts: $75-$400<br>5 to under 20 cts: $150-$550 | Good | Good | Good |

(Price charts continued on next page)

*Prices compiled from *The Guide*, Gemworld International, Inc., and adjusted to retail based on keystone.

| FAMILY | POPULAR NAME | COLOR(S) | APPROX. RETAIL COST PER CARAT JANUARY 1993 | BRILLIANCE | WEARABILITY | AVAILABILITY |
|---|---|---|---|---|---|---|
| Tourmaline | Chrome | Deep green | 1 to under 3 cts: $150-$1,400<br>3 to under 5 cts: $300-$1,600 | Good | Fair to good | Scarce |
| | Indicolite | Inky blue to blue green | 1 to under 5 cts: $50-$1,000<br>5 to under 10 cts: $150-$1,200 | Good | Fair to good | Good |
| | Paraiba | Wide range of "neon" blue, green, blue-green & purplish | under 1 ct: $300-$1,000<br>1 ct-3 cts: $750-12,500 | Excellent | Fair to good | Under 1 ct: fair<br>Over 1 ct in fine quality, scarce |
| | Pink | Pink or rose | 1 to under 5 cts: $50-$450<br>5 to under 10 cts: $120-$650 | Good | Fair to good | Good |
| | Rubellite | Red to violet | 1 to under 5 cts: $50-$650<br>5 to under 10 cts: $250-$1,100 | Good | Fair to good | Good |
| | Verdelite | Green—all shades except chrome tourmaline | 1 to under 3 cts: $40-$240<br>3 to under 5 cts: $50-$320<br>5 to under 20 cts: $100-$500 | Good | Fair to good | Good |
| | | Yellow, orange, and brown varieties | 1 to 5 ct: $50-$400 | Good | Fair to good | Fair |
| | Bicolor & tricolor | Red/black, red/green, red/green/colorless | 1 to under 5 cts: $50-$400<br>5 to under 10 cts: $100-$600 | Good | Fair to good | Good |
| Zircon | Zircon | Pastel blue (usually heat-treated) | 1 to under 5 cts: $50-$450<br>5 to under 10 cts: $100-$700 | Good | Fair–not recommended for rings | Large: scarce |
| | | Green to Yellow green | 1 to under 5 cts: $30-$200<br>5 to under 10 cts: $80-$300 | Good | " " | Good |
| | | Colorless (usually heat-treated) | Comparable to green | Good | " " | Good |
| | | Orange to golden brown | Comparable to green | Good | " " | Good |
| | | Red to brownish red | Prices unknown (rare) | Good | " " | True red: scarce<br>Other reds: good |
| | | Yellow to yellow brown | Comparable to green | Good | " " | Good |

| Zoisite | | | | | | |
|---|---|---|---|---|---|---|
| Tanzanite | Strong blue to weak violet, blue violet | 1 to under 3 cts: $240-$680<br>3 to under 5 cts: $400-$1,040<br>5 to under 20 cts:<br>$440-$1,600 | Good | Poor for rings | Good | |
| Green | Blue-green to grey-green | 1 to under 3 cts: $200-$1,000 | Good | Good | Good | Small: fair<br>Large: scarce |

[1] Beryl also comes in red, green (different from emerald green), lilac, salmon, and orange. Most are still not easily available, but some, such as the lovely orange variety, can be found for under $75. a carat and offer excellent value.

[2] Cabochon-cut rubies, sapphires and emeralds usually cost much less; finest gems can cost much more.

[3] Natural pearls are very rare and much more expensive than cultured. Pricing information is insufficient to provide guidelines.

[4] 3/4 *round* pearls which may *appear* to be fully round, sell for approximately 50% less than full round pearls.

[5] Undrilled. Drilled pearls (such as those mounted on "posts") sell for much less than undrilled pearls.

---

# Opal Price Guide*
## Approx. Retail Cost Per Carat

There are numerous varieties of opals and wide ranges in quality. Quality differences are often difficult for the amateur to distinguish, but may significantly affect price. The following prices provide only a guide. For more detailed information see Selected Readings.

## White Base, Gray Base and Jelly Opal

| | Commercial | Good | Fine | Extra Fine |
|---|---|---|---|---|
| 1 to under 7 cts | $8-16 | $16-50 | $50-150 | $150-350 |
| 7 to under 15 cts | $16-50 | $50-100 | $100-220 | $220-350 |

## Boulder Opal

| | Commercial | Good | Fine | Extra Fine |
|---|---|---|---|---|
| Small (1-5 cts) | $20 & up | $100-1,800 | $1,800-5,000 | $5,000-10,000 |
| Medium (5-10 cts) | $20 & up | $900-2,200 | $2,200-11,000 | $11,000-20,000 |
| Large (10-15 cts) | $20 & up | $1,200-4,000 | $4,000-15,000 | $15,000-50,000 |
| Very Large (over 15 cts) | $20 & up | $2,000-6,000 | $6,000-20,000 | $20,000-80,000 |

(Price charts continued on next page)

*Prices compiled from *The Guide*, Gemworld International, Inc. and adjusted to retail based on keystone.

## Black Opal

| | Commercial | Good | Fine | Extra Fine |
|---|---|---|---|---|
| 1 to under 5 cts | $100 & up | $300-1,400 | $1,400-8,000 | $8,000-20,000 |
| 5 to under 10 cts | $100 & up | $300-1,400 | $1,400-8,000 | $8,000-20,000 |
| 10 to 15 cts | $100 & up | $300-1,400 | $1,400-6,400 | $6,400-16,000 |

NOTE: The finest black opals can cost more than prices given here, but opals of this quality are very rare.

## Semi-Black & Crystal Opal

| | Commercial | Good | Fine | Extra Fine |
|---|---|---|---|---|
| 1 to under 5 cts | $70 & up | $300-1,200 | $1,200-3,000 | $3,000-5,000 |
| 5 to under 10 cts | $70 & up | $300-1,200 | $1,200-4,000 | $4,000-7,000 |
| 10 to 15 cts | $70 & up | $300-1,200 | $1,200-3,600 | $3,600-6,400 |

## Crystal Opal

| | Commercial | Good | Fine | Extra Fine |
|---|---|---|---|---|
| 1 to under 5 cts | $70 & up | $150-500 | $500-1,000 | $1,000-2,000 |
| 5 to under 10 cts | $70 & up | $150-500 | $500-1,000 | $1,000-2,400 |
| 10 to 15 cts | $70 & up | $150-500 | $500-1,000 | $1,000-2,000 |

## Semi-Crystal Opal

| | Commercial | Good | Fine | Extra Fine |
|---|---|---|---|---|
| 1 to under 5 cts | $30 & up | $70-250 | $250-500 | $500-1,200 |
| 5 to under 10 cts | $30 & up | $70-250 | $250-500 | $500-1,200 |
| 10 to 15 cts | $30 & up | $70-250 | $250-500 | $500-1,200 |

*Prices compiled from *The Guide*, Gemworld International, Inc., and adjusted to retail based on keystone.

# 16

## Colorful Choices In Colored Gemstones

### The Big Three—Emerald, Ruby, & Sapphire

#### Emerald

Emerald is the green variety of the mineral beryl and one of the most highly prized of all the gems. Aside from being the birthstone for May, it was historically believed to bestow on its wearer faithfulness and unchanging love, and was thought to enable the wearer to forecast events.

The highest-quality emerald has the color of fresh young green grass—an almost pure spectral green, possibly with a very faint tint of blue, as in the finest emerald from Colombia, which is considered by connoisseurs to be the world's finest. Flawless emeralds are rare, so their "flaws" have come to serve almost as "fingerprints," while flawless emeralds are immediately suspect. Although a hard stone, emerald will chip easily since it tends to be somewhat brittle, so special care should be given in wearing and handling.

Because of emerald's popularity and value, imitations are abundant. Glass, manufactured complete with "flaws," and doublets or triplets, like "aquamarine emeralds" and "Tecla emeralds" (see chapter 14), are often encountered. New products such as the "Lannyte Emerald Doublet" are also entering the market; when properly represented, they can make an interesting jewelry choice, but a second or third party may fail to mention that they are "doublets."

Also, fine synthetic emeralds are being produced (see chapter 13) with nearly the same color, hardness, and brilliance as genuine emerald. These synthetics are not inexpensive themselves, except by comparison to a genuine emerald of equivalent quality.

Techniques to enhance color and reduce the visibility of flaws are also frequently used. A common practice is to boil the emerald in oil (sometimes tinted green), a practice that goes back to early Greek times. This is a widely accepted trade practice, since it is actually good for the stone in light of its fragile nature. Oiling hides some of the whitish flaws, which are actually cracks, filling the cracks so they become less visible. The oil becomes an integral part of the emerald unless it is subjected to some type of degreasing procedure. The development and use of the ultrasonic cleaner has brought to light the extensiveness of this practice. *Never clean emeralds in an ultrasonic cleaner.*

A good friend of mine took her heirloom emerald ring to her jeweler for a "really good cleaning." Luckily for the jeweler, she never left the store and was standing right there when the ring was put into the cleaner and removed. She couldn't believe her eyes. She was shocked by the loss of color and the "sudden appearance of more flaws." The ultrasonic cleaner had removed the oil that had penetrated the cracks, and an emerald several shades lighter and more visibly flawed emerged. Had she not been there, she would never have believed the jeweler hadn't pulled a switch.

Oiling is considered an acceptable practice, but be sure the price reflects the actual quality of the stone. If necessary, most emeralds can be "re-oiled."

As with all highly desired gems, the greater the value and demand, the greater the occurrence of fraudulent practices. Examples of almost every type of technique to simulate emerald can be found—color alteration by using green foil on closed backs, use of synthetics, substitution of less valuable green stones, doublets, or other composites, etc. Therefore, be especially cautious of bargains, deal with reputable jewelers when planning to purchase, and always have the purchase double-checked by a qualified gemologist-appraiser.

## Ruby

Prized through the ages, even by kings, as the "gem of gems . . . surpassing all other precious stones in virtue," ruby is the red variety of the mineral corundum. Historically, it has been symbolic of love and passion, considered to be an aid to firm friendship, and believed to ensure beauty. Today's birthstone for July, ruby's color ranges from purplish or bluish red to a yellowish red. The finest color is a vivid, almost pure spectral red with a very faint undertone of blue, as seen in Burmese rubies, which are considered the finest (see pages 109-110). The ruby is very brilliant and very hard, ranking 9 on Mohs' scale (an internationally recognized standard that ranges from 1 for very soft to 10 for the very hardest). Ruby is also very durable and wearable, characteristics that make it an unusually fine choice for any piece of jewelry.

Translucent varieties of ruby are also seen, and one variety exhibits a six-ray star effect when cut as a cabochon. This variety is called *star ruby* and is one of nature's most beautiful and interesting gifts. But, as with so many other beautiful gifts once produced only in nature, these lovely gems are now duplicated in *synthetic* star rubies, and numerous "faked" star rubies are also the products of mankind's attempts at mimicry.

Here again, remember that the greater the value and demand, the greater the use of techniques to "improve" or to simulate. Among rubies, as among other gemstones, examples of almost every type of deceptive technique can be found—color enhancement, synthesis, substitutes, doublets, triplets, misleading names, and so on. The newest laboratory-grown synthetic rubies, like those made by Ramaura and Chatham, are so close to natural ruby in every aspect that many are actually passing for genuine, even among gemologists. When getting a very fine, valuable ruby, be sure to verify genuineness with a gemologist who has both many years' experience in colored gems and an astute knowledge of the marketplace today. We would recommend having the jeweler or gemologist also obtain a colored gemstone report from a major gem-testing laboratory.

Here again, be especially cautious of bargains. Deal with reputable jewelers when planning to purchase, and have the purchase double-checked by a qualified gemologist-appraiser.

## Sapphire

The "celestial" sapphire, symbol of the heavens, guardian of innocence, bestower of truth and good health, preserver of chastity, is in fact the mineral corundum. While we know it best in its blue variety, which is highly prized, it comes in essentially every color; red corundum is ruby. As with ruby, its sister stone, sapphire is characterized by hardness, brilliance, and availability in many beautiful colors, all of which make it probably the most important and most versatile of the gem families.

Blue sapphires can be among the most valuable members of the sapphire family—especially stones from Burma and Kashmir, which are closest to the pure spectral blue. Fine, brilliant, deep blue Burmese sapphires will surely dazzle the eye and the pocketbook, as will the Kashmir, which is a fine velvety-toned deep blue. Many today tend to be too dark, however, because of the presence of too much black and poor cutting (cutting deep for additional weight), but the deep blues can be treated to lighten the color.

The Ceylon (Sri Lanka) sapphires are a very pleasing blue, but are a less deep shade than the Burmese or Kashmir, instead tending to fall more on the pastel side.

We are also seeing many Australian sapphires, which are often a dark blue, but with a slightly green undertone, as are those from Thailand; both sell for much less per carat. They offer a very affordable alternative to the Burmese, Kashmir, or Ceylon, and can still be very pleasing in their color. Blue sapphires also come from Tanzania, Brazil, Africa, and even the United States. Montana sapphires are very collectible because of their unusual shades of color, and because many are *natural* color, that is not subjected to any treatment. For those who want a gem that is truly "natural," Montana sapphire may be the choice for you.

With sapphire, origin can have a significant effect on price, so if you are purchasing a Kashmir, Burmese, or Ceylon sapphire, that should be noted on the bill of sale.

Like ruby, the blue sapphire may be found in a translucent variety that may show a six-rayed star effect when cut into a cabochon. This variety is known as *star sapphire,* of which there are numerous synthetics (often referred to in the trade as "Linde," pronounced Lin´dee).

In addition to blue sapphire, we are now beginning to see the appearance of many other color varieties in the latest jewelry designs—especially yellow and pink, and in smaller sizes some beautiful shades of green. These are known as *fancy* sapphires. Compared to the cost of blue sapphire and ruby, these stones offer excellent value and real beauty.

A beautiful and rare variety called *padparadscha* (a type of lotus flower) is also in demand. The true padparadscha should exhibit a *pink and orange color simultaneously.* Depending upon the richness of color, brilliance, and size, these can be very expensive. A lovely but more common and more affordable variety is available today which is really a rich orange color. It is often sold as padparadscha but the rarer and more costly gem will always exhibit a strong pink with the orange.

Inevitably, evidence abounds of every technique known to improve the perceived quality and value of the sapphire—alteration of color, synthesis, composites, and misleading names. Techniques have been developed to treat natural sapphires to remove a certain type of flaw (needle inclusions) and to change the color—for example, to create a "Ceylon" sapphire that never came from Sri Lanka but whose color looks like that of a Ceylon. Be especially alert to the new diffusion-treated blue sapphire, which is blue on the surface only. Also, watch out for the new *true* doublets flooding the market. As always, we urge you to be especially cautious of bargains, deal with reputable jewelers, and have your stone double-checked by a qualified gemologist-appraiser.

# Other Popular Colored Gems

## Alexandrite

Alexandrite is a fascinating transparent gem that appears grass green in daylight and raspberry red under artificial light. It is a variety of chrysoberyl reputedly discovered in Russia in 1831 on the day Alexander II reached his majority; hence the name. In Russia, where the national colors also happen to be green and red, it is considered a stone of very good omen. It is also considered Friday's stone or the stone of "Friday's child."

Unlike other stones, which mankind has known about and admired for thousands of years, Alexandrite is a relatively recent gem discovery. Nonetheless, it has definitely come into its own and is presently commanding both high appeal and high prices. While fairly common in small sizes, it has become relatively scarce in sizes of two carats or more. A fine three-carat stone can cost $45,000 today. If you see an alexandrite that measures more than half inch in width, be suspicious of a fake. Alexandrite is normally cut in a faceted style, but some cat's-eye type alexandrites, found in Brazil, would be cut as a cabochon to display the eye effect. These are usually small; the largest we've seen was approximately three carats.

Prior to 1973, there were really no good synthetic alexandrites. While some varieties of synthetic corundum and synthetic spinel were frequently sold as alexandrite, they really didn't look like the real thing but were hard to differentiate since so few buyers had ever seen genuine stones. They are, however, easy for a gemologist to spot. In 1973 a very good synthetic alexandrite was produced, which is not easy to differentiate from natural stones. While a good gemologist today can identify the synthetics, when they first appeared on the market many were mistaken for the real thing. Be especially careful to verify the authenticity of your alexandrite, since it might have been mistakenly identified years ago, and passed along as authentic to you today. It could save you a lot of money!

## Amber

Amber is not a stone, but rather an amorphous, fossilized tree sap. It was one of the earliest substances used for personal adornment. Modestly decorated pieces of rough amber have been found in Stone Age excavations and are assumed to have been used as amulets and talismans—a use definitely recorded throughout history before, during, and since the ancient Greeks. Because of its beautiful color and the ease with which it could be fashioned, amber quickly became a favorite object of trade and barter and personal adornment. Amber varies from transparent to semitranslucent, and from yellow to dark brown in color; occasionally it's seen in reddish and greenish brown tones. In addition, amber can be dyed many colors. Occasionally, one can find "foreign" fragments or insects that were trapped in the amber, which usually increases its value because of the added curiosity factor.

Plastics are the most common amber imitations. But real amber, which is the lightest gem material, may be easily distinguished from most plastic when dropped into a saturated salt solution—amber will float while plastic sinks. One other commonly encountered "amber" type is "reconstructed" amber—amber fragments compressed under heat to form a larger piece. An expert can differentiate this from the real under magnification.

Amber can be easily tested by touching it in an inconspicuous place with a hot needle (held by tweezers). The whitish smoke that should be produced should smell like burning pine wood, not like medicine or disinfectant. If there is no smoke, but a black mark occurs, then it is *not* amber. Another test is to try to cut a little piece of the amber with a sharp pointed knife, at the drill hole of the bead; if it cuts like wood (producing a shaving), it is *not* amber, which would produce a sharp, crumbly deposit.

With the exception of those pieces possessing special antique value, the value of amber fluctuates with its popularity, which in part is dictated by the fashion industry and the prevalence of yellow and browns in one's wardrobe. Nonetheless, amber has proved itself an ageless gem and will always be loved and admired.

## Amethyst

Amethyst, a transparent purple variety of quartz, is one of the most popular of the colored stones. Once believed to bring peace of mind to the wearer, it was also thought to prevent the wearer from getting drunk, and if the circle of the sun or moon was engraved thereon, amethyst was believed to prevent death from poison.

Available in shades from light to dark purple, this February birthstone is relatively hard, fairly brilliant, and overall a good, versatile, wearable stone, available in plentiful supply even in very large sizes (although large sizes with deep color are now becoming scarce). Amethyst is probably one of the most beautiful stones available at a moderate price; buyers should be careful, however, because "fine" amethyst is being produced synthetically today. Most synthetics can be identified by a skilled gemologist.

Amethyst may fade from heat and strong sunshine. Guard your amethyst from these conditions and it should retain its color indefinitely. We are hearing stories from customers across the country, however, complaining of newly purchased amethyst jewelry fading over just a few months, from *deep purple* to *light lavender*. This should not happen, and may result from an unacceptable color treatment. If your stone fades this quickly, return it to your jeweler.

## Andalusite (Poor Man's Alexandrite)

Andalusite is now offering interesting new possibilities for jewelry. Brazil is the primary source of these fascinating, fairly hard, and fairly durable stones. Andalusite is very interesting because it may exhibit several colors—an olive green in one direction, a rich reddish brown from another direction, and grayish green from yet another direction. In an emerald cut it may look primarily green while exhibiting an orange color at the ends of the emerald shape. In a round cut you may see the green body color with simultaneous flashes of another color. One benefit andalusite has over alexandrite is that you don't have to change the light in which it is being seen to experience its colors; merely changing the perspective does the trick. A rare and sometimes expensive emerald green variety may exhibit a bright yellow simultaneously, or when viewed from different angles. A pink variety does not exhibit this kind of color phenomenon. While andalusite is not readily available yet, it is finding a market, especially among men.

## Aquamarine

To dream of aquamarine signifies the making of new friends; to wear aquamarine earrings brings love and affection. Aquamarine, a universal symbol of youth, hope, and health, blesses those born in March. (Prior to the fifteenth century it was considered to be the birthstone for those born in October.)

Aquamarine is a member of the important beryl family, which includes emerald, but aquamarine is less brittle and more durable than its green counterpart. Aquamarine ranges in color from light-blue to bluish green to deep blue, the latter being the most valuable and desirable. It is a very wearable gem, clear and brilliant, and, unlike emerald, is available with excellent clarity even in very large sizes, although these are becoming scarce today. Aquamarines are still widely available in sizes up to 15 carats, but 10-carat sizes with fine color and clarity are becoming scarce and are more expensive. Long considered a beautiful and moderately priced gem, it is now entering the "expensive" classification for stones in larger sizes with a good deep blue color.

Several words of caution for those interested in this lovely gem. First, you may want to think twice before buying a pale or shallow-cut stone, since the color will become paler as dirt accumulates on the back. These stones need constant cleaning to keep them beautiful. Second, be careful not to mistake blue topaz for aquamarine. While topaz is an equally beautiful gem, it is usually much less expensive since it is usually treated to obtain its desirable color. For those who can't afford an aquamarine, however, blue topaz is an excellent alternative—as long as it is properly represented and priced. Finally, note that many aquamarine-colored synthetic spinels are erroneously sold as aquamarine.

## Benitoite

This exquisitely beautiful and rare gem is seldom seen in jewelry, but is very popular among collectors and connoisseurs. Discovered in San Benito, California—hence the name *benito-ite*—it was recently selected as the official state stone of California and we are beginning to see more of it in fine jewelry houses there.

Benitoite ranges from colorless to dark blue (often with a violet tint) to violet. A rare pink variety has also been identified. Benitoite can display "fire," the dispersion of white light into the rainbow colors, comparable to a diamond, and is also very brilliant. Some might easily mistake it at a glance for a blue diamond. It lacks diamond's incredible hardness, however, and is more comparable to amethyst or tanzanite in hardness. It is difficult to find benitoite in sizes over one carat; only about five stones per year are cut which weigh two carats or more; only one every five years yields a stone five carats or more. Benitoite's rarity keeps it very expensive—a fine one-carat stone could easily cost $3,000—and two-carat sizes with fine color are extremely rare and even more costly. The largest fine benitoite known weighs just over 7³/4 carats, and is on display at the Smithsonian Institution in Washington, D.C.

For jewelry, benitoite is a relatively wearable stone, but given its rarity and value, we recommend that it be set in a somewhat protective mounting so that it is not easily subjected to accidental scratching or wear.

## Beryl (Golden Beryl and Morganite)

As early as A.D. 1220 the virtues of beryl were well established in legend. Beryl provided help against foes in battle or litigation, made the wearer unconquerable, but at the same time friendly and likable, and also sharpened the wearer's intellect and cured laziness. Today beryl is still considered important, but primarily for aesthetic reasons. The variety of colors in which it is found, its wonderful clarity (except for emerald), its brilliance, and its durability (again with the exception of emerald) have given the various varieties of beryl tremendous appeal.

Most people are familiar with the blue variety of beryl, aquamarine, and the green variety, emerald. Few as yet know the pink variety, morganite, and the beautiful yellow to yellow green variety, referred to as golden beryl. These gems have only recently found their place in the jewelry world but are already being shown in fabulous pieces made by the greatest designers. While not inexpensive, they still offer excellent value and beauty.

Beryl has also been found in many other colors—lilac, salmon, orange, sea green, as well as colorless. While most of these varieties are not as yet available to any but the most ardent rock hound, the orange varieties are fairly common and can still be found for under $125 per carat. Some orange varieties are heated to produce the more popular pink color and then sold as morganite.

The rarest color is *red*, which is even more rare than emerald, and comparable in cost. Until recently, it was known only to serious collectors and was called "Bixbite," after the man who discovered it. The gem variety of red beryl was discovered in Utah, still its only known source. But thanks to the discovery of a new deposit, we are now beginning to see this exciting gemstone in the jewelry market. It faces a major problem, however—what to call it. Some dealers are calling it "red emerald" because it is the same basic material as emerald and because it is truly comparable to emerald in rarity, beauty, and value. Whatever the name by which it is called—red emerald, red beryl, or "Bixbite"—it is a beautiful gem that should be loved and cherished by anyone lucky enough to own one.

## Bloodstone (Heliotrope)

Believed by the ancient Greeks to have fallen from heaven, this stone has held a prominent place throughout history, and even into modern times, as a great curative. It was (and still is in some parts of the world) believed capable of stopping every type of bleeding, clearing bloodshot eyes, acting as an antidote for snakebite, and relieving urinary troubles. Today there are people who wear bloodstone amulets to prevent sunstroke and headache, and to provide protection against the evil eye.

The birthstone for March, bloodstone is a more or less opaque, dark green variety of quartz with specks of red jasper (a variety of quartz) spattering red throughout the dark green field. Particularly popular for men's rings (perhaps they need more protection from illness?) bloodstone is most desirable when the green isn't so dark as to approach black and the red flecks are roundish and pronounced. It is moderately durable and is fairly readily available and inexpensive.

## Chrysoberyl and Cat's-Eye

The chrysoberyl family is very interesting because all three of its varieties—alexandrite, cat's-eye, and chrysoberyl—while chemically alike, are quite distinct from one another in their optical characteristics and bear no visible resemblance to each other.

Chrysoberyl in its cat's-eye variety has long been used as a charm to guard against evil spirits, and one can understand why, given the pronounced eye effect; the eye, so legend has it, could see all and it watched out for its wearer. But it was also believed that to dream of cat's-eye signified treachery. On still another level, it symbolized long life for the wearer, perhaps as a result of being protected from the evil eye.

Cat's-eye is a hard, translucent gem ranging in color from a honey yellow or honey brown to yellowish green to an almost emerald green. It has a velvety or silk-like texture, and when properly cut displays a brilliant whitish line of light right down the center, appearing almost to be lighted from inside. Genuine cat's eye should not be confused with the common quartz variety, which is often brown, and called tiger eye; the latter has a much less striking eye and weaker color altogether. This phenomenon is produced only in cabochons (cabs).

To see the effect properly, the stone should be viewed under a single strong light source, coming if possible from directly overhead. If the line is not exactly in the center, the stone's value is reduced. The line does shift from side to side when the stone is moved about—probably another reason ancient people believed it capable of seeing all and guarding its wearer.

The stone called chrysoberyl, on the other hand, is a brilliant, transparent, very clear, and very durable stone found in yellow, yellow green, and green varieties. This is another stone that still offers excellent value. It's a real beauty, very moderately priced, and just beginning to be appreciated and used in contemporary jewelry.

## Chrysoprase and Carnelian

Chrysoprase has long been the subject of marvelous stories. In the 1800s, it was believed that a thief sentenced to be hanged or beheaded would immediately escape if he placed a chrysoprase in his mouth. Of course, it might be hard to obtain the stone unless he just happened to carry one around! And Alexander the Great was believed to have worn a "prase" in his girdle during battle, to ensure victory.

Chrysoprase is an inexpensive, highly translucent, bright, light-to dark-green variety of quartz. While its color is often very uniform and can be very lovely in jewelry, for many years these gems have been dyed to enhance their color, where necessary. Chrysoprase is another stone that is usually cut in cabochon style. It has become very popular for jewelry as a fashion accessory. Do not confuse it with jade, however. It is sometimes called "Australian jade" and is sometimes misrepresented as real jade.

If you're the timid sort, carnelian is the stone for you. "The wearing of carnelians is recommended to those who have a weak voice or are timid in speech, for the warm-colored stone will give them the courage they lack so that they will speak both boldly and well," reports G. F. Kunz, a turn-of-the-century gemologist and historian.

This stone is especially revered by Moslems, because Muhammad himself wore a silver ring set with a carnelian engraved for use as a seal.

Napoleon I, while on a campaign in Egypt, picked up with his own hands (apparently from the battlefield) an unusual octagonal carnelian, upon which was engraved the legend, "The Slave Abraham Relying Upon The Merciful [God]." He wore it with him always and bequeathed it to his nephew.

Carnelian, one of the accepted birthstones for August, is a reddish orange variety of quartz. A moderately hard, translucent to opaque stone, its warm uniform color and fair durability have made it a favorite. It is often found in antique jewelry and lends itself to engraving or carving (especially in cameos). It is still a relatively inexpensive stone with great warmth and beauty and offers an excellent choice for jewelry to be worn as an accessory with today's fashion colors.

## Coral

Coral, which for twenty centuries or more was classed with precious gems and can be found adorning ancient amulets alongside diamond, ruby, emerald, and pearl, had been "experimentally proved" by the sixteenth century to cure madness, give wisdom, stop the flow of blood from a wound, calm storms, and of course enable the traveler to safely cross broad rivers. It was also known to prevent sterility. This was certainly a powerful gem!

Red coral symbolizes attachment, devotion, and protection against plague and pestilence. And one unique quality: it loses its color when a friend of the wearer is about to die! There is a catch to coral's potency, however. To effectively exercise its power, it should not be altered by man's hands but should be worn in its natural, uncut state. This perhaps is why one often sees this stone in necklaces or pins in its natural state.

Coral lost its popularity for a while, but has been steadily gaining in popularity in recent years. It is a semitranslucent to opaque material that, formed from a colony of marine invertebrates, is primarily a skeletal calcium carbonate gem. The formations as seen in the water look like tree branches. Coral occurs in a variety of colors—white, pink, orange, red, and black. One of the most expensive varieties, very popular in recent years and used extensively in fine jewelry, is angel skin coral. This is a whitish variety highlighted with a faint blush of pink or peach. Today the rarest variety, and the most expensive, is blood coral, also called noble or oxblood coral. This is a very deep red variety and shouldn't be confused with the more common orangy red varieties. The best red comes from the seas around Italy; the whites from Japanese waters; the blacks (which we personally don't find very attractive, and which are also different chemically) from Hawaii and Mexico.

Coral is usually cabochon cut, often carved, but is also fairly frequently found in jewelry fashioned "in the rough" (uncut) in certain countries where the belief persists that coral's magical powers are lost with cutting. It is a fairly soft stone, so some caution should be exercised when wearing it. Also, because of its calcium composition, you must be careful to avoid contact with acid, such as vinegar in a salad that you might toss with your hands.

Also, be a cautious buyer for this gem as for others; glass and plastic imitations are commonplace.

## Garnet

If you are loyal, devoted, and energetic, perhaps the garnet is your stone. Or if not, perhaps you should obtain some! Red garnets were "known" to promote sincerity, stop hemorrhaging or other loss of blood, cure inflammatory diseases, and cure anger and discord. And if you engrave a well-formed lion image upon a garnet, it will protect and preserve health, cure the wearer of all disease, bring him honors, and guard him from all perils in traveling. All in all, quite a worthwhile stone.

The garnet family is one of the most exciting families in the gem world. A hard, durable, often very brilliant stone, available in many colors (greens, reds, yellows, oranges), it offers far greater versatility and opportunity for the jewelry trade than has yet been capitalized upon. Depending upon the variety, quality, and size, lovely garnets are available for under $40 per carat or more than $5,000 per carat. Garnet can also be mistaken for other, usually more expensive, gems; green garnet, tsavorite, is one of the most beautiful, and all but a few would assume it was an emerald of the finest quality. In fact, it is clearer, more brilliant, and more durable than emerald itself. There is also a rarer green garnet, called demantoid, which costs slightly more than tsavorite but which, although slightly softer, has more fire. These gems offer fine alternatives to the person desiring a lovely green gem who can't afford emerald. While still rare, expensive gems themselves, these garnet varieties are far less expensive than an emerald of comparable quality. Garnet also occurs in certain shades of red that have been taken for some varieties of ruby. And in yellow it has been confused with precious topaz.

Garnet is found in almost every color and shade *except blue*. It is best known in a deep red variety, sometimes with a brownish cast, but it is commonly found in orangish brown shades, and brilliant wine red shades as well. Other colors include orange, red purple, violet, and pink. A nontransparent variety, grossularite, has a jade-like appearance and may be mistaken for jade when cut into cabochons or carved.

A star garnet found in the United States is a reddish to purple variety that displays a faint four-rayed or six-rayed star, similar to the six-rayed star ruby but not as pronounced.

## Hematite and Marcasite

Hematite is a must for the lawyer, for it ensures for its wearer "alertness, vivacity, and success in litigation." It is also believed to ensure sexual impulse, so if you know of someone with a problem, this may make a "thoughtful" gift.

Hematite is an iron oxide (like iron rust), a metallic, opaque stone found in iron-mining areas. It takes a very brilliant, metallic polish that can look almost like silver, or almost pure black, or gunmetal blue. It was and is popular for use in carving hollow cameo portraits known as intaglio.

Marcasite, the tiny, glittering stone with a brassy-colored luster often seen in old belt buckles and costume jewelry, is a relative of hematite. But *most* "marcasite" seen in jewelry is *not* marcasite, but pyrite (fool's gold)—another brassy-colored metallic mineral.

## Iolite

This is a transparent, usually very clean, blue gem, ranging from deep blue to light gray blue to yellowish grey. It is sometimes called dichroite, and in its sapphire blue color is sometimes referred to as *water sapphire* or *lynx sapphire*. It is a lovely, brilliant stone but not as durable as sapphire. We are just beginning to see this stone in jewelry, and it is still a good value. It is abundant, still very low priced, and one of the most attractive jewelry options for the near future.

## Jade

Jade has long been revered by the Chinese. White jade (yes, white) was believed by the early Chinese to quiet intestinal disturbances, while black jade gave strength and power. A very early written Chinese symbol for "king" was a string of jade beads, and jade beads are still used in China as a symbol of high rank and authority. Jade is also an important part of the Chinese wedding ceremony (the "jade ceremony" holds a prominent place here), for jade is considered "the concentrated essence of love."

Jade is a very tough, although not too hard, translucent to opaque gem, often seen in jewelry and carvings. There are really two types of jade—jadeite and nephrite—which are really two separate and distinct minerals differing from one another in weight, hardness, and color range. Both are called "jade."

Jadeite, the most expensive, more desirable variety, was the most sought after by the Chinese after 1740. It is *not* found in China, however, but in Burma. Some fine jadeite also comes from Guatemala. It is found in a much wider range of colors than nephrite: green, mottled green and white, whitish gray, pink, brown, mauve, yellow, orange, and lilac. In fact, it occurs in almost every color. But with the exception of green, which comes in shades that vary from light to a beautiful emerald green, colored jade is usually pale and unevenly tinted. The most desirable color is a rich emerald green sometimes referred to as imperial jade. Smooth, evenly colored pieces of this jadeite are highly prized, and, in fact, can be classed as precious stones today. The mottled pieces of irregular green, often seen carved, are less valuable, but still more rare and valuable than nephrite jade.

Nephrite jade, the old and true Chinese jade, resembles jadeite but is slightly softer (yet slightly tougher and thus less easily broken) and has a much more limited range of color. Usually fashioned in cabochon cut, or round beads, or in carvings, it is regularly seen in dark green shades sometimes so dark as to look black, hence, black jade. Nephrite green is a more sober green than the apple green or emerald green color of good jadeite. It is closer in color to a dark, sage green or spinach green. Nephrite may also be a creamier color, as in mutton fat jade. Any fine Chinese carving that is more than 230 years old is carved from nephrite (jadeite was unknown to the Chinese before 1740).

Nephrite has been found in many countries, including the United States, where in the late nineteenth century Chinese miners panning for gold in California discovered large boulders of nephrite jade that they sent back to China to be cut or carved. It is also common in Wyoming, Alaska, and British Columbia.

Nephrite jade is much more common than jadeite and is therefore much less expensive. But it is a lovely, popular stone, used extensively in jewelry and carvings.

One must be careful, however, in purchasing jade. You will often see "imperial" jade that is nothing more than a cheap jade that has been dyed. Much of it is treated (usually this means dyed) to enhance its value. The dyeing, however, may be very temporary. Black jade is either dyed or very dark green nephrite that looks black. There are also numerous minerals that look like jade and are sold as jade under misleading names, such as "Virginia jade" (a blue green mineral called amazonite, common in Virginia); "Mexican jade" (jade-colored or dyed onyx marble); "Potomac jade" (diopside, a green mineral). "Pennsylvania jade," "Korean jade," and "new jade" are all serpentine, a soft green stone, similar in appearance to some varieties of jade. In fact, much of the intricately and beautifully carved jade is actually serpentine, which can be scratched easily with a knife.

Soapstone may also look like jade to the amateur, especially when beautifully carved. This stone is so soft that it can easily be scratched with a pin, hairpin, or point of a pen. It is much less expensive than comparable varieties of jade, as well as softer and less durable.

Jade is a wonderful stone and imperial jade is breathtaking; no wonder it was the emperor's stone! But jade has long been "copied"—misrepresented and altered. Just be sure you know you are buying what you think you are buying.

## Labradorite and Sunstone (Feldspar)

Labradorite is a fascinating stone that is starting to appear in some of the more distinctive jewelry salons, especially in beads and carved pieces. A member of the feldspar family, the most frequently seen variety is a grayish, almost opaque stone, within which startlingly brilliant flashes of peacock blue, greens, and/or yellows are visible at certain angles.

A beautiful, shimmering red to orange variety (and occasionally green or bi-color) known as *sunstone* is also beginning to enter the jewelry scene. Mined in Oregon, major US retailers such as Tiffany are featuring this wonderful, truly American gem.

Labradorite is usually cut in cabochon style, but sunstone also occurs in a transparent material that makes a beautiful faceted gem. There are some glass imitations, but they don't come close to the real thing. This is a stone that is still relatively inexpensive and one to consider seriously if you want something striking and unusual.

## Lapis Lazuli

Lapis, a birthstone for December, has been highly prized since ancient Babylonian and Egyptian times. An amulet of "great power" was formed when lapis was worked into the form of an eye and ornamented with gold; in fact, so powerful that sometimes these eyes were put to rest on the limbs of a mummy. In addition, it was recognized as a symbol for capacity, ability, success, and divine favor.

Genuine lapis is a natural blue opaque stone of intense, brilliant, deep blue color. It sometimes possesses small, sparkling gold- or silver-colored flecks (pyrite inclusions), although the finest quality is a deep, even blue with a purplish tint or undertone and no trace of these flecks. Occasionally it may be blue mottled with white.

Don't confuse genuine lapis with the cheaper "Swiss lapis" or "Italian lapis," which aren't lapis at all. These are natural stones (usually quartz) artificially colored to look like lapis lazuli. Genuine lapis is often represented as "Russian lapis," although it doesn't always come from Russia. The finest lapis comes from Afghanistan.

Lapis has become very fashionable, and the finest-quality lapis is becoming more rare and more expensive. This has resulted in an abundance of lapis that has been "color-improved." It is often fashioned today with other gems—pearls, crystal, coral—that make particularly striking fashion accessories.

Sodalite is sometimes confused with the more expensive, and rarer, lapis and used as a substitute for it. However, sodalite rarely contains the silvery or golden flecks typical of most lapis. It may have some white veining, but more commonly it just exhibits the fine lapis blue without any markings. The lapis substitutes do transmit some light through the edges of the stone; lapis does not, since it is opaque.

Dyed chalcedony (quartz), glass, and plastic imitations are common. One quick and easy test to identify genuine lapis is to put a drop of hydrochloric acid on the stones; this will immediately produce the odor of a rotten egg. This test should be administered only by a professional, however, since hydrochloric acid can be dangerous.

## Malachite and Azurite

Malachite must have been the answer to a mother's prayer. According to legend, attaching malachite to the neck of a child would ease its pain when cutting teeth. Also, tied over a woman in labor, it would ensure an easier, faster birth; and it could also cure diseases of the eye. More important, however, it was believed capable of protecting from the evil eye and bringing good luck.

Malachite is also popular today, but perhaps more because of the exquisite color and a softness that makes it very popular for carving. Malachite is a copper ore that comes in a brilliant kelly green, marked with bands or concentric striping in contrasting shades of the same basic green. It is opaque and takes a good polish, but it is soft and should not be worn in rings. This softness, however, makes it a favorite substance for use in carved bases, boxes, beads, statues, spheres, and so on. It is also used in pins, pendants, and necklaces (usually of malachite beads).

Azurite is also a copper ore, but it occurs in a very vivid deep blue, similarly marked. Occasionally one will come across both the green and the blue intermingled in brilliant combinations of color and striking patterns. Both malachite and azurite make beautiful jewelry and lovely carvings.

A particular note of *caution:* Never clean malachite or azurite with any product containing ammonia. In seconds the ammonia will remove all of the polish, which will significantly reduce the stone's beauty.

## Moonstone (Feldspar)

Moonstone is definitely a good luck stone, especially for lovers. As a gift the moonstone holds a high rank, for it is believed to arouse one's tender passion and to give lovers the ability to foretell their future—good or ill. To get this information, however, legend has it that the stone must be placed in the mouth while the moon is full. Perhaps a more important use, however, was in amulets made of moonstone, which would protect men from epilepsy and guarantee a greater fruit-crop yield when hung on fruit trees. The stone, in fact, assisted all vegetation.

The name "moonstone" is probably derived from the myth that one can observe the lunar month through the stone—that a small white spot appears in the stone as the new moon begins and gradually moves toward the stone's center, getting always larger, until the spot finally takes the shape of a full moon in the center of the stone.

Moonstone is a member of the feldspar family. It is a transparent, milky-white variety in which can be seen a floating opalescent white or blue light within the stone's body. It is a popular stone for rings because as the hand moves the effect of the brilliant light color is more pronounced. The bluer color is the finer and more desirable, but it is becoming rare in today's market, particularly in large sizes.

There are some glass imitations of moonstone, but compared to the real thing they are not very good.

## Obsidian

Obsidian was widely used by the Mexicans, probably because of its brilliant polished surface, for making images of their god Tezcatlipoca, and for polishing into mirrors used to divine the future. It has also been found in Egypt, fashioned into masks.

Obsidian is a semitranslucent to opaque glass that is smoky brown to black and sometimes a mixture of both. It is *natural* glass, not man-made. It is formed by volcanic activity, and is also called "volcanic glass." One variety, snowflake obsidian, exhibits white spots resembling snowflakes against or mingled with the black; some obsidian exhibits a strong iridescence; and some obsidian exhibits a sheen from within, as seen in moonstone.

Jewelry made from obsidian, which is available in great quantity and is very inexpensive, is a popular fashion accessory. It is particularly popular in Mexican and Indian jewelry, and is seen fairly extensively in the West and in Mexico. One must exercise some caution, however, because obsidian is glass and can be scratched or cracked easily.

## Onyx

Onyx is not a good-omen stone, and it is certainly not one for young lovers, since it is believed to bear an evil omen, to provoke discord and separate them. Worn around the neck, it was said to cool the ardors of love. The close union and yet strong contrast between the layers of black and white in some varieties may have suggested onyx's connection with romance. It was also believed to cause discord in general, create disharmony among friends, bring bad dreams and broken sleep to its wearer, and cause pregnant women to give birth prematurely.

But there isn't complete agreement as to its unlucky nature. Indians and Persians believe that wearing onyx will protect them from the evil eye, and that when placed on the stomach of a woman in labor it would reduce the labor pain and bring on earlier delivery. So you choose—good or bad?

Onyx is a lovely banded, semitranslucent to opaque quartz. It comes naturally in a variety of colors—reds, oranges, reddish orange, apricot, and shades of brown from cream to dark, often alternating with striking bands of white. The banding in onyx is *straight,* while *curved* bands occur in the variety of quartz known as agate. Onyx is used extensively for cameo and other carving work. It is also frequently dyed.

The "black onyx" that is commonly used in jewelry isn't onyx at all, and isn't naturally black. It is chalcedony (another variety of quartz) dyed black. It is *always* dyed, and may be banded or solid black.

Do not confuse the quartz variety of onyx with cave onyx, which is found in the stalactites and stalagmites of underground caves. Cave onyx is a different material altogether. It is much softer, lacks the color variety, and is much less expensive than quartz onyx.

## Opal

The opal has suffered from an unfortunate reputation as being an evil stone and bearing an ill omen. Ominous superstitions surround this wonderful gem, including the belief that misfortune will fall on those who wear it. But its evil reputation has never been merited and probably resulted from a careless reading of Sir Walter Scott's *Anne of Geierstein,* in which the ill-fated heroine received an opal before her untimely death.

Among the ancients, opal was a symbol of fidelity and assurance, and in later history it became strongly associated with religious emotion and prayer. It was believed to have a strong therapeutic value for diseases of the eye, and worn as an amulet it would make the wearer immune from them as well as increase the powers of the eyes and the mind. Further, many believed that to the extent the colors of red and green (ruby and emerald) were seen, the wearer would also enjoy the therapeutic powers of those stones: the power to stop bleeding from the ruby or the power to cure kidney diseases from the emerald. The black opal was particularly highly prized as the luck stone of anyone lucky enough to own one!

This stone, whose brilliance and vibrant colors resemble the colors of the fall, is certainly appropriate as a birthstone for October. When we try to describe the opal, we realize how insufficient the English language is. It is unique among the gems, displaying an array of very brilliant miniature rainbow effects, all mixed together.

Its most outstanding characteristic is this unusual, intense display of many colors flashing out like mini-rainbows. This effect is created by opal's formation process, which is very different from that of other gems. Opal is composed of hydrated silica spheres. The mini-rainbows seen in most opals result from light interference created by these spheres. The arrangement of the spheres, which vary in size and pattern, is responsible for the different colors.

Opal is usually cut flat or in cabochon, since there is no additional brilliance to be captured by faceting. In opals, color is everything. The more brilliant the color, the more valuable the gem. It is probably truer of opal than any other stone that the more beautiful the stone and its color, the more it will cost.

The finest of all is the black opal. Black opals are usually a deep gray or grayish black with flashes of incredibly brilliant color dancing around within and about the stones as they are turned. One must be careful when purchasing a black opal, however, to ensure that it is not a doublet or triplet, a stone composed of two or three parts of some material fused or glued together. There are many such doublets on the market because of the black opal's rarity, beauty, and extremely high cost; a black opal the size of a lima bean could cost $25,000 today. The black opal doublet provides an affordable option to one who loves the stone but can't afford a natural. But it also provides another opportunity for misrepresentation that can be very costly to the consumer.

Generally speaking, purity of color, absence of dead spots (called *trueness*), flawlessness, and intensity or brilliance of color are the primary variables affecting value. Opals with an abundance of red are usually the most expensive; those strong in blue and green are equally beautiful but not as rare, so their price is somewhat less. Some opals are very transparent and are classified as "jelly," "semi-jelly," or "water" opals. One of the rarest is the "harlequin" opal, which displays color patterns resembling a checker-board.

While there are imitations and synthetics, for the most part their quality is such that they are not yet worth considering. The synthetic opal, nonetheless, is being used extensively. Also, since the color of black opals can be improved by treatment, treated opals are encountered frequently. So the usual precautions are in order: make sure you know what you are getting and before buying, shop around. This holds truer for opal, perhaps, than any other stone.

One word of caution must also be offered: Opals require special care because some tend to dry and crack. Avoid exposure to anything that is potentially drying. And, believe it or not, rubbing it periodically with an oil-moistened cloth—such as olive oil—will help preserve it. *Do not soak it;* soaking some opals for only a few hours can cause them to lose some or nearly all of their fire.

## Peridot

Today's birthstone for August, peridot was also a favorite of the ancients. This lovely transparent yellowish green to deep chartreuse stone was quite a powerful gem. It was considered an aid to friendship and was also believed to free the mind of envious thoughts. (Which is probably why it was an aid to friendship.) Because of its yellowish green color, it was also believed to cure or prevent diseases of the liver and dropsy. And, if that's not enough, if worn on the left arm it would protect the wearer from the evil eye.

Peridot is also popular today, but probably more for its lovely shade of green than its professed powers. While not particularly brilliant, the richness of its color can be exceptional. It comes in shades of yellowish green to darker, purer green colors. Unfortunately, because of its rarity most people never see peridot in the deeper, purer green color that is so prized.

Peridot is still widely available in small sizes but larger stones are becoming scarce, so prices are now fairly high for good quality material in higher carat weights.

Some caution should be exercised in wearing peridot. It is not a very hard stone and may scratch easily. Also, some stones—like green sapphire or green tourmaline—can look like peridot and be mistaken or misrepresented.

## Quartz

The most versatile of any of the gem families, quartz includes among its members more variety and a larger number of gems than any other three mineral families together. In the gem trade the old saying, "If in doubt, say quartz," still holds true.

The quartz minerals, for the most part, are relatively inexpensive gems that offer a wide range of pleasing color alternatives both in transparent and nontransparent varieties (from translucent to opaque). They are reasonably hard stones, and while not very brilliant in the transparent varieties, still create lovely, affordable jewelry.

Some of these gems have been discussed in separate sections, but we will provide a list here with brief descriptions of most of the quartz family members.

### Transparent Varieties

*Amethyst* (see page 163). Lilac to purple.

*Citrine,* often called quartz topaz, citrine topaz, or topaz, all of which are misleading. The correct name for this stone is citrine. It is yellow, amber to amber brown. This is the most commonly seen "topaz" in today's marketplace and is, unfortunately, too often confused with precious topaz because of the careless use of the name. While a pleasing stone in terms of color and fairly durable, citrine is slightly softer and has less brilliance than precious topaz. It also lacks the subtle color shading, the pinker yellow or pinkish amber shades, which lend to precious topaz a distinctive color difference. Much citrine is made by heat-treating purple amethyst.

Citrine is much less expensive than precious topaz. It should never be represented as topaz, which technically is "precious" or "imperial" topaz. Unfortunately, it often is. For example, "topaz" birthstone jewelry is almost always citrine (or a worthless synthetic).

So the question to ask the seller is, "Is this citrine or precious topaz?" Get the answer in writing if you are told, "Precious topaz."

Citrine is plentiful in all sizes, and can be made into striking jewelry, especially in very large sizes, for a relatively small investment, while precious topaz of fine quality is scarce in sizes over seven carats, and *very* expensive.

*Praseolite.* A pale green transparent variety produced by heating amethyst.

*Rock crystal.* Water clear. Used in old jewelry for rondelles, a type of small bead resembling a doughnut. Faceted crystal beads were also common in older jewelry. Today, however, *crystal* usually refers to glass.

*Rose quartz.* Light to deep pink. This stone has been very popular for many years for use in carved pieces—beads, statues, ashtrays, fine lamp bases, and pins and brooches. Rarely clear, this stone is usually seen in cabochon-cuts, rounded beads, or carvings rather than in faceted styles. Once very inexpensive, it is becoming more costly, particularly in the finer deep pink shades. But the color of rose quartz is especially pleasing and offers an excellent choice for use in fashion accessory jewelry.

You must be somewhat cautious with rose quartz, however, because it tends to crack more easily than most other varieties of quartz if struck or exposed to a blow. The inclusions or internal fractures that are also responsible for the absence of clarity in this stone cause it to be slightly brittle.

*Smoky quartz.* A pale to rich smoky brown variety, sometimes mistaken for or misrepresented as smoky topaz or topaz. Also very plentiful and becoming popular for use in very large sizes for beautiful brooches, large dinner rings, and so forth.

### Translucent to Opaque Varieties

*Agate and chalcedony.* All colors and varieties of markings are seen in this wonderful ornamental gem. Among them you'll find, to mention a few: banded agate; moss agate, a fascinating white or milky agate that looks as though it actually has black, brown, or green moss growing within; eye agate, which has an eyeball effect; or plume agate, which looks like it's filled with beautiful feather plumes. The colors and "scenes" in agate are infinite. While agate is usually an inexpensive stone, some varieties or special stones with very unusual scenes or markings can be quite expensive.

*Carnelian, sard, and sardonyx* are reddish, orange, apricot, and brown varieties of chalcedony and are often seen in cameo or other carving work. Black onyx is a dyed chalcedony; chrysoprase is green chalcedony, often dyed green.

The unusual colors and markings of agate made it very highly regarded by the ancients and revered throughout history, even to the present day. It was believed to make wearers "agreeable and persuasive and give them God's favor." Other virtues claimed for agate wearers include giving the wearer victory and strength and also protection from tempests and lightning, guarding its wearer from all dangers, enabling him to overcome all terrestrial obstacles, and imparting to him a bold heart.

Wearing agate ornaments was also seen as a cure for insomnia and could ensure good dreams. In the middle of the 1800s and continuing to the present in some parts of the world, amulets made from eye agate (brown or black agate with a white ring in the center) were so popular that agate cutters in Germany had time for cutting little else. The "eye" was believed to take on the watchfulness of one's guardian spirit and protect the wearer from the evil eye by neutralizing its power. At one time these amulets commanded an incredible price.

Whatever their real power, these are fascinating stones, some quite mesmerizing in their unusual beauty. They are often seen in antique jewelry as well as in contemporary pieces. One must be careful, however, to exercise some caution in wear to protect from knocks, as some varieties are more fragile than others. Also, agate is frequently dyed, so it is important to ask whether the color is natural, and to be sure that it is not another less valuable stone, dyed to look like a special variety of agate.

*Aventurine.* A lovely pale to medium green semitranslucent stone with tiny sparkling flecks of mica within. This stone makes very lovely cabochon or bead jewelry at a very affordable price. It is occasionally misrepresented as jade; although the mica flecks are sometimes so small that they cannot be seen easily, they provide an immediate and reliable indicator that the material is aventurine quartz. Be aware, however, that there are some fairly good glass imitations in the marketplace.

*Bloodstone* (see page 166). Dark green with red spots.

*Cat's-Eye.* A pale yellowish green stone that when cut in cabochon style produces a streak of light down the center that creates an eye effect. This phenomenon is a result of the presence of fiberlike inclusions. This stone's center line is weaker, its color paler, and its cost much less than true cat's-eye from the chrysoberyl family. But it is nonetheless an attractive stone that makes attractive, affordable jewelry.

*Chrysocolla.* The true chrysocolla is a very soft copper mineral, too soft for jewelry use. However, quartz that has been naturally impregnated or stained with chrysocolla has good hardness and the same brilliant blue green, highly translucent color. Chrysocolla is becoming a very popular stone for jewelry, and its price is starting to reflect increased demand.

*Chrysoprase* (see page 167). A bright light to dark green, highly translucent stone, often of very even color. Sometimes misrepresented or confused for jade.

*Jasper.* Opaque red, yellow, green, and brown (or sometimes gray). Usually strongly marked in terms of the contrast between the green and other colors in an almost blotchlike or veinlike pattern. The red and green combination is the most popular, although there are more than fifty types of jasper of various colors and patterns.

Jasper was believed in ancient cultures to bring rain and also to protect its wearer from the bites of poisonous creatures. It was believed to have as diverse a power as the colors and veins in which it came, so there were many uses and magical powers associated with it.

Jasper offers interesting color contrast and variety, and is being used increasingly in today's fashion accessory jewelry.

*Petrified wood.* Sections of trees or limbs that have been replaced by quartz-type silica and transformed into a mineral after centuries of immersion in silica-rich water under extreme pressure. Usually red, reddish brown, or brown. Not often seen in jewelry.

*Tiger-eye.* A golden, yellowish, reddish, and sometimes bluish variety of quartz that produces a bright shimmering line (or lines) of light, which when cut in a cabochon will produce an eye. The eye will move when the stone is turned from side to side. It is inexpensive, but very popular for fashion accessory jewelry and men's cuff links and rings.

## Rhodochrosite

Rhodochrosite is a newcomer to the jewelry business. While sought by rock hounds for many years and a favorite of beginning lapidaries, rhodochrosite appeared only occasionally outside of rock and mineral shows frequented by hobbyists. A member of the carbonate mineral group, rhodochrosite is a relatively soft stone occurring in both a rare transparent and a more common nontransparent variety. For practical purposes, we will discuss the latter, more readily available form.

A lovely red to almost white color, often with agatelike curved lines creating a design in contrasting shades of red or pink, rhodochrosite may occasionally occur in an orangy tone, but this is poorer-quality material. The finest color is a medium to deep rose, preferably with curved banding. It has long been popular for certain ornamental objects (spheres, boxes, eggs) but only recently for jewelry. Today, necklaces using rhodochrosite beads alternating with other stones or gold beads are becoming particularly popular. We will see more rhodochrosite on the market in coming years. It is soft, however, and some caution should be used in wearing to avoid unnecessary abuse.

## Scapolite

This is an interesting gem that is beginning to appear in more jewelry as it becomes more available. Rediscovered in Brazil after a forty-year hiatus and also recently discovered in Kenya, scapolite is a nice, transparent, fairly durable stone occurring in a range of colors from colorless to yellow, light red, orange to greenish to bluish gray, violet, and violet blue. The orange, light red, and whitish specimens may also occur as semitransparent stones, which may show a cat's-eye effect (chatoyancy) when cut into cabochons.

The most likely to appear in jewelry are the violets and yellows, and possibly orange cat's-eyes. They might easily be mistaken for yellow beryl or certain quartz minerals like amethyst or citrine.

The bottom line here is that we will have to wait and see what trends evolve around this stone, as its availability will determine future use and cost.

## Serpentine

Serpentine derives its name from its similarity to the green, speckled skin of the serpent. Amulets of serpentine were worn for protection from serpent bites, stings of poisonous reptiles, and poison in general. A king was reputed to have insisted that his chalice be made of serpentine, as it was believed that if a poisoned drink were put into a serpentine vessel, the vessel would sweat on the outside. The effectiveness of medicine was increased when drunk from a serpentine vessel.

Serpentine is often used as a jade substitute. It is a translucent to semitranslucent stone occurring in light to dark yellowish green to greenish yellow. One variety is used for decorative wall facings and table and counter surfaces, but some of the more attractive green varieties so closely resemble jadeite or nephrite jade that they are used in carvings and jewelry, and are often misrepresented as jade. Common serpentine is also sometimes dyed a jadelike color. One lovely green variety, williamsite, which is a very pleasing deep green, often with small black flecks within, is often sold as "Pennsylvania jade." It is pretty, but it is not jade. Another variety of serpentine, bowenite, is also sold today as "Korean jade" or "new jade." Again, it is pretty but is not jade. Serpentine is softer than jade, less durable, and much more common, which its price should reflect.

It is a lovely stone in its own right, and makes a nice alternative to jade. While it has been around for a long time (too often, however, represented as jade), we are just beginning to see this stone used frequently in necklaces and other fine jewelry under its own name.

## Sodalite

This stone has already been discussed under lapis. It is a dark blue semitransparent to semitranslucent stone used frequently as a substitute for the rarer, more expensive lapis. While it may have some white veining, it does not have the golden or silver flecks that are characteristic of lapis. If you do not see these shiny flecks, suspect that the stone is probably sodalite.

## Spinel

Spinel is one of the loveliest of the gems but hasn't yet been given due credit and respect. It is usually compared to sapphire or ruby, rather than being recognized for its own intrinsic beauty and value. There is also a common belief that spinel (and similarly zircon) is synthetic rather than natural, when in fact it is one of nature's most beautiful products. This misconception probably arose because synthetic spinel is seen frequently on the market whereas *genuine* spinel is not often seen.

Spinel occurs in red orange (flame spinel), light to dark orangy red, light to dark slightly grayish blue, greenish blue, grayish green, and dark to light purple to violet. It also occurs in yellow and in an opaque variety—black. When compared to the blue of sapphire or the red of ruby, the color is usually considered less intense (although some red spinel can look very much like some ruby on the market now), yet its brilliance can be greater. If you appreciate these spinel colors for themselves, they are quite pleasing. The most popular are red (usually a more orange-red than ruby red) and blue (sometimes resembling a strong Bromo-Seltzer-bottle blue).

Spinel may be confused with or misrepresented as one of many stones—ruby, sapphire, zircon, amethyst, garnet, synthetic ruby/sapphire or synthetic spinel—as well as glass. The synthetic is often used to make composite stones such as doublets. Spinel is a fairly hard, fairly durable stone, possessing a nice brilliance, and still a good value.

This stone is becoming more and more popular today, and may, therefore, become more expensive if current trends continue.

## Spodumene (Kunzite and Hiddenite)

Spodumene is another gem relatively new to widespread jewelry use. The most popular varieties are kunzite and hiddenite.

Kunzite is a very lovely brilliant stone occurring in delicate lilac, pinkish, or violet shades. Its color can fade in strong light, and so it has become known as an "evening" stone. Also, while basically hard, it is nonetheless brittle and can break easily if it receives a sharp blow from certain directions. It is not recommended for rings for this reason unless set in a protective mounting. But it is a lovely gem, whose low cost makes it attractive in large sizes, and an excellent choice for lovely, dramatic jewelry design.

Hiddenite is rarer. Light green or yellow green varieties are available, but the emerald green varieties are scarce. As with kunzite, it is hard but brittle, so care must be exercised in wear.

Spodumene also occurs in many other shades of color, all pale but very clear and brilliant. Only blue is currently missing but who knows what may yet be discovered in some part of the world? Spodumene is still fairly inexpensive and is an excellent choice for contemporary jewelry design. Be careful, however, as it can be confused with and sold for more expensive topaz, tourmaline, spinel, or beryl. Also, synthetic corundum or spinel can be mistaken for this gem.

## Sugilite

Named for the Japanese petrologist who discovered it, Ken-ichi Sugi, sugilite first appeared on the jewelry scene in the late 1970s, sold as Royal Azel and Royal Lavulite. Best known today as sugilite, its lovely, deep rich purple to purple-red color is unique. An opaque gem, it is usually cut in cabochons or beads, although it is also popular for inlay work (intarsia) by top artisans. Sugilite belongs to the manganese family and most comes from Africa. The finest color is already becoming scarce, so it is difficult to predict the future for this interesting newcomer.

## Tanzanite (see *Zoisite*)

## Titanite (Sphene)

This is another "new" gem that is beginning to appear and offers some interesting possibilities for the jewelry market. While it has been highly regarded for many years, its relative scarcity prevented its widescale use in jewelry. Today, however, new sources have been discovered and we are beginning to see greater availability.

This is a beautiful, brilliant stone, with a diamondlike (adamantine) luster and fire that is even greater than in diamond. Unfortunately, it is soft. Its colors range from grass green to golden yellow to brown.

There is need for some caution because of this stone's softness. We suggest that it is especially suitable for pendants, earrings, brooches, and protective ring settings.

## Topaz

True topaz, symbol of love and affection, aid to sweetness of disposition, and birthstone for November, is one of nature's most wonderful and least-known families. The true topaz is rarely seen in jewelry stores. Unfortunately, most people know only the quartz (citrine) topaz, or glass, and in the past almost any yellow stone was called topaz. A very beautiful and versatile stone, topaz is a hard, brilliant stone with a fine color range, and it is much rarer and much more expensive than the stones commonly sold as topaz. It is also heavier than its imitators.

Topaz occurs not only in the transparent yellow, yellow brown, orangy brown, and pinky brown colors most popularly associated with it, but also in a very light to medium red now found naturally in fair supply, although many are produced through heat treatment. It also is found in a very light to medium deep blue, also often the result of treatment, although it does occur naturally on a fairly wide scale. Other topaz shades include very light green, light greenish yellow, violet, and colorless.

Blue topaz has become very popular in recent years, most of it treated; unfortunately, there is no way yet to determine which have been treated and which are natural. The blue form closely resembles the finest aquamarine, which is very expensive today, and offers a very attractive, and much more affordable, alternative to it. Some of the fine, deeper blue treated topazes have been found to be radioactive and, according to the Nuclear Regulatory Commission, may be injurious to the wearer. In the United States all blue topaz must be tested for radiation levels; the GIA now provides this service to the jewelry trade. However, be very careful when buying blue topaz outside the United States. If you do, you may be wise to have it tested when you get home.

There are many misleading names to suggest that a stone is topaz when it is not, for example, "Rio topaz," "Madeira topaz," "Spanish topaz," and "Palmeira topaz." They are types of citrine (quartz) and should be represented as such.

The true topaz family offers a variety of color options in lovely, clear, brilliant, and durable stones. This family should become more important in the years ahead.

## Tourmaline

Tourmaline is a gem of modern times, but nonetheless has found its way to the list of birthstones, becoming an "alternate birthstone" for October. Perhaps this honor results from tourmaline's versatility and broad color range. Or perhaps from the fact that red-and-green tourmaline, in which red and green occur side-by-side in the same stone, is reminiscent of the turning of October leaves.

Whatever the case, tourmaline is one of the most versatile of the gem families. It is available in every color, in every tone, from deep to pastel and even with two or more colors appearing in the same stone, side-by-side. There are bicolored tourmalines (half red and the other half green, for example) and tricolored (one-third blue, one-third green, and one-third yet another color). The fascinating "watermelon" tourmaline looks just like the inside of a watermelon—red in the center surrounded by a green "rind." Tourmaline can also be found in a cat's-eye variety.

One of the most exciting gemological discoveries of this century was the discovery of a unique variety of tourmaline in Paraiba, Brazil. These particular beauties, referred to as "Paraiba" or "Hetorita" after the man who discovered them, have colors so intense and come in such a wide range of green, blue, and lilac shades that they are referred to as the *neon* tourmalines. Unfortunately, demand has been unprecedented for these particular tourmalines, and supply has dwindled. The result is that many of the finest Paraibas are very expensive and some rival the finest sapphires in price. For anyone who loves these colors, they are worth seeing just for their own sake. If jewelers in your area don't have these stones, they can contact the *American Gem Trade Association* in Dallas, Texas, regarding where to obtain them.

It is indeed surprising that most people know of tourmaline simply as a common "green" stone. Nothing could be more misleading. Today, we are finally beginning to see other lovely varieties of this fascinating gem in the jewelry market. In addition to the exciting new "Paraiba," other popular varieties include:

- Chrome—A particularly rare green hue
- Indicolite—Deep indigo blue, usually with a green undertone
- Rubellite—Deep pink to red, as in ruby

While many tourmalines are very inexpensive, the chrome, indicolite, and rubellite varieties are priced (depending on size and quality) anywhere from $300 to $1,000 per carat or more. And the incomparable Paraiba varieties can sell for $2,000 to $3,000 per carat for a top quality one-carat stone—up to $8,000 per carat for a five-carat stone, if you can find one. So much for the "common and inexpensive" myth!

Tourmaline is a fairly hard, durable, brilliant, and very wearable stone with a wide choice of colors. It is also still available in large sizes. It is a stone that without question will play a more and more important role in jewelry in the years ahead.

## Turquoise

A birthstone for December, and ranking highest among all the opaque stones, turquoise—the "Turkish stone"—is highly prized throughout Asia and Africa, not only for its particular hue of blue (a beautiful robin's-egg or sky blue) but more important for its supposed prophylactic and therapeutic qualities. The Arabs consider it a lucky stone and have great confidence in its benevolent action. Used in rings, earrings, necklaces, head ornaments, and amulets, it protects the wearer from poison, reptile bites, eye diseases, and the evil eye. It was also believed capable of warning of impending death by changing color. Also, the drinking of water in which turquoise has been dipped or washed was believed to cure bladder ailments. Buddhists revere the turquoise because it is associated with a legend in which a turquoise enabled Buddha to destroy a monster. Even today it is considered a symbol of courage, success, and love. It has also long been associated with American Indian jewelry and art.

Turquoise is an opaque, light to dark blue or blue green stone. The finest color is an intense blue, with poorer qualities tending toward yellowish green. The famous Persian turquoise, which can be a very intense and pleasing blue, is considered a very rare and valuable gem.

All turquoises are susceptible to aging and may turn greenish or possibly darker with age. Also, care must be taken when wearing, both to avoid contact with soap, grease, or other materials that might discolor it, and to protect it from abuse, since turquoise scratches fairly easily.

But exercise caution when buying turquoise. This is a frequently simulated gem. Very fine glass imitations are produced that are difficult to distinguish from the genuine. Very fine adulterated stones, and reconstructed stones (from turquoise powder bonded in plastic) saturate the marketplace, as does synthetic turquoise. There are techniques to quickly distinguish these imitations or simulations, so, if in doubt, check it out (and get a complete description on the bill of sale: "genuine, natural turquoise").

## Zircon

Known to the ancients as "hyacinth," this gem had many powers, especially for men. While it was known to assist women in childbirth, for men it kept evil spirits and bad dreams away, gave protection against "fascination" and lightning, strengthened their bodies, fortified their hearts, restored appetite, suppressed fat, produced sleep, and banished grief and sadness from the mind.

Zircons are very brilliant transparent stones available in several lovely colors. Unfortunately, many consumers suffer from a strange misconception that zircon is a synthetic or man-made stone rather than a lovely natural creation. Perhaps this belief is based on the fact that they are frequently color treated, as in the blue zircons so often seen. Zircons also occur naturally in yellow, brown, orange, and red.

Many might mistake the colorless zircon for diamond because of its strong brilliance, which coupled with its very low cost, makes colorless zircon an interesting alternative to diamonds as a stone to offset or dress up colored stones. But care needs to be exercised because zircon is brittle and will chip or abrade easily. For this reason, zircon is recommended for earrings, pendants, brooches, or rings with a protective setting.

## Zoisite (Tanzanite)

Zoisite was not considered a gem material until 1967, when a beautiful rich, blue to purple blue, transparent variety was found in Tanzania (hence tanzanite). Tanzanite can possess a rich, sapphire blue color, possibly with some violet red or greenish yellow flashes. A gem *green* variety has recently been discovered, which is being called "green tanzanite" or "chrome tanzanite." The green can be a very lovely shade, ranging from a slightly yellowish green to gray green to a bluish green. Supply is still limited, so time will tell whether or not this green variety will be readily available to the public.

This lovely gem can cost over $2,000 per carat today in larger sizes. But one must be cautious. It is relatively soft, so we do not recommend tanzanite for rings (unless it's set in a very protected setting) or for everyday wear in which it would be exposed to knocks and other abuse.

# 17

## Pearls

*The richest merchandise of all, and the most sovereign
commodity throughout the whole world, are these pearls.*

Pliny, A.D. 105

Next to the diamond, there is no gem that has fascinated
mankind more than the pearl. The oldest known natural
pearl necklace is more than 4,000 years old. Today's birthstone for
June, the pearl was long believed to possess a special mystical quality,
symbolized by the glow that seems to radiate from its very center.
This glow signified to the ancient world a powerful inner life. In fact,
Roman women are believed to have taken pearls to bed with them to
sweeten dreams! Over time, the pearl has acquired strong associations with love, success, happiness, and the virtues of modesty,
chastity, and purity, which make it a popular choice for brides on
their wedding day.

Pearls offer more versatility than perhaps any other gem—they go
well with any style, in any place; they can be worn from morning to
evening; they look smart and attractive with sportswear, add an
"executive" touch to the business suit, or add elegance to even the
most glamorous evening gown. They are also available in a wide
variety of types, sizes, shapes, colors, and price ranges. They offer
limitless possibilities for creative stringing, which adds up to greater
versatility as well as greater affordability.

Pearls have become an essential for any well-dressed woman
today, yet most buyers feel overwhelmed and intimidated by all the
choices, and the widely differing prices. But with just a little knowledge, you'll be surprised by how quickly you can learn to see and
understand variations in characteristics and quality.

# What Is a Pearl?

A pearl is the gem produced by oysters (the non-edible variety) in saltwater, or by a freshwater mollusc. In either case, a small foreign object (such as a tiny sea parasite from the ocean floor) finds its way into the shell, and then into the tissue of the mollusc. If the intruder becomes trapped, and the oyster can't rid itself of it, the foreign body becomes an "irritant." To ease the discomfort this irritant creates, the mollusc takes defensive action, and produces a blackish substance called conchiolin, over which another substance, a whitish substance called "nacre," is secreted. The nacre is composed of microscopic crystals, each crystal aligned perfectly with the others so that light passing along the axis of one is reflected and refracted by the others to produce a rainbow-like glow of light and color. The pearl is the result of the build-up of layer after layer of this nacre. The thicker the nacre, the more beautiful the pearl.

# The Pearl Market Is a "Cultured" Pearl Market Today

Most pearls sold today are *cultured* pearls. Natural—or "Oriental" pearls, as they are sometimes called—have become one of the rarest of all gems, with prices to match. Cultured pearls are much more affordable.

One way to understand the difference between a natural pearl and a cultured pearl is to think of the natural pearl as a product of the oyster working alone, and the cultured pearl as a product of humans "helping" nature. In the natural pearl, the "irritant" around which the oyster secretes the nacre and produces the pearl is a foreign object which *accidentally* finds its way into the oyster tissue. In the cultured pearl, humans implant the irritant—a mother-of-pearl bead called the "nucleus." After the initial implantation, however, the process by which the cultured pearl is produced is very similar to that in the natural pearl—the oyster produces "nacre" to coat the irritant, layer after layer building up and producing the pearl. The oyster produces the "nacre;" the oyster produces the finished pearl. The pearl producers wash the oyster periodically, control available food, try to maintain constant water temperature and control pollutants, but the oyster itself still has control of the pearl product it produces.

The primary physical difference between the resulting products—natural and cultured pearls—is in the thickness of the nacre. Even though it takes several years to raise the oyster and produce a fine cultured pearl, the pearls are nonetheless harvested much sooner than comparable natural pearls, often when the nacre thickness reaches only $1/_2$ millimeter. The nacre on the natural pearl is much thicker because it has taken many more years to produce.

Natural pearls are often less perfectly round than fine cultured pearls, and in strands or jewelry containing numerous pearls, naturals usually appear much less uniform in color and shape than do cultured pearls. The reason for greater uniformity in cultured pearls is that, given the larger quantity of cultured pearls available, it is easier to find and carefully match pearls.

Fine natural pearls are rare and valuable and, for the most part, always have been. Never take anyone's word that their pearls are natural, even "inherited" pearls. Most of the time these inherited heirlooms turn out *not* to be natural, or even cultured, but *fake*. Imitation pearls have been around for centuries. Even Mrs. Harry Winston and the Duchess of Windsor owned and wore fake pearls. Of course, they also had "real" pearls in the safe!

If you are buying a strand of pearls represented to be natural, make sure they are accompanied by an identification report from a reliable lab. Natural pearls must be x-rayed to confirm authenticity. Always be sure to have proper documentation, no matter who the owner, or how wealthy, or how old the piece.

## Cultured Versus Imitation Pearls

Both cultured and natural pearls are produced by the oyster or mollusc. Imitation pearls have never seen the inside of an oyster. They are entirely artificial, made from round glass or plastic beads dipped in a bath of ground fish scales and lacquer, or one of the new plastic substances. The difference between real and simulated pearls can usually be seen when the two are compared side by side. One of the most obvious differences is in the luster. Give it the *luster test;* the real pearl will have a depth of luster that the fake cannot duplicate. The fake usually has a surface "shine" but no inner "glow." Look in the shaded area—in the real pearl you see a clearly defined reflection; in the fake pearl you will not.

### Use the tooth test to separate the fake

There are some fine imitations today that can be very convincing. Some have actually been mistaken for fine cultured pearls. An easy, reliable test in most cases is the "tooth test." Run the pearl gently along the edge of your teeth (the upper teeth are more sensitive, and also be aware that the test won't work with false teeth). The genuine pearl will have a mildly abrasive or gritty feel (think of sand at the seaside—real pearls come from the sea), while the imitation will be slippery smooth (like the con artist, slippery smooth signifies a fake!). Try this test on pearls you know are genuine, and then on known imitations to get a feel for the difference. You'll never forget it!

The tooth test may be unreliable when applied to the Majorica pearl, however. This is an imitation pearl which might easily be mistaken for genuine. An experienced jeweler or gemologist can quickly and easily identify the Majorica for you.

## The Factors That Affect Pearl Quality and Value

Now that you understand the differences between natural, cultured, and imitation pearls, let's talk about quality differences. Regardless of the type of pearl, or whether it is natural or cultured, five factors are evaluated to determine its quality.

1. *Luster and Orient.* This is the sharpness and intensity of the images reflected from the pearl's surface (luster) and the underlying iridescent play of colors (orient) which distinguishes the pearl from all other gems. The degree of luster and orient is one of the most important factors in determining the quality and value of the pearl. High luster is perhaps the first thing one notices when looking at a fine strand of pearls. The higher the luster and orient, the finer the pearl. Luster is usually judged from "sharp" (high) to "dull" (low). When judging luster and orient, look at the *shadow* area of the pearl, not the shiny, reflective area (don't confuse "shine" with the deep iridescent glow created by the combination of luster and orient).

2. *Color.* Color is usually considered the most important factor affecting value and cost. There are two elements involved in evaluating color: body color and overtone. The "body color" refers to the basic color, i.e., white, yellow, black. The "overtone" refers to the presence of a secondary color (its "tint"), such as the

"pinkish" overtone in fine white pearls. Color refers to the combination of the body color and overtone. Very white pearls with a rose-colored overtone (tint) are the rarest and the most expensive. The creamier the color becomes, the less costly they are. However, today the "rose" tint is often imparted to the pearl through artificial means. If you use a loupe to examine the drill hole, you may be able to detect the color enhancement if you can see the line of demarcation between the mother-of-pearl nucleus and the nacre; if the pearl has been tinted, the line will show a pinkish coloration.

Cultured pearls are available in many colors—gray, black, pink, blue, gold—but often these colors have been produced by surface dyes or irradiation techniques. White pearls that have been drilled for jewelry use (as in a necklace) and then tinted or dyed can usually be detected easily by a qualified gemologist. With rare black pearls it may be necessary to send them to a gem-testing laboratory with sophisticated equipment in order to be sure.

3. *Cleanliness* (surface texture or perfection). This refers to the pearl's freedom from such surface blemishes as small blisters, pimples, spots, or cracks. Imperfections may also appear as dark spots, small indentations, welts or blisters, or surface bumps. While occasional small blemishes are not uncommon, if large or numerous they are unsightly. A pearl with sizable or numerous blemishes may also be less durable. The cleaner the skin, the better. Also, the closer the blemish to the drill hole, the less it detracts from both appearance and value.

4. *Shape.* Shape in pearls is divided into three categories: spherical, symmetrical, and baroque. The rarest and most valuable is the spherical or round pearl; these are judged on their degree of "sphericity" or roundness. While perfectly round pearls are extremely rare, the closer to perfectly round, the finer and more expensive the pearl. Button pearls and pear-shaped pearls are symmetrical pearls, and are judged on evenness and good symmetry, that is, whether they have a nice, well proportioned shape. Symmetrical pearls are less expensive than round pearls, but much more expensive than baroque pearls, which refers to irregularly shaped pearls. Any strand of pearls should be well matched for shape, and when worn give the appearance of uniformity.

5. *Size.* Natural pearls are sold by weight. They are weighed in "grains," with four grains equal to one carat. Cultured pearls are sold by millimeter size (one millimeter equals approximately $1/25$ inch): their measurement indicates the number of millimeters in the diameter of the pearl. Two millimeter dimensions—length and width—may be given if the pearl is not round. The larger the pearl, the greater the cost. A 2 millimeter cultured pearl is considered very small, whereas those over 9 millimeters are considered very large. Large cultured pearls are rarer, and are more expensive. There is a dramatic jump in the cost of cultured pearls after seven and a half millimeters. The price jumps upward rapidly with each half-millimeter from 8 millimeters up.

Another factor affecting the value of any pearl item which has been strung, as in a necklace, is the precision which went into the matching of the pearls; this is called the "make." Consider how well matched the strand is in size, shape, color, luster, and surface texture. Graduated pearls also require careful sizing. Failure to match carefully will detract from both the appearance of the item and its value.

# Types of Pearls

The best-known pearl is the round pearl produced by saltwater oysters. The most famous of these is Japan's Akoya pearl. The finest Akoyas are more perfectly round than other pearls and have the highest luster, which makes them very desirable. Unfortunately, for those who prefer very large pearls, they rarely exceed 10 millimeters in diameter, and when they do, they command a stellar price.

## Biwa and other freshwater pearls

Biwa pearls are grown in fresh water (lakes and rivers) and derive their name from Lake Biwa in Japan, where very fine pearls are cultivated. Until recently, the term "Biwa" was often used for any freshwater pearl. Today it is used only for those from Lake Biwa.

Freshwater pearls are grown in many countries, including the United States, Japan, China, and Ireland. Common mussel-type molluscs are used. The process does not require the insertion of a mother-of-pearl bead, so the pearls grow much faster and, unlike the saltwater oyster, which normally produces only one or two pearls, each mussel can simultaneously produce many. As a result, most freshwater pearls are much less expensive than their saltwater counterparts.

The most familiar freshwater pearls have long, narrow, rice-shaped outlines, generally with a "wrinkled" surface, although the surface can be smooth. They can also be round, but these are rare and expensive.

Some of the world's most prized—and most beautiful— pearls are *natural* freshwater pearls. These are very expensive and can compare to the price of natural saltwater pearls. Frequently whiter than the natural saltwater pearl, these are the pearls that were so cherished by the Romans—pearls found in the rivers of the European countries they conquered. The only reason the Roman legions ever ventured into England, it is rumored, was to search for the rare and beautiful *pink* freshwater pearls found in Scotland!

Cultured freshwater pearls also occur in interesting shapes, as do the natural; in fact, natural "angel-wing" pearls from the Mississippi River and other nearby rivers and lakes are very collectible. Cultured pearl producers are experimenting with culturing freshwater pearls in special shapes, such as "crosses."

Freshwater pearls occur in a wide range of colors—a much wider variety than round, saltwater pearls—which give them a special allure. Colors include light, medium, and dark orange, lavender, purple, violet, blue, rose, and gray. Large natural freshwater pearls in unusual colors can be *very* expensive. Freshwater pearls may also be dyed. Be sure to ask if the color is natural.

Another interesting feature of freshwater pearls is that they can be worn singly or grouped in alternating colors, either hanging straight or twisted for an even more interesting effect. In addition to the versatility offered by the many color options, freshwater pearls (with the exception of round) are very inexpensive, so one can afford to buy many strands and create an almost endless variety of looks.

## Baroque pearls

A baroque pearl, technically, is any pearl that is not "round" and has an interesting irregular shape (don't confuse with a round pearl that is simply "out-of-round"—it must have a distinctive enough shape to be interesting and attractive). They are produced by both saltwater and freshwater molluscs and can be natural or cultured. They have a distinctive appeal because of their very beautiful tints of color and iridescent flashes. Their irregular shape renders them far less valuable than round pearls. Nonetheless, they make beautiful, versatile fashion accessories.

# Today's Pearl Market Is Filled with Variety

In addition to these general pearl classifications, there are many other interesting varieties of pearls from which to choose. Here are some of the most popular.

*Button pearls.* A type of saltwater pearl which has a shape that resembles a "squash" or the pope's cap. With a shape that can be distinctive and interesting, they are always peg-mounted or glued into settings and are usually used for earrings or rings. They are less expensive than fine, round pearls.

*Tear-drop pearls.* Sometimes called "pear-shaped," these pearls are very lovely and highly desirable. In large sizes, especially in matched pairs, and when truly symmetrical, these pearls can be very expensive.

*Half-pearls.* Usually small pearls (two to three millimeter) which have been cut in half to use for border decoration, as in a continuous row of pearls surrounding a cameo or center stone. They are inexpensive, but create a lovely effect.

*Three-quarter pearls.* A round pearl which has had approximately one quarter of it cut off due to a blemish or imperfect shape. These are mounted in cups to conceal the bottom and create the illusion of a full round pearl. Be suspicious of any pearl set in a cup that seems disproportionately large; it may contain a three-quarter pearl. These are frequently used in earrings. They are much less expensive than a full round pearl.

*Seed pearls.* Very, very tiny round, natural pearls, usually under two millimeters in size. Seed pearls are often seen in antique jewelry.

*Keshi pearls.* Very small pearls which are a by-product of producing cultured pearls. They resemble seed pearls in appearance, but are less expensive.

*Mabé pearls* (Mobe). A dome-shaped pearl, available in a variety of shapes, the most common being round or pear-shaped. This is an *assembled* "blister" pearl (a hollow blister that forms on the side of the interior of the oyster, which is removed and then filled). It has a very thin nacre coating, an epoxy center, and a mother-of-pearl backing. These pearls are produced very inexpensively, and require extra care, but they provide a very large, attractive look at affordable prices, compared to other pearls of comparable size. They are especially popular for earrings and rings.

*Solid blister pearl.* A dome-shaped pearl similar to the mabé but **not** assembled, this type of pearl is produced in freshwater lakes in Tennessee. It's available in several shapes, and has a distinctive look created by a mother-of-pearl background, retained from the shell lining when the pearl is removed. These pearls also have an unusually high luster and a lovely iridescent play-of-color across the surface. They are more expensive than mabé pearls, but also more durable.

*South Sea pearls.* Most are produced in the waters off Australia, Indonesia, and the Philippines in saltwater oysters. A much larger variety than the Japanese oyster, many exceed a foot in diameter. South Sea pearls usually start at about 10 millimeters in size, and go up from there. Pearls from 11 to 14 millimeters are the average. Pearls over 16 millimeters are considered very large. The South Sea specimens are often less perfectly round and have a less intense luster than their smaller Japanese counterpart, but they are very beautiful and very expensive. The rarest, most expensive color is a warm pinkish-white, but the silvery-white is perhaps more in demand and therefore also expensive. Yellow-whites also exist, but these are the least popular and sell for much less. "Fancy" intense yellows (truly rich yellow, not in any way to be confused with off-white or yellow-white) and a wide variety of hues including many "golden" tones, are now in great demand. These are less expensive than the finest whites, but they can still be expensive. South Sea pearls are rare in fine qualities, and more expensive than most other pearls.

*Burmese pearls.* Very large cultured pearls (10 millimeters and up) grown in a particular type of large oyster found only off the coasts of Burma. They are classified as "South Sea" pearls, and for many years these oysters produced the rarest, finest, and most valuable pearls in the world. The best possess an exceptionally high luster, unmatched by any other South Sea pearl, and a fine pink-white color. In recent years the quality of Burmese pearls has been deteriorating, however, because of a complicated political situation reducing availability of skilled technicians and disrupting quality control. Very few fine Burmese pearls are being produced today, and most are mixed in with other "South Sea" pearls.

*Tahitian Black Pearls.* Large pearls produced by a black-lipped saltwater oyster unique to the waters of Polynesia. They range from gray to black in color, and the color is natural; both *natural pearls* with natural black color, and *cultured pearls* with natural black color have been found. These varieties are distinctive because of their unusual shades of color, including tones of gray, blue-gray, gun-metal gray, brown-black, or greenish-black. The color in the Tahitian black pearl, however, is often not uniform throughout. The stone can be black on one end, and much lighter on the other end. The rarest and most expensive color for Tahitian black pearls is black with an irridescent peacock-green overtone. Tahitian black pearls are seldom smaller than eight millimeters. They are rarely perfectly round. Teardrop-shaped baroque pearls are more common. As with other South Sea pearls, these are rare and expensive. Remember, however, not to confuse "natural" black color with being a "natural" pearl; most are cultured. In addition, beware of "irradiated" or "dyed" black pearls, which are common and inexpensive.

# Choosing Your Pearls

When buying pearls, it's important to take the time to compare various types, sizes, and qualities to develop an eye for differences. Here are some suggestions you might find helpful:

- *Compare the quality factors* as you shop. Pay attention to differences in luster and orient, color/tint, cleanliness, roundness and size. Pay special attention to the luster and orient. This is the most important quality factor you should learn to judge.

  You should also weigh the innumerable variables in quality against each other: if luster is good, roundness may be poor; if roundness is good, luster may be poor; if luster and color are good, they may not have clean surfaces; shape may be good but matching in the strand may be poor. You can learn a great deal about pearl quality simply by looking.

- *Examine pearls against your own neck and face* to be sure the color of the pearls suits your skin and hair coloring.

- *Ask whether or not the color is natural,* especially when considering colored pearls (gray, blue, black, etc.). Pearls of natural color often sell for much more than white pearls, whereas dyed pearls should sell for much less. If the color is natural, be sure it is so stated on the bill of sale.

- *Compare size.* As you shop, ask what size the pearls are, and compare differences in cost for the same quality in different sizes. A *double* strand of smaller pearls may create an equally lovely look, and cost less than a single strand of larger pearls.

- *Be sure to ask whether or not the pearls are genuine or simulated,* and be sure that "genuine cultured" or "genuine natural" is in writing on the bill of sale. Don't be afraid to use the "tooth test;" it won't harm the pearls (but remove lipstick first).

Shopping around can be of tremendous help before you buy pearls. It will help you become familiar with the wide range of pearls available within your price range; it will also develop your eye to distinguish quality differences, and help you decide what color, size, and shape is best for you. If you take the time to follow our advice, your pearls will give you unending pleasure and pride.

Pearl beds being tended in freshwater lakes in Tennessee. American Pearl Company founder, John Latendresse, is the leading pioneer in American cultured pearl production.

# 4

# Design & Style
## Getting the Look You Want

## *Platinum - Rarest and Purest of Precious Metals*

**Platinum's** whiteness, strength and maleability have made it a favorite of fine jewelers since its turn-of-the-century debut. With platinum, jewelers of that era discovered they could create lighter, more delicate settings than ever imagined — the lacey, intricate designs for which Edwardian jewelry remains unparalleled. Today platinum is equally popular for sophisticated, contemporary design.

*Left:* Platinum, a natural for this modern *tension* ring by designer Steven Kretchmer

*Below:* Skilled contemporary designers use platinum today to *reproduce* heirloom looks

*Above:* Platinum keepsakes from days-gone-by

Modern designers: Scott Keating *(top)* and Etienne Perret *(right)* forge dramatic and playful new looks in platinum.

# Gold — *A Favorite From Ancient Times...*

Prized and coveted for personal adornment since earliest history, gold remains a popular choice for jewelry, for both men and women.

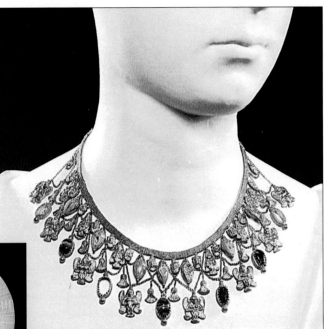

Gold, always popular for diamonds, makes an especially good choice to enrich the color of many colored gems.

*Above:* Classic diamond and sapphire bracelet
*Inset:* Popular gold and colored gemstone insert/guard rings

*Right, top and bottom:* Contemporary styles in yellow gold, yellow and white gold combined with gemstone accents

# ...to the Present.

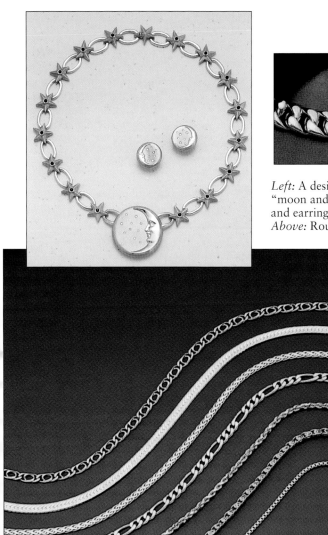

*Left:* A designer's interpretation of the "moon and stars" in this gold necklace and earrings
*Above:* Round curb link necklace

## Some popular chains and necklace styles:

Open herringbone

Triple herringbone

Fancy wheat

Figaro

Diamond-cut rope

Diamond-cut queen

Box

*Right:* Distinctive, 18K gold *reversible* necklace offers versatility with two great looks in one necklace

*Below:* Ancient *Makume Gane* technique used to create a unique new look in jewelry

# Pearls — Lustrous Beauty For Every Mood

Whatever your personality, whatever the event, pearls fit the occasion.

Gem quality, round pearl earrings

A rainbow assortment of freshwater pearls

Striking contemporary gold and pearl ring

One of the new shapes available in cultured pearls today

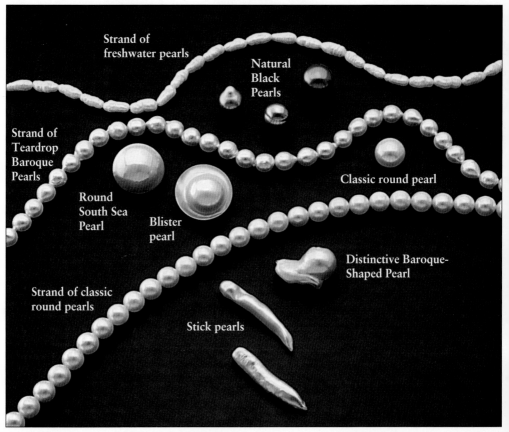

Strand of freshwater pearls

Natural Black Pearls

Strand of Teardrop Baroque Pearls

Round South Sea Pearl

Blister pearl

Classic round pearl

Strand of classic round pearls

Stick pearls

Distinctive Baroque-Shaped Pearl

# *Pearls*

*Left:*
American (Tennessee)
freshwater,
cultured solid blister
pearls (domé™),
stick pearls and
irridescent natural
abalone pearl

Freshwater cultured "coin"
pearls from Tennessee

Baroque natural pearls

Natural round pearls

*Left:* Rare natural color
black cultured pearl
necklace of exceptional
quality and size

*Left, inset:* natural black
color cultured pearl
pendant/enhancer

# Fine Jewelry Design — Art You Can Wear

Fine jewelry designers are gaining recognition as artists in the truest sense. Major design competitions – such as *Spectrum* and *Diamonds of Distinction* are recognising their accomplishments. Here are examples of work created by some of the most exciting contemporary American designers. Note the interesting use of different textures and finishes in the metalwork, and the wide variety of gemstone materials used.

*Right:* Striking combination of cabochon and faceted gemstones in this ring by William Richie

*Above:* A one-of-a-kind neckpiece holding fantasy cut colored gemstone by Michael Good

A combination pendant and brooch by Ruud Kahle

Whimsical Abstracts:
*Left:* Brooch by
Phil Delano
*Right:* Brooch/enhancer
by Julie Hinds

Gold, diamond, black onyx and gemstone brooch by Jean - Francois Albert

Contemporary yet classic earrings by Eric J. Walls

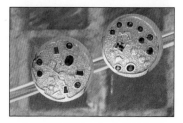

Unique stacking rings by Eric Russell

Fanciful hearts by Cheryl Stern

*Above: Makume Gane* technique provides a distinctive gold setting for gemstones in these rings by George Sawyer

Colored gemstone cabochons combined with distinctive sculpted gold create luscious-looking rings by Elisabeth Rand

Brooches have become an essential fashion accessory. Here are two dramatic creations:
*Top:* Susan Saunders
*Bottom:* Richard Kimball

Sleek contemporary ring by Eddie Sakamoto

Ring with contemporary yet ancient feel by Whitney Boin

Contemporary gold and trilliant-shaped gemstone stacking rings by Whitney Boin

Diamond, gold and colored gemstones in this hinged *Scissors* bracelet by Paul Klecka

# *Popular Diamond Ring styles For Her...*
## *...and for Him*

Numerous small diamonds used in a distinctive design can create an important look on a limited budget

*Above:* The use of trilliant-cut diamonds gives these classic designs a fresh, new look.

A striking duo — marquises combined with baguettes

Classic Tiffany-style solitaire

Fanciful ring using *fancy colored* and colorless diamonds

*Left:* Classic *Anniversary* bands

*Above:* Use of contrasting metal textures, black onyx and diamonds creates a bold new look

*Left and right:* Interesting styles designed to highlight smaller center-stones and create a more dramatic look

# 18

---

# Rare & Precious:
## Gold and Platinum

## Gold—The Timeless Choice

Gold jewelry is very popular today and available in more styles, colors, and finishes than ever before. It is also a very popular choice for setting gemstones. But it is very important to understand gold, and differences that affect price, in order to avoid confusion about the wide range of prices that seems to pervade the market for what may *appear* to be the "same thing." As with gems, wherever there are significant price differences there are usually quality differences. The key to getting good value in gold is understanding what accounts for differences in quality and price.

## What is Gold?

Gold is one of the world's most precious metals. It is so soft and workable that one ounce can be stretched into a five-mile-long wire, or hammered into a sheet so thin that it could cover a hundred square feet. It is one of our rarest metals, and since pure gold doesn't rust or corrode, it can last forever. Interestingly, gold is present almost everywhere around us—in the earth's crust, in seas and rivers, and in plants—but it is very difficult and expensive to extract. Approximately two and a half to three tons of ore are needed to extract one ounce of gold.

### Most gold used in jewelry is an alloy

Gold is the most popular metal used for jewelry today. The simple gold wedding band probably accounts for more of the world's gold than any other single type of jewelry. But pure gold is very soft so it is usually mixed with other metals to make it stronger and prevent it from bending too easily. When two or more metals are mixed together, we call the resulting product an *alloy*. Most gold used in jewelry is an alloy—and the metals added to the gold are also called "alloys."

## What is a karat? Or is it carat?

In jewelry, the term *carat* (or, karat) has a double meaning: *carat* is used as a measurement of weight for gemstones, with one carat weighing $1/5$ gram; *carat* is also used in countries around the world to indicate the amount of pure gold in a piece of gold jewelry. In the United States, however, when using the word to indicate gold content rather than gemstone weight, it is spelled with a *K*—hence "karat"— to avoid confusion. Jewelry should always be marked to indicate how much pure gold it contains.

In the United States a karat mark, abbreviated to K or KT, indicates the amount of pure gold present in the metal. The word *karat* (carat) is derived from the word for the fruit of the carob tree: in Italian, carato; in Arabic, qirat; in Greek, keration. The seeds of the fruit were used in ancient times for weighing gems. Also, the pure gold Byzantine coin called the *solidus* weighed 24 karats. Therefore, a 24 karat mark (24K or 24KT) became the mark used to indicate that something was pure gold.

To understand the concept as applied to gold, imagine that "pure gold" is a pie divided into 24 equal "slices" or parts. Each karat equals one part of the pie. So, 24K would mean that 24 parts (out of a total of 24) are gold. In other words, 24K would be 100 percent gold—or, pure gold. In 18-karat gold jewelry, 18 parts are pure gold and six are another metal (or, $18/24 = 3/4 = 75$ percent pure gold); in 12-karat, 12 parts are pure gold, 12 parts another metal ($12/24 = 1/2 = 50$ percent pure gold). And so on.

In some cultures, 24-karat gold jewelry is required for certain jewelry pieces, but it's generally agreed that 24 karat, or pure gold, is too soft for jewelry use. In some parts of the world, 18- or 20-karat is preferred because of its brighter yellow color and because it is considered "purer" and more precious. In the United States we prefer 14- or 18-karat gold because it is more durable than higher karat gold. We caution clients about the risk of high karat gold (20-, 22-, or 24-karat) for a gem-studded setting because prongs can be too easily bent open accidentally, resulting in loss of stones.

In some countries, such as Italy, the percentage of pure gold is indicated by a number representing how many parts—out of a total of 1,000 parts—are pure gold. *One thousand* parts would be the equivalent of 24-karat; *Seven hundred fifty* means that 750 parts out of 1,000 are pure gold: $^{750}/_{1,000} = {}^{75}/_{100} = {}^{3}/_{4} = 75$ percent pure gold. This corresponds to 18K.

The following chart shows how different international gold markings correspond to one another:

| Gold Marks | | |
| --- | --- | --- |
| American Marking (karatage) | Pure Gold content (Fineness in percent) | European Marking |
| 24K | 100 | 1,000 |
| 22K | 91.6 | 916 |
| 20K | 83 | 833 |
| 19K (used in Portugal) | 79.2 | 792 |
| 18K | 75.0 | 750 |
| 15K (seen in antiques) | 62.5 | 625 |
| 14K | 58.3 | 585 |
| 12K | 50.0 | 500 |
| 10K | 41.7 | 417 |
| 9K | 37.5 | 375 |

## A word about Russian marks

Old timepieces made in Russia were marked to indicate the content based on its equivalent to a "zolotnik." A piece marked 96 contained as much gold as 96 zolotniks, which equals pure gold; 72 equals 18K (750); 56 equals 14K (585).

## To be called gold, what is the minimum gold content?

Many countries have established minimum standards that must be met for items to be legally called "gold." The laws governing the actual content of gold required in a piece of jewelry, however, vary. In the United States, to be called "gold," the item must be at least 10K; in England and Canada, 9K; in Italy and France, 18K.

# The Many Colors of Gold

Pure gold is always yellow. But because pure gold is too soft for most jewelry use, and must be mixed with other metals (alloys) to increase its hardness, the color can also be modified by adding varying amounts of these other metals. Those usually added to gold for jewelry use include copper, zinc, silver, nickel, platinum, and palladium (a metal in the platinum family). Depending upon which alloys are used, a variety of colors can be produced. Another practice is to plate 14K gold jewelry with 18K for an 18K look, that is, a stronger yellow color. White gold is also frequently plated with rhodium, a rare and more expensive metal from the platinum family, to create a whiter, brighter finish.

Using some combination of one or more of the metals shown below will result in various colors.

| COLOR | COMPOSITION |
|---|---|
| Yellow Gold | Gold, Copper, Silver |
| White Gold | Gold, Nickel,* Zinc, Silver, Platinum, Palladium |
| Green Gold | Gold, Silver (much more than in yellow gold), Copper, Zinc |
| Pink (red) Gold | Gold, Copper (sometimes a small amount of silver is used) |

\* Note: some people are allergic to nickel and should not wear white gold containing nickel. For this reason, a white gold alloyed with palladium is being used by some manufacturers. White gold that contains palladium will be more expensive than yellow gold or white gold containing another alloy. But it is still less expensive than platinum.

*What causes skin discoloration with some gold jewelry?* Pure gold doesn't tarnish and won't discolor the skin, but *alloys* in the gold can *corrode* and produce discoloration to the skin in contact with the gold, especially under moist or damp conditions. Fats and fatty acids present in perspiration can set up a corrosive reaction, and the problem can be worse in warm, humid areas, especially where chloride (salt) is in the air.

Smog can also be a problem. Smog fumes can introduce chemicals that cause the alloys in gold to tarnish. The tarnish then rubs off, discoloring skin or clothing.

*Cosmetics may be culprit.* Another common cause of discoloration is metallic abrasion caused by some makeup. Some makeup contains compounds that are actually harder than the jewelry with which it comes into contact. As the harder compounds rub against the jewelry, they cause tiny particles of metal to flake off, forming a darkish looking dust. When this dust makes contact with a soft, absorbent surface such as skin or clothing, it forms a black smudge.

There are several possible solutions to the problem of skin discoloration. First, get into the habit of removing jewelry often and cleansing the skin that has been in contact with it with soap and water. Keep your jewelry clean as well, and wipe it periodically with a soft cloth to remove tarnish. Next, try using an absorbent body powder, one free of abrasives, on all areas of your skin that are in contact with jewelry.

Pay attention to the design of jewelry you select if skin discoloration seems to be a problem—wide shanks can cause perspiration, and rings with an inner concave surface can cause moisture and contaminants to *collect,* causing both discoloration and dermatitis.

Finally, try switching to a higher gold content or to a different manufacturer. The higher the gold content, the less likely it is that discoloration will occur because in the higher karat gold there is less of the alloy—such as copper, silver, nickel—that might corrode. People who have a problem wearing 14K gold jewelry may find that the problem disappears with 18K gold.

Sometimes simply changing to a similar product made by a different manufacturer may solve the problem. For example, a 14K yellow gold bracelet made by one manufacturer may cause discoloration, while a similar bracelet made by another manufacturer may not. This does not mean that one product is inferior to the other. Manufacturers often use different combinations of alloys, or different percentages or ratios of alloys. They may look the same, but you might find you can wear one manufacturer's line better than that of another.

Since different metals, and different ratios, are used to produce different colors, discoloration may result when wearing one particular *color* of gold, but not when wearing other colors. If there seems to be a problem when wearing white gold, try a white gold alloyed with platinum rather than nickel, since platinum won't corrode.

# Determining Value Requires More than a Scale!

• **Weight** is one factor that goes into determining the value of a piece of gold jewelry. Gold is usually sold by weight, in grams or penny-weights. There are 20 pennyweights to one ounce; if you multiply grams by 0.643, you will have the number of pennyweights. Weight is important because it is an indication of the actual amount of pure gold in the piece. However, it is only one factor to consider. When buying gold from a gold manufacturer, for example, factored into the price-per-gram is the cost of gold PLUS the cost for labor and workmanship. The price always takes into consideration: 1) the type of *construction*, 2) the means of *production*, and 3) how the piece is *finished*.

• **Design and construction** is important not only because of the piece's finished look, but also because specific details in the overall design and construction affect comfort, wearability, and ease in putting the piece on or taking it off. Good design requires excellent designers, and extra care and attention to small mechanical details. This adds to the cost of any piece of jewelry.

In addition, jewelry design is also becoming recognized as an "art," and jewelry designers as "artists." Some award-winning designers command top dollar, as do top painters, sculptors, and other artists. A piece of gold jewelry made by a fine designer, especially if it is a one-of-a-kind or limited-edition piece, will sometimes sell for much more than another piece of mass-produced gold jewelry of the same weight and gold content.

In looking at a piece of gold jewelry, you must also consider the type of construction necessary to create a particular design or look. Is the construction simple or complex? Did the piece require extensive labor or minimal labor? Did it require special skill, talent, or equipment?

To ignore the design and construction factors and assign a value to a piece of gold jewelry based on gold content (i.e. 14K, 18K, etc.) and weight alone would be equivalent to placing a value on a painting based on the cost of paint and canvas alone.

• **Production** can affect price significantly. Is the piece produced by machine or by hand? The type of construction required to create a particular design may require that it be made entirely, or in part, by hand, while others can be completely made by machine. Some designs may be produced either way, but those done by hand will have a different look, feel, and cost.

• **Finish** is where we take into account the care and labor costs associated with the actual finishing of the piece. For example, are there any special skills or techniques required to put on the final touches that make the piece distinctive, such as engraving, milgraining, hammering, or granulation? Here we also need to note whether or not the piece has been carefully polished to remove any scratches that might diminish its beauty, or rough edges that might be abrasive or catch or snag on fabric. Consider whether the item was hand polished or machine polished; some pieces are machine made, but finished by hand. We must also take into consideration any special finishes to the metal itself, such as a florentine, matte, or sand-blasted finish. Each step in the process, and each special step or skill required, adds—sometimes dramatically—to the cost.

### Adding it all up

Many pieces of gold jewelry look alike at first glance. When examined carefully, however, it often becomes clear where the differences lie, both in quality and cost. Ask your jeweler to help you understand these differences by comparing different qualities for you. Only after carefully evaluating all of these factors can you appreciate gold jewelry and recognize cost differences and real value.

## Is That "Bargain" Really a Bargain?

Beware of *underkarating,* which is a serious problem around the world. If a piece of gold jewelry is underkarated, it means that the jewelry is marked to indicate a certain gold content, but actually contains less than is indicated. Needless to say, retailers who knowingly sell underkarated gold jewelry create the impression that they are giving you a bargain because their prices are so low, but if there is actually less gold (and more alloy, so the piece would have a comparable weight to others you might be considering), you aren't getting any bargain. Unfortunately, most people never learn that they have bought underkarated gold. We know of people who bought gold jewelry marked 14K or 18K and found out later that it was only 8K or 10K—or less! Thus, it is very important to buy gold jewelry from a reputable source, one that makes the effort to check its gold shipments carefully.

*Look for a manufacturer's registered trademark.* Being sure gold is properly represented in terms of its value is what really matters; you should get what you pay for. Buying from a reliable source is the first step. In addition, be sure to look for a manufacturer's registered trademark, a mark stamped near the karat mark. To avoid being held liable themselves, more and more jewelers are buying only from manufacturers willing to stamp what they make with their own mark, a mark registered with the U.S. Patent and Trademark Office. Buying gold with a "manufacturer's trademark" is one way to help assure you get what you pay for, since the product can be traced to a specific manufacturer, whose name and reputation are on the line.

Fine, expensive gold jewelry should always be tested. While testing for *exact gold content* requires assaying, it is usually relatively easy to detect any underkarating that is serious enough to affect the value of a specific piece of jewelry and the price paid. Any jeweler or gemologist-appraiser can make such a determination, in most cases, quickly and easily with only a gold tester or by using the streak test. You should be aware that with an electronic gold tester, some very heavily plated pieces might give a false reading indicating gold when the piece is only base metal. For this reason the streak test is better, but the person doing the test must be sure to take a file or carbide scriber and make a very deep scratch in order to penetrate the plating for an accurate test.

There are strict laws pertaining to gold content and marks used to indicate it. Take the time to understand what you are buying, buy only from a reputable source, and be sure to have it tested. If you do, your gold jewelry will give you a lifetime of pleasure.

# Platinum: Cool, Classic, & Contemporary

Platinum, which has been used in jewelry since the turn of the century, became especially popular during the Edwardian period because its malleable character made it a natural for the intricate and lacy work style of the day.

Platinum is frequently used in the finest jewelry and to set the most valuable gems because it's more "workable" and easier to move the prongs or setting around the stone, thereby reducing the risk of accidentally damaging it. Long a favorite for classic looks and for the finest diamond settings, platinum is now evolving as the metal of choice for new design trends—sleek, bold, contemporary looks for brooches, necklaces, chains, and earrings. Sometimes platinum is alloyed with another metal to create an interesting color, or used alongside gold to create an innovative look.

## Nothing is purer than platinum

Platinum is even more rare and valuable than gold. The platinum family is composed of six elements—platinum, palladium, iridium, osmium, rhodium, and ruthenium. These six silvery-white metals are generally found together in nature, with platinum and palladium the most abundant, and osmium, rhodium, and ruthenium the rarest.

Platinum is rarer and heavier than other precious metals and as the purest, it's sometimes referred to as the "noblest." Most platinum jewelry also contains small amounts of the rarer and more expensive elements iridium or ruthenium for added strength.

Because platinum is so pure, it rarely causes allergic reactions. This is greatly appreciated by those sensitive people who experience reactions to or skin discoloration from jewelry containing base metals. In addition, platinum is somewhat stronger than other precious metals.

Platinum is not identified by karat marks. In the United States, the abbreviations *PT* or *plat* indicate platinum. In Europe the numerical marks *950* or *PT950* indicate platinum. The finest jewelry often uses platinum mixed with 10 percent iridium or ruthenium for added strength. This costs more since these are rarer and costlier metals.

# Rhodium Plating

Rhodium, another member of the platinum family, is the brightest and most reflective of all the platinum metals. Rhodium is also harder and whiter than platinum and, because it is so durable, doesn't wear off quickly, as does gold plating. As a result, it is often used to coat gold and platinum jewelry.

Rhodium plating should be considered especially for people who have allergic reactions to 10K or 14K gold, since it can help eliminate reaction to the alloys.

# Yellow Gold, White Gold, or Platinum: Which One?

To decide whether or not you want yellow gold, white gold, or platinum, you must first decide which *color* metal you prefer. This selection usually depends on personal preference, skin tone, and the color of other jewelry you may own. If your choice is yellow gold, keep in mind that it is available in several different shades, including a pure yellow, a pinkish yellow, and a greenish yellow.

If you decide yellow is the color you want, then you must decide whether to get 14-karat or 18-karat. Certainly, 14-karat is more affordable than 18-karat; it is also harder. But the yellow won't be as bright. If you prefer a brighter yellow, we recommend that you ask your jeweler for a 14-karat gold with an 18-karat finish, that is, an 18-karat coating over the 14 karat. After several years the finish may wear off, but it can be replated for a minimal charge.

If you prefer a white metal, your choice may be more difficult. Even though white gold and platinum may be similar in appearance, they are very different metals. As we mentioned, platinum is much more expensive, so if you're on a limited budget, white gold may be the sensible choice. White gold is very hard and very resistant to scratching but may exhibit a brownish or yellowish cast which *must* be covered by rhodium plating. As we mentioned, this plating will eventually wear off, although it can easily be replated.

One significant disadvantage of white gold is that it is more *brittle* than platinum or yellow gold. So if you decide on white gold, be sure to have your jeweler check the setting—especially prongs—at least once a year.

Platinum is somewhat softer and more malleable than white gold, making it an ideal choice for very intricate settings that require intensive labor. It is much easier to use platinum for pavé work, that is, designs in which the stones are set as closely together as possible. With platinum, the jeweler can also make a safer setting because a larger prong can be used, since platinum conforms so easily to the shape of the stone, reducing risk of damage. Over time, platinum also holds up better than gold because it is more durable and doesn't wear down or abrade like gold.

One disadvantage of platinum is that many jewelers do not have the proper equipment to work with it. This, combined with platinum's cost, results in a more limited variety of styles from which to choose. If you like basic classic design, you shouldn't have a problem finding a setting you like. But if you need custom work to get the look you want, it can add substantially to the cost of the finished piece.

In the final analysis, it is up to the individual to weigh the relative advantages and disadvantages of gold or platinum. Whichever precious metal you select, there are many beautiful styles and designs from which to choose. And if you are having something custom made, many fine jewelers and designers will work in both metals.

# 19

# Choosing the Setting

The setting you choose will be determined primarily by your personal taste. Nevertheless, it is a good idea to be familiar with a few of the most common settings so that you have a working vocabulary and some idea of what is available.

*Bezel setting.* With a bezel setting, a rim holds the stone and completely surrounds the gem. Bezels can have straight edges, scalloped edges, or can be molded into any shape to accommodate the stone. The backs can be open or closed. One advantage of the bezel setting is that it can make a stone look larger. The bezel setting can also conceal nicks or chips on the girdle. It can also protect the girdle of the stone from chips and nicks.

Keep in mind that if you use yellow gold in a bezel setting, the yellow of the bezel surrounding the stone will be reflected into the stone, causing white stones to appear less white. On the other hand, a yellow gold bezel can make a red stone such as ruby look even redder or an emerald look greener.

A variation on the bezel setting is the *collet* setting. The collet setting has a similar appearance to the bezel setting but involves the use of gold *tubing*.

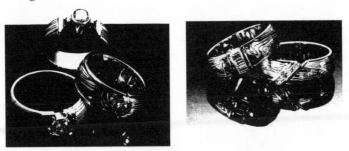

Notice *collet* settings (left) and *channel*-settings (right).

215

*Prong setting.* Prong settings are perhaps the most common type of setting. They come in an almost infinite variety—four-prong, six-prong, and such special styles as the Belcher, Fishtail, or six-prong Tiffany. In addition, prongs can be pointed, rounded, flat, or V-shaped. Extra prongs provide added security for the stone and can make a stone look slightly larger. However, too many prongs holding too small a stone can overpower the stone and make the setting look heavy. When setting a marquise, heart-shape, or pear-shape stone, we recommend that the point or points be held by a V-shaped prong, which will best protect the point(s). For emerald-cut stones which have canted corners, straight, flat prongs are the best choice.

A pear-shaped diamond showing a V-shaped prong holding the *point* and two normal prongs holding the upper portion.

*Gypsy setting.* In this type of setting, the shank (the metal part of a ring that goes around the finger) is one continuous piece that gets broader at the top, and is shaped on top into a dome. At the center of the domed top is an opening, into which the stone is inserted. There are no prongs. The look is very smooth and clean, and popular for men's jewelry.

*Illusion setting.* The illusion setting is used to make the mounted stone appear larger by surrounding it with metal, often worked to create an interesting design.

*Flat-top* and *bead* settings. In a flat-top setting a faceted stone is placed into a hole in the flat top of the metal and then held in place by small chips of metal attached at the stone's girdle. Sometimes these metal chips are worked into small beads, so this setting is sometimes called a bead setting.

*Channel setting.* This setting is used extensively today, especially for wedding bands. The stones are set into a channel with no metal separating them. In some cases the channel can continue completely around the ring, so that the piece has a continuous row of stones.

*Bar setting.* This setting, which resembles a channel setting, combines the contemporary and classic look. It is used in a circular band and, rather than using prongs, each stone is held in the ring by a long thin bar, shared between two stones.

*Pavé setting.* This setting is used for numerous small stones set together in a cluster with no metal showing through. The impression is that the piece is entirely *paved* with stones. The setting can be flat or domed-shaped, and can be worked so that the piece almost appears to be one large single stone. Fine pavé work can be very expensive.

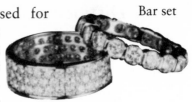
Bar set

*Cluster setting.* A cluster setting usually consists of one large stone and several smaller stones as accents. A cluster setting is designed to create a lovely larger piece from several small stones.

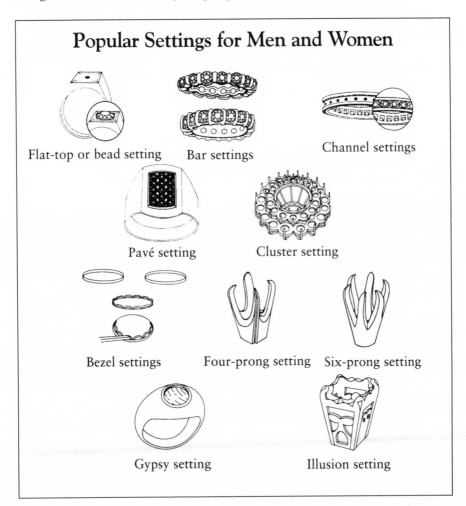

# Popular Settings for Men and Women

Flat-top or bead setting

Bar settings

Channel settings

Pavé setting

Cluster setting

Bezel settings     Four-prong setting   Six-prong setting

Gypsy setting          Illusion setting

# Distinctive Contemporary Settings

Today there are many interesting and distinctive designs offering something for everyone. Fine "casting" houses produce top quality settings that simply await the stones to finish them off. Some firms produce "semi-mounts," settings complete with side stones, awaiting only your center stone. These can provide affordable and easy solutions to creating a new ring, or remounting stones from something else.

An increasing number of custom jewelry designers also cater to today's market (see color section). International jewelry design competitions such as the Spectrum Awards designer competition sponsored by the American Gem Trade Association (AGTA), or the Diamonds-International Awards sponsored by the Diamond Information Center, provide a showcase for their work. The result is an almost limitless choice, ranging from bold sculpted gold and platinum combinations to intricate antique reproductions.

# Settings to Suit Your Lifestyle

It is important to consider your lifestyle when selecting any piece of jewelry. Be realistic about the wear-and-tear a ring or bracelet might take and remember that no piece of jewelry is indestructible. Remember, even diamond, the hardest natural substance known, can chip or break if exposed to a sharp accidental blow.

Active outdoor types, for example, might be better off avoiding jewelry like a ring containing a marquise or pear-shape stone since both these shapes have points. Points are more vulnerable to chipping or breaking, which could result from the kind of sudden or sharp blow an active person might subject a stone to.

In addition, the shank as well as the prongs of a ring will show the effects of wear; any detailing on a ring will blur over time, as the result of gardening, playing on the beach, mountain-climbing, handling ski equipment or bicycles, or any other kind of repeated contact or use.

Classic four- or six-prong settings serve a less active generation well, but may not be as well suited to today's woman. If your daily schedule features a great deal of activity, you would be wise to consider a sturdier jewelry style, keeping in mind that sturdy and graceful are not mutually exclusive. For example, a bezel setting might be better suited to your activity level. This choice won't detract from a gemstone's brilliance, yet it will afford you and your fine gems greater security.

Since everyday activities can loosen a setting as easily as more strenuous ones can, it is important to have a reputable jeweler check mountings and settings once every six months. Chlorine attacks soldering links and stress points, so if you swim regularly in a chlorinated pool, take your jewelry off first.

In terms of ring design, while rings are usually round, fingers aren't. Top-heavy rings will turn on the finger unless the diameter, or outline, is square or stirrup-shaped to conform to the shape of the finger. Also, remember that rings worn together side by side quickly begin to wear on each other.

## Tips for Selecting the Right Style

1. Set a realistic budget range to eliminate confusion and temptation that can result in disappointment.
2. Shop around and familiarize yourself with current styles to educate your eye and learn what really appeals to you.
3. Try on different styles—jewelry looks different when you see it *on*. This holds true of rings especially. I've seen many men and women insist they don't like a particular ring in a showcase, and then love it when they try it on.
4. If you're trying to achieve an impressive look with smaller stones, consider interesting jackets for earrings, or inserts or wraps for rings. These enable you to slip your ring or studs into another piece (usually gold, platinum, or silver, sometimes with stones) and instantly create a larger look.
5. If selecting an engagement ring, remember that you will also be wearing a wedding band. Be sure to select a style that will complement the type of wedding band you are considering.

# 5

# Important Advice
# Before You Buy

# 20

---

# What to Ask
# When Buying the Stone

Asking the right questions is the key to knowing what you're getting when it comes to buying gemstones. It is also the only way you can be sure what you are comparing when considering gems from different jewelers. Be sure the jeweler can answer your questions, or can get the answers for you. Then, be sure the jeweler is willing to put the answers *in writing* on your bill of sale. Finally, verify the facts—double-check that the stone is as represented—by having it examined by a qualified gemologist-appraiser. In this way you'll be able to make an informed choice about quality and value, you'll have no doubt about what you are getting, and you'll begin to develop a solid relationship with the jeweler from whom you make the purchase, based on confidence and trust. And, in the event the stone is not as represented, you'll know in time—and have the information you need—to get your money back.

## Questions to Ask When Buying a Diamond

You should always have very specific information before purchasing a fine diamond weighing one carat or more. For smaller stones, the information may not be so readily available, since most jewelers don't take the time to grade them precisely. An experienced jeweler, however, should be able to provide information regarding quality for stones from a half carat and up, or offer to find it for you. Indeed, some laboratories are now providing grading reports for diamonds from 0.47 carats and up.

Also keep in mind that since it is not possible to grade mounted diamonds accurately, we recommend that fine diamonds weighing one carat or more be purchased unmounted, or removed from the setting and then remounted. In jewelry containing numerous small diamonds, the stones are graded before they are set and the information may be on the sales tag. If not, it is extremely difficult to know for sure what the true quality is, and much can be concealed by a setting. We recommend buying such pieces only from a knowledgeable jeweler with a good reputation.

Here are the basic questions to ask and information that needs to be included on the bill of sale of your diamond:

1. *What is the exact carat weight?* Be sure the stone's *weight* is given, not its *spread* (see chapter 7).
2. *What is its color grade?* And what grading system was used? (see chapter 5).
3. *What is its clarity (flaw) grade?* Again, ask what system was used (see chapter 6).
4. *What shape is it?* Round, pear, marquise? (see chapter 4).
5. *Is it well cut for its shape?* How would the "make" be graded: ideal, excellent, good? (see chapter 2).
6. *What are the exact millimeter dimensions of the stone?*
7. *Is this stone accompanied by a diamond grading report or certificate?* Ask for the full report (see chapter 8).

Be sure to find out what system was used to grade the stone. If GIA terms are used, ask if GIA standards and methods have been applied to grading the stone.

Be sure to get the *exact* millimeter dimensions of the stone; the dimensions can be approximated if the stone is mounted. For a round stone, be sure you are given *two* dimensions for the stone's diameter; since most are not round, you need the highest and lowest. For fancy shapes, get the dimensions of the length and width. Always get the dimension from the table to the culet as well, that is, the depth of the stone.

Be especially careful if the diamond is being taken out on consignment, on a jeweler's memorandum or sales slip, or on a contingency sale. Having the measurements in writing helps protect you from being accused of switching should you have to return the stone for any reason.

Always ask if the stone has a certificate or diamond grading report and, if so, make sure it accompanies the stone; if you are taking the stone on approval, ask for a copy of the report. If there is no report or certificate, find out who determined the color and flaw grades; make sure the seller puts that information on the bill of sale, and insist that the sale be contingent upon the stone's actually having the grades represented.

## Additional Questions to Help You Make Your Selection

*Is it large enough?* This is a valid question and one you should be honest with yourself about. If you think the diamond is too small, you won't feel good about wearing it. Remember that such other factors as clarity and color can be juggled several grades with little visible difference, and this might enable you to get a larger diamond. And remember that the color and type of setting can also help you achieve a larger look.

*Does this stone have a good make?* Does this stone have good proportions? How do its proportions compare to the "ideal?" Remember, much variance can exist and a stone can still be a beautiful, desirable gem even if it does not conform to the ideal. Nonetheless, you won't want a stone with poor proportions, so if you have any question about the stone's brilliance and liveliness—if it looks lifeless or dull in spots—you should ask specifically about the proportioning of the cut. In addition, you should ask if there are any cutting faults that might make the stone more vulnerable to chipping or breaking, as, for example, an extremely thin girdle would.

*Has this stone been clarity enhanced?* Be sure to ask whether or not the diamond has been laser treated, or fracture-filled (see chapter 6). If it is accompanied by a GIA report, the report will indicate lasering, if present. However, GIA won't issue a report on a fracture-filled stone and some jewelers don't know how to detect them. If there is no GIA report, be sure to ask explicitly, and get a statement in writing that the diamond is or is not clarity enhanced, whichever the case may be. Getting this fact in writing may save you a big headache should you learn later that the stone is enhanced.

*Does this stone show any fluorescence?* If a diamond fluoresces blue when viewed in daylight or under daylight-type fluorescent light, it will appear whiter than it really is. This can be a desirable quality so long as the stone has not been graded or classified incorrectly. A diamond may also fluoresce yellow, which means that in certain light its color could appear worse than it actually is. If the stone has a diamond grading report, any fluorescence will be indicated there. If there is no report, and if the jeweler can't tell you whether or not the stone exhibits any fluorescence, the stone's color grade may be incorrect.

# Special Tips When Buying a Diamond

## Ask the jeweler to clean the stone

Don't hesitate to ask to have the stone cleaned before you examine it. Cleaning will remove dirt, grease, or indelible purple ink. Cleaning is best done by steaming or in an ultrasonic cleaner. Cleaning also helps to ensure that you'll see the full beauty of the stone; diamonds can become very dirty just from customers handling them, and, as a result, look less brilliant and sparkling than they really are.

## View the stone against a dead white background

When looking at unmounted stones, look at them only against a *dead-white background* such as white blotter paper or a white business card, or on a grading trough. Examine the stone against the white background so that you are looking at it through the side, not down through the table (see chapter 5). Tilt the stone toward a good light source; daylight fluorescent lamp is best. If the stone shows any yellow body tint when viewed through the girdle, if it is not as colorless as an ice cube, then the diamond is not "white" or "colorless."

## Get the facts on a bill of sale

Ask that all the facts concerning the stone be put on the bill of sale. These include the carat weight, the color and flaw grades, the cut, and the dimensions. Also, be sure you obtain the report on any "certificated" stone, as diamonds accompanied by laboratory reports are sometimes called.

## Verify facts with a gemologist

If a stone is one carat or larger and not accompanied by a respected laboratory report, make the sale contingent on verification of the facts by a qualified gemologist, gem-testing lab, or the GIA. While the GIA will not estimate dollar value, it will verify color, flaw grade, make, fluorescence, weight, and other physical characteristics.

### Weigh the Facts

Decide what is important to you and then weigh the facts. Most people think color and make are the most important considerations when buying a diamond, but if you want a larger stone, you may have to come down several grades in color, or choose a slightly spread stone, or select one of the new shapes that look much larger than traditional cuts. The most important thing is to know what you're getting, and get what you pay for.

# What to Ask When Buying a Colored Gemstone

As with diamonds, it's very important to ask the right questions to help you understand the differences in gems you may be considering. Asking the following questions should help you to gain a greater understanding of the differences, determine what's right for you, and have greater confidence in your decision.

1. *Is this a genuine, natural stone, or a synthetic?* Synthetic stones are *genuine,* but not *natural* (see chapter 13).

2. *Is the color natural?* Most colored gemstones are routinely color-enhanced (see chapters 13, 14). However, stones such as lapis should not be, and you must protect yourself from buying dyed material that will not retain its color permanently. See information on specific gems (chapters 16, 17) to determine whether or not this is an important question for you to ask.

   Be especially cautious when buying any blue sapphire; make sure you ask whether or not the stone has been checked for diffusion treatment. Today, with diffused sapphire being found mixed in parcels of natural sapphires and *unknowingly* set into jewelry, it's possible that one may be sold inadvertently. (See chapter 14.)

3. *Clarify what the name means.* Be particularly careful of misleading names (see chapter 14). When a stone is described with any *qualifier* such as *Rio* Topaz (which is not topaz), ask specifically whether or not the stone is genuine. Ask why the qualifier is being used.

4. *Is the clarity acceptable, or do too many inclusions detract from the beauty of the stone?* Are there any flaws, inclusions, or natural characteristics in this stone that might make it more vulnerable to breakage with normal wear? This is a particularly important question when considering a colored stone (see chapter 12).

While visible inclusions are more common in colored gems than in diamonds, and their existence has much less impact on value than they have on diamond value, value is nonetheless reduced if the inclusions or blemishes affect the stone's durability, or are so numerous that they mar its beauty.

Be especially careful to ask whether or not any inclusion breaks the stone's surface, since this may weaken the stone, particularly if the imperfection is in a position normally exposed to wear, like the top of the stone or around the girdle. This would reduce the stone's value significantly. On the other hand, if the flaw is in a less vulnerable spot, where it can be protected by the setting, it may be of minimal risk and have little effect on value.

A large number of inclusions will usually detract noticeably from the beauty, especially in terms of liveliness, and will also generally weaken the stone and make it more susceptible to any blow or knock. Such stones should be avoided unless the price is right and you're willing to assume the risk.

Also, certain gems, as we've mentioned, are more brittle than others, and may break or chip more easily, even without flaws. These stones include opal, zircon, and some of the new and increasingly popular gems, such as iolite (water sapphire) and tanzanite. This does not mean you should avoid buying them, but it does mean you should give thought to how they will be worn and how they will be set. Rings and bracelets are particularly vulnerable, since they are more susceptible to blows or knocks; brooches, pendants, and earrings are less vulnerable.

5. *Do you like the color? How close is the color to its pure spectral shade? Is it too light? Too dark? How does the color look in different types of light?* Learn to look at color critically. Become familiar with the rarest, and most valuable, color of the gem of your choice. But after you do this, decide what you really like, for yourself. You may prefer a color that might be less rare, and therefore more affordable. Be sure the color pleases you—don't buy what you think you *should* buy unless you really like it.

6. *Is the color permanent?* This question should be asked in light of new treatments (such as diffusion) and also because color in some stones is prone to fading. Two examples are amethyst and kunzite (one of the new and increasingly popular gems). Just which ones will fade and which ones won't, and how long the process might

take, no one can know. This phenomenon has never affected the popularity of amethyst and we see no reason for it to affect kunzite's popularity, but we feel the consumer should be aware of it. There is evidence that too much exposure to strong sunlight or intense heat contributes to fading in these stones, so we suggest avoiding sun and heat. It may be wise to wear these gems primarily for "evening" or "indoor" activities.

7. *Does the stone need a protective setting?* The setting may be of special importance when considering stones like tanzanite, opal, or emerald. They require a setting that will offer some protection—for example, one in which the main stone is surrounded by diamonds. A design in which the stone is unusually exposed, such as in a high setting or one with open, unprotected sides, would be undesirable.

8. *Does the stone have a pleasing shape? Does it have a nice "personality?"* This will be determined by the cutting. Many colored gems are cut in fancy shapes, often by custom cutters. Fine cutting can enrich the color and personality, and increase the cost. However, with colored gems brilliance and sparkle are less important than the color itself. The most critical considerations must focus on color, first and foremost. Sometimes a cutter must sacrifice brilliance in order to obtain the finest possible color. But if the color isn't rich enough or captivating enough to compensate for less brilliance, ask if the jeweler has something that is cut better and exhibits a little more sparkle. Keep in mind, however, that the more brilliant stone may not have the precise color you like, and that when buying a colored gem, *color* is the most crucial factor. Unless you find the stone's personality unappealing, don't sacrifice a beautiful color for a stone with a less appealing color just because it may sparkle more. Compare, and decide based upon what you like, and what you can afford.

When considering a pastel colored gem, remember that if it is cut too shallow (flat), it can lose its appeal quickly (but only temporarily) with a slight build-up of greasy dirt on the back; the color will fade and liveliness practically disappear. This can be immediately remedied by a good cleaning.

9. *What are the colorless stones?* In a piece of jewelry where a colored stone is mounted with colorless stones to accentuate or highlight its color, ask, "What are the colorless stones?" Do not assume

they are diamonds. They may be diamonds, zircons, man-made diamond imitations such as CZ or YAG, or synthetic white spinel (spinel is frequently used in the Orient).

# Special Tips to Remember When Buying a Colored Stone

*When looking at unmounted stones, view them through the side as well as from the top.* Also, turn them upside down on a flat white surface so they are resting on the table facet and you can look straight down through the stone from the back. Look for evenness of color versus color zoning—shades of lighter or darker tones creating streaks or planes of differing color.

*Remember that color is the most important consideration.* If the color is fine, the presence of flaws or inclusions doesn't detract from the stone's value as significantly as with diamonds. If the overall color or beauty is not seriously affected, the presence of flaws should not deter a purchase. But, conversely, flawless stones may bring a disproportionately higher price per carat due to their rarity, and larger sizes will also command higher prices. In pastel colored gems, or stones with less fine color, clarity may be more important.

*Be sure to check the stone's color in several different types of light*—a spotlight, sunlight, or fluorescent or lamplight—before making any decision. Many stones change color—some just slightly, others dramatically—depending upon the light in which they are viewed. Be sure that the stone is a pleasing color in the type of light in which you expect to be wearing it most.

If considering a stone with rich, deep color—especially if it is for special occasions and likely to be worn mostly at night—be sure it doesn't turn *black* in evening light. Some stones, like sapphire, can look like black onyx in evening light.

*Remember to give special attention to wearability.* If you are considering one of the more fragile stones, think about how the piece will be worn, where, and how frequently. Also, pay special attention to the setting and whether the stone is mounted in a way that will add protection, or allow unnecessary, risky exposure to hazards.

# Get the Facts on the Bill of Sale

If a colored stone is over one carat and exceptionally fine and expensive, make the sale contingent on verification of the facts by a qualified gemologist, appraiser, or gem-testing lab such as GIA or American Gemological Laboratories (AGL).

Always make sure that any item you purchase is clearly described in the bill of sale exactly as represented to you by the salesperson or jeweler. For diamonds, be sure each of the 4Cs is described in writing. For colored gems, essential information also includes the following:

- The identity of the stone or stones and whether or not they are genuine or synthetic, and not in any way a composite (doublet, triplet).

- A statement that the color is natural, if it has been so represented; or, in the case of sapphire, a statement that the stone either *is* surface diffused, or that it *is not* surface diffused.

- A statement describing the overall color (hue, tone, intensity).

- A statement describing the overall flaw picture. This is not always necessary with colored stones. In the case of a flawless or nearly flawless stone it is wise to note the excellent clarity. In addition, note any unusual flaw that might prove useful for identification.

- A statement describing the cut or make. This is not always necessary, but may be useful if the stone is especially well cut, or an unusual or fancy cut.

- The carat weight of the main stone or stones plus total weight if there is a combination of main and smaller stones.

- If the stone is to be taken on approval, make sure that the *exact* dimensions of the stone are included, as well as any other identifying characteristics. The terms and period of approval should also be clearly stated.

## Other Information that Should be Included for Jewelry

- If the piece is being represented as being made by a famous designer or house (Van Cleef and Arpels, Tiffany, Caldwell, Cartier, etc.) and the price reflects this, the name of the designer or jewelry firm should be stated on the bill of sale.

- If the piece is represented as antique (technically, an antique must be at least a hundred years old) or as a "period" piece from a popular, collectible period like Art Deco, Art Nouveau, Edwardian (especially if made by a premier artisan of the period), this information should be stated on the bill of sale, with the approximate age or date of manufacture, and a statement describing "condition."

- If made by hand, or custom-designed, this should be indicated on the bill of sale.

- If the piece is to be taken on approval, make sure millimeter dimensions—top to bottom, as well as length, width, or diameter—are provided, as well as a full description of the piece. Also, check that a time period is indicated, such as "two days," and before you sign anything, be sure that you are signing an approval form and not a binding contract for its purchase.

# 21

## How to Select a Reputable Jeweler

It's very difficult to give advice on this matter since there are so many exceptions to any rules we can suggest. Size and years in business are not always absolute indicators of the reliability of a firm. Some one-person jewelry firms are highly respected; others are not. Some well-established firms that have been in business for many years have built their trade on the highest standards of integrity and knowledge; others should have been put out of business years ago.

One point worth stressing is that for the average consumer, price alone is not a reliable indicator of the integrity or knowledge of the seller. Aside from variations in quality, which often are not readily discernible by the consumer, significant price differences can also result from differences in jewelry manufacturing processes. Many jewelry manufacturers sell mass-produced lines of good quality jewelry to jewelers all across the country. Mass-produced items, many of which are beautiful, classic designs, are usually much less expensive than hand-made, one-of-a-kind pieces, or those on which there is a limited production. The work of some designers may be available in only a few select establishments, and may carry a premium because of skill, labor, reputation, and limited distribution. Handmade or one-of-a-kind pieces are always more expensive, since the initial cost of production is paid by one individual rather than shared by many, as in mass-produced pieces.

Furthermore, depending upon the store, retail markups also vary, based on numerous factors unique to each retailer, including differences in insurance coverage, security costs, credit risks, education and training costs, special services such as in-house design and custom jewelry production and repair, customer service policies, and more.

The best way to select wisely is by shopping around. Go to several fine jewelry firms in your area and compare the services they offer, how knowledgeable the salespeople seem, the quality of their products, and pricing for specific items. This will give you a sense of what is fair in your market area. As you do so, however, remember to ask the right questions to be sure the items are truly comparable, and pay attention to design and manufacturing differences as well. As part of this process, it may be helpful to consider these questions:

- *How long has the firm been in business?* A quick check with the Better Business Bureau may reveal whether or not there are significant consumer complaints.

- *What are the gemological credentials of the jeweler, manager, or owner?* Is there a gemologist on staff? Does the store have its own laboratory?

- *What special services are provided?* Are custom design services, rare or unusual gemstones, educational programs, Gemprint, or photographic services for your jewelry available?

- *How would you describe the store window?* Is the jewelry nicely displayed? Or is the window a mélange of incredible bargains and come-on advertising to lure you in?

- *How would you describe the overall atmosphere?* Is the sales staff's manner professional, helpful, tasteful? Or hustling, pushy, intimidating?

- *What is the store's policy regarding returns?* Full refund or only store credit? How many days? What basis for return?

- *What is the repair or replacement policy?*

- *Will the firm allow a piece to be taken "on memo"?* It won't hurt to ask. Some jewelers will. However, unless you know the jeweler personally this is not often permitted today, since too many jewelers have suffered from stolen, damaged, or switched merchandise.

- *To what extent will the firm guarantee its merchandise to be as represented?* Be careful here. Make sure you've asked the right questions and get complete and accurate information on the bill of sale, or you may find yourself stuck because of a technicality.

If the jeweler can't or won't provide the necessary information, we recommend you go to another store, no matter how much you've fallen in love with the piece. And, if you're making the purchase on a contingency basis, put the terms of the contingency on the bill of sale.

Never allow yourself to be intimidated into accepting anyone's claims. Beware of the person who says, "Just trust me" or who tries to intimidate you with statements such as "Don't you trust me?" A trustworthy jeweler will not have to ask for your trust; he or she will earn it through knowledge, reliability, and a willingness to give you any information you request—in writing.

Again, in general, you will be in a stronger position to differentiate between a knowledgeable, reputable jeweler and one who isn't if you've shopped around first. Unless you are an expert, visit several firms, ask questions, examine merchandise carefully, and then you be the judge.

## If You Want to File a Complaint

If you have a complaint about a firm's practices or policies, please contact the Better Business Bureau in your city. In addition, if any jeweler has misrepresented what was sold to you, please contact the Jeweler's Vigilance Committee (JVC), 1185 Avenue of the Americas, Suite 2020, New York, New York 10036. This group can provide invaluable assistance to you, investigate your complaint, and take action against firms believed to be guilty of fraudulent activity in the jewelry industry.

# 22

## A Word About Gemstone Investment

### Caution!

Caution is the only word we can apply to gem investment. If you have taken the time to read any of this book, you should now fully understand that the world of gems is very complex, that fraud and misrepresentation can be costly, and that the average consumer lacks the knowledge and experience to make sound judgments on the purchase of expensive gems without the assistance of a qualified gemologist-appraiser.

It is for this reason primarily that we recommend that gems and jewelry be purchased first and foremost for the pleasure they will bring to the purchaser/wearer, or as something to be handed down to future generations. The investment consideration, while it is certainly a valid consideration, in most cases should remain secondary.

Gemstones have been attracting investors by startling numbers since the late 1970s. While gems have a magical allure, and some investors have done well with them, few people outside the gem trade possess sufficient knowledge about the gems themselves—and their value—to make sound decisions in this arena. Fewer still have the means to liquidate such investments.

We have never recommended gems as investments for the average consumer. But since "investment" is a word the public continues to apply to gem and jewelry purchases, we think it important to discuss some of the pros and cons. Before we begin, however, let's take a look at what has occurred over the last two decades, including fraudulent investment scams to be on guard against.

During the late 1970s gem prices were pushed to unprecedented levels. Numerous gemstone investment companies appeared, as did fraudulent investment schemes. Prices for diamonds began to plummet in 1981, followed shortly thereafter by price declines for other gems. Consumer losses were significant. Many gem investment companies went out of business.

The gem market stabilized and strengthened as people returned to buying jewelry to wear, to give as a token of love, or as a special gift or memento. People seemed to have learned that investing in gems is not a quick and easy way to make money.

In the mid-eighties interest in gemstone speculation reappeared. Published figures began to give gems renewed investment allure but the frequently simplistic presentation of rewards without full discussion of the risks was extremely misleading. Such claims created a fertile market for the proliferation of fraudulent gemstone investment companies between 1985 and 1993. The result is that once again gems have lost their sparkle for thousands of unsuspecting victims.

# Fraudulent Gemstone Telemarketing: A Serious Problem

Today, prospective buyers must be especially careful not to fall victim to sophisticated telephone marketing schemes offering gemstones as investments. Americans have been the primary targets for a number of Canadian-based companies. The Toronto Fraud Squad estimates that companies behind these schemes have already made over a billion dollars in net profit and are beginning to expand operations into Europe and Asia.

Normally the scam begins with a telephone call offering an opportunity to buy gems at prices represented to be wholesale or below. Impressive, professional-looking documentation is provided, gems are shipped in sealed plastic or lucite containers for security, accompanied by seemingly reliable reports from a gem-testing laboratory. The brokerage firm promises to re-sell the gems at the appropriate moment, for handsome profits. Unfortunately, the stones are never sold and the victims are left holding stones for which—they learn too late—they paid prices far in excess of full retail.

In most cases, victims are lucky to recover 10 percent of their investment. By the time they realize what has happened, there is usually nothing that can be done. The company is either no longer in business, or hiding behind international boundaries: In the United States, activity is handled from Canada; in the UK, from Antwerp or

Amsterdam. The complexity of international laws makes it virtually impossible for the average person to bring legal action.

# Gemstone Investment: Not for the Average Investor

Gemstone investment can be profitable, but schemes such as this telemarketing operation illustrate the need for extreme caution. In light of our concern about the growing potential for renewed speculation, and a concomitant increase in fraudulent schemes, we would like to refer any reader seriously considering gem investment to our chapter "Gemstones" in the *Encyclopedia of Investments* (Warren, Gorham and Lamont, New York City, 1989). It is much broader in scope than what we can offer here, and was written for the serious investor, rather than the average, casual consumer. Reprints of the chapter, including updates, may be obtained from GemStone Press, Box 237, Woodstock, VT 05091 ($10.00 including postage/handling).

If one takes the time to become knowledgeable about the gem industry, is interested in a long-term investment (over five years), and is willing to locate, retain, and work with a knowledgeable, reputable gem consultant, gems can offer an exciting, sparkling, and very enjoyable area for speculation. But entered casually, without knowledge of the industry and the risks, this investment may lose its sparkle quickly.

If you can't resist the temptation of gem investment, and if a contemplated investment can be professionally evaluated before you close the deal, it may have merit. There are certainly some strong facts to support gem investment . . .

# Some Facts in Support of Gem Investment

*Over a 20-year period, gem prices have increased significantly for rare gemstones.* While the finest-quality diamonds in 1-carat sizes and up suffered a severe decline in late 1980–early 1981 (after unprecedented appreciation from 1978 to 1980), on an average basis diamonds were still a very sound investment, and smaller diamonds of very good quality, and stones of good quality generally, held very well even during the decline of the finest-quality larger stones.

*Gems can be used and enjoyed without adversely affecting value, unlike most other beautiful things people buy and use (autos, furs, furniture, etc.).*

*Historically, there has always been a market for gems.* Good stones are not trendy and don't go in and out of fashion, like some fine-art investments, where an artist is popular today and never heard of in a few years.

*Gems have portability—they are easily moved and stored, so they are readily available to the owner, easy to show when the need arises.*

## Some Facts that May Discourage Gem Investment

*Extreme care must be taken to verify the authenticity of the gem being considered and to determine its precise quality/value.* For this reason we advise against consideration of sealed merchandise.

*Gems are not a short-term investment.* In most cases, depending upon the price you have paid (the average consumer buys at retail, not at wholesale) and the rate of appreciation, there is a minimum five-year period simply to break even.

*Liquidity can be a problem.* Since you are not a jeweler, your own credibility will be suspect where the average consumer is concerned, so it may be very difficult to find a buyer for your gem.

Jewelers may be interested in buying "off the street," but the seller usually gets less than the current wholesale price in such transactions. This is not because the jeweler is trying to take advantage so much as a matter of simple economics. When the jeweler has a customer for a specific piece, he can always go to his dealer to obtain what he needs. Not only does he not risk tying up his money until he actually has a customer, but he may also charge the cost to his account and carry his cost for an extra thirty days or more, earning that extra interest on the money in the bank. Therefore, the only incentive for him to tie his money up in a cash transaction off the street, for which he may or may not even have an immediate customer, is if the price is attractive enough—usually *half the wholesale cost.* Yet another consideration is his own protection—he has no way to determine whether merchandise bought off the street is stolen property, which could end up confiscated by police (in which case he loses whatever he paid for the goods). There may be exceptions made if the piece is particularly fine or rare or unusual in some way, but the norm is as stated above.

Investment-house buy-back guarantees are *no* guarantee. Some of the new investment firms guarantee buy-back after a prescribed time period. Unfortunately, you have no way of knowing where they will be after the prescribed period of time.

# 6

# Important Advice
# After You Buy

# 23

## Choosing the Appraiser & Insurer

### Why Is It Important to Get an Appraisal?

Whether you have bought a diamond or a colored gemstone ring, getting a professional appraisal and keeping it updated is critical. An appraisal is necessary for four reasons: to verify the facts about the jewelry you have purchased (especially important with the abundance of new synthetic materials and treatments); to obtain adequate insurance to protect against theft, loss, or damage; to establish adequate information to legally claim jewelry recovered by the police; and, if items are lost or stolen, to provide sufficient information to make sure that they are replaced with jewelry that actually is of "comparable quality," if that is what your insurance policy provides.

The need for appraisal services has increased greatly because of the high incidence of theft and sharp increases in the prices of diamonds and colored gems. It has become a necessity to have any fine gem properly appraised, particularly prior to making a purchase decision, given today's costs and the potential for financial loss if the gem is not accurately represented.

It is also important, given recent rising prices, to update value estimations from old appraisals; this will ensure adequate coverage should gems that have been in your possession for several years or more be lost or stolen. In addition, current and accurate appraisals may be needed in connection with inheritance taxes, gifts, or in the determination of your net worth.

### How to Find a Reliable Appraiser

The appraisal business has been booming over the past few years and many jewelry firms have begun to provide the service themselves.

We must point out, however, that there are essentially no officially established guidelines for going into the gem appraising business. Anyone can
represent himself as an "appraiser." While many highly qualified professionals are in the business, some others lack the expertise to offer
these services. So it is essential to select an appraiser with care and
diligence. Further, if the purpose of the appraisal is to verify the identity or genuineness of a gem, as well as its value, we recommend that
you deal with someone who is in the business of gem identification
and appraising and not primarily in the business of selling gems.

To assist you in finding a reliable gem testing laboratory, we have
provided a selected list of laboratories that issue internationally recognized reports on page (251). To find a reliable gemologist-appraiser in your community, contact the following:

The American Society of Appraisers
Box 17265, Washington, DC 20041
(703) 478-2228
Ask for a current listing of *Master Gemologist Appraisers*

The American Gem Society
5901 West 3rd Street, Los Angeles, CA 90036-2898
(213) 936-4367
Ask for a list of *Certified Gemologist Appraisers*

The Accredited Gemologists Association
6034 W. Courtyard Drive, Suite 305
Austin, TX 78730
(512) 328-9411
Ask for a list of *Certified Gem Laboratories* or *Certified Master
    Gemologists*

The International Society of Appraisers
P.O. Box 726
Hoffman Estates, IL 60195
(708) 882-0706
Ask for a list of *Certified Appraisers of Personal Property*

In addition, when selecting a gemologist-appraiser, keep the following suggestions in mind:

*Obtain the names of several appraisers and then compare their
credentials.* To be a qualified gemologist-appraiser requires extensive
formal training and experience. You can conduct a preliminary check
by telephoning the appraisers and inquiring about their gemological
credentials.

*Look for specific credentials.* The Gemological Institute of America and the Gemological Association of Great Britain provide internationally recognized diplomas. GIA's highest award is GG (Graduate Gemologist) and the Gemmological Association of Great Britain awards the FGA—Fellow of the Gemmological Association (FGAA in Australia; FCGA, Canada). Some hold this honor "With Distinction." In Germany, the DGG is awarded; in Asia, the AG. Make sure the appraiser you select has one of these gemological diplomas. In addition, when seeking an *appraiser*, look for the title "Certified Gemologist Appraiser," which is awarded by the American Gem Society, or "Master Gemologist Appraiser," which is awarded by the American Society of Appraisers. Some fine gemologists and appraisers lack these titles because they do not belong to the organizations awarding them, but these titles currently represent the highest awards presented in the gemological appraisal field. Anyone holding these titles should have fine gemological credentials and adhere to high standards of professional conduct.

*Check the appraiser's length of experience.* In addition to formal training, to be reliable a gemologist-appraiser needs extensive experience in the handling of gems, use of the equipment necessary for accurate identification and evaluation, and activity in the marketplace. The appraiser should have at least several years' experience in a well-equipped laboratory. If the gem being appraised is a colored gem, the complexities are much greater and require more extensive experience. In order to qualify for CGA or MGA titles, the appraiser must have at least several years experience.

*Ask where the appraisal will be conducted.* An appraisal should normally be done in the presence of the customer, if possible. This is important in order to ensure that the same stone is returned to you, and to protect the appraiser against charges of "switching." Recently we appraised an old platinum engagement ring that had over twenty years' filth compacted under the high, filigree-type box mounting typical of the early 1920s. After cleaning, which was difficult, the diamond showed a definite brown tint, easily seen by the client, which she had never noticed when the ring was dirty. She had just inherited the ring from her deceased mother-in-law, who had told her it had a blue-white color. If she had not been present when this ring was being cleaned and appraised, it might have resulted in a lawsuit, for she would certainly have suspected a switch. This particular situation does not present itself often, but appraisers and customers alike need to be diligent and watchful.

If there are several pieces, the process can be very time-consuming. It normally takes about a half hour per item to get all of the specifications, and it can take much longer in some cases. It may require several appointments to do a proper job.

# Appraisal Fees

This is a touchy and complex subject. As with any professional service, there should be a suitable charge. Fees should be conspicuously posted or offered readily on request so that the customer knows beforehand what to expect to pay for this service. Fees are essentially based on the expertise of appraisers and the time required of them, as well as secretarial work required to put the appraisal in written form, since all appraisals should be done in writing. While it used to be standard practice to base appraisal fees on a percentage of the appraised value, this practice is no longer acceptable. Today, all recognized appraisal associations in the United States recommend that fees be based on a flat hourly rate, or on a per-carat charge for diamonds.

There is usually a minimum appraisal fee, regardless of value. The hourly rate charged by a professional, experienced gemologist-appraiser can range from $50 to $150, depending on the complexity of the work to be performed and the degree of expertise required. Find out beforehand what the hourly rate is and what the minimum fee will be.

For multiple-item appraisals, special arrangements are usually made. For appraisals containing many items, such as an estate appraisal, an hourly rate of $50 to $75 is normal. For certification or special gemological consulting requiring special expertise, rates can easily be $125 to $150 per hour. Extra services, such as photography, radiography, Gemprint, or spectroscopic examination of fancy colored diamonds, will require additional fees.

Be wary of appraisal services offering appraisals at very low rates, and of appraisers who continue to base their fee on a percentage of the "appraised valuation." The Internal Revenue Service, for example, will not accept appraisals performed by appraisers who charge a "percentage-based" fee.

Mr. Bonanno usually takes a photograph of the piece he is appraising, except for simple watches and simple rings. On the photograph he notes the approximate magnification, the date, and the owner's name, and he signs it using his personal embossing seal to make an impression over his name. This provides a means of identifying merchandise that may have been stolen, lost, or damaged, and will also aid in duplicating the piece should the customer so desire. The photograph may also be used for the U.S. Customs Service should the customer be a world traveler.

With the information provided here, the consumer will know how to evaluate the appraiser and make sure that accurate, complete documentation is provided.

# Protecting Your Diamond With Gemprint

Gemprint is a unique service offered by many jewelers and appraisers. While not totally foolproof (re-cutting the diamond may affect Gemprint's reliability), it is playing an increasingly important role in the recovery and return of lost and stolen diamonds, and we recommend it where available.

Gemprint offers a means to identify a diamond, even one already mounted, by taking a photograph of the pattern of reflections created when a low-level laser beam hits the gem. Each diamond produces a unique pattern, which is documented by this service. As with human fingerprints, no two gemprints are ever alike.

The process takes only a few minutes and the cost is nominal ($35 to $50). Two gemprints are taken. One is given to the customer, accompanied by a numbered certificate of registration. The second is filed in the Gemprint Central Registry.

If the stone is ever lost or stolen, the owner sends a notice-of-loss form to Gemprint, which immediately puts out a computerized alert to police departments across the country. Police can then verify with the registry the identification of recovered diamonds, many of which are thereby returned to the rightful owner.

As another safeguard, Gemprint also checks each new registration against its lost-and-stolen file before confirming and storing the registration. Gemprint can also be useful in situations where a diamond, or diamond jewelry, has been left for repair, cleaning, or resetting, to assure the owner that the right stone has been returned.

Some insurance companies give 10 percent off the annual premium paid to insure a Gemprinted diamond. Gemprint is available in about 650 locations in the United States. For the location nearest you contact: Gemprint, Ltd., 10 Lower Spadina, Toronto, Ontario, Canada, 416-597-6740.

# Choosing An Insurer

Once you have a complete appraisal, the next step is obtaining adequate insurance. Most people do not realize that insurers differ widely in their coverage and reimbursement or replacement procedures. Many companies will not reimburse the "full value" provided in the policy, but instead exercise a "replacement" option by which they offer a *cash sum less than the amount for which the jewelry is insured,* or offer to replace it for you. Therefore, it is important to ask very specific questions to determine the precise coverage offered. We recommend asking at least the following:

- *How do you satisfy claims?* Do you reimburse the insured amount in cash? If not, how is the amount of the cash settlement determined? Or do you replace the jewelry?

- *What involvement do I have in the replacement of an item?* What assurance do I have that the replacement will be of comparable quality and value?

- *What is your coverage on articles that cannot be replaced?*

- *Exactly what risks does my policy cover?* All risks? Mysterious disappearance? In all geographic areas? At all times?

- *Are there any exemptions or exclusions?* What if the loss involves negligence?

- *What are the deductibles, if any?*

- *What documentation do you expect me to provide?*

To help with insurance claims keep a "photo inventory" of your jewelry. Take a photo and store it in a safe place, (a bank safe deposit box). In case of theft or fire, a photo will be useful to help you remember what is missing and identify it, if recovered. A photo is also useful for insurance documentation.

# Appendix

# A Selected List of Laboratories that Provide Internationally Recognized Reports of Genuineness and Quality

American Gemological Laboratory
580 Fifth Avenue
New York, NY 10036

Gemmological Lab, Gubelin
Denkmalstrasse, 2
Ch-6006 Luzern, Switzerland

GIA Gem Trade Laboratory
Gemological Institute of America
580 Fifth Avenue
New York, NY 10036

GIA Gem Trade Laboratory
Gemological Institute of America
1660 Stewart Street
Santa Monica, CA 90404

Hoge Raad voor Diamant (HRD)
Hoveniersstraat, 22
B-2018 Antwerp, Belgium

Schweizerische Stiftung fur Edelstein-Forschung (SSEF)
Lowenstrasse, 17
Ch-8001 Zurich, Switzerland

# Selected Readings

Arem, Joel E. *Color Encyclopedia of Gemstones*. New York: Van Nostrand Reinhold, 1987. Excellent color photography makes this book interesting for anyone. An invaluable reference for the gemologist.

Ball, S.H. *A Roman Book on Precious Stones*. Los Angeles: Gemological Institute of America, 1950. Very interesting from a historical perspective, especially for the knowledgeable student of gemology.

Becker, Vivienne. *Antique and Twentieth Century Jewellery*. London: N.A.G. Press, 1987. A beautifully illustrated classic focusing on 18th-20th century collectible jewelry.

Blauer, Ettagale. *Contemporary American Jewelry Design*. New York: Van Nostrand Reinhold, 1991. Beautifully illustrated and informative book revealing the work of many of America's most talented jewelry designers.

Bruton, E. *Diamonds*. 2nd Edition. Radnor, PA: Chilton, 1978. An excellent, well-illustrated work for amateur and professional alike.

Cavenago-Bignami Moneta, S. *Gemmologia*. Milan: Heopli, 1965. One of the most extensive works on gems available. Excellent photography. Available in Italian only. Recommended for advanced students.

Cody, Andrew. *Australian Precious Opal; A Guide Book for Professionals,* Melbourne: Mount Press Pty. Ltd., 1991. Superb book on all types of Australian opal and evaluation. Many excellent photos.

Desautels, Paul E. *The Jade Kingdom*. New York: Van Nostrand Reinhold, 1986. Important resource on world occurrences, history, uses and identification.

Downing, Paul B. *Opal Identification and Value*. Tallahassee, FL: Majestic Press, 1992. Excellent book on opals for the serious opal lover. Includes retail price guides.

Farn, Alexander E. *Pearls: Natural, Cultured & Imitation*. Oxford: Butterworth-Heinemann Ltd., 1991. The definitive volume; covering pearl evolution, biology, science, and trade.

Federman, David. *Modern Jeweler's Consumer Guide to Colored Gemstones*. New York: Van Nostrand Reinhold, 1989. Good general reference covering many popular gemstones, supply and demand, and interesting historical tidbits.

Gubelin, Edward and J.L. Koivula. *Photoatlas of Inclusions in Gemstones*. Zurich: ABC Editions, 1986. Recommended for the serious student of gemology. Most comprehensive collection of inclusions ever photographed.

Hurlbut, Cornelius and R.C. Kammerling, *Gemology,* New York: John Wiley & Sons, 1991. Excellent, well-organized textbook for beginning through advanced students.

Keverne, Roger. Editor. *Jade,* New York: Van Nostrand Reinhold, 1991. Superb, encyclopedic work on jade with lavish illustrations. A must for anyone who loves jade. 450 lavish photos.

Keller, Peter C. *Gemstones and Their Origins.* New York: Van Nostrand Reinhold, 1989. A very interesting, well illustrated resource covering geological origins and mining of gems.

Kunz, G.F. *The Curious Lore of Precious Stones.* Reprinted 1972, with *The Magic of Jewels and Charms.* New York: Dover Publications.

————. *Gems and Precious Stones of North America.* Reprinted 1968. New York: Dover Publications. Very interesting for both beginner and advanced.

Liddicoat, R.T. *Handbook of Gem Identification.* 12th Edition. Los Angeles: Gemological Institute of America, 1989. Textbook for the student of gemology.

Matlins, Antoinette Leonard & Bonanno, A.C. *Gem Identification Made Easy: A Hands-On Guide to More Confident Buying and Selling.* Woodstock, VT: GemStone Press, 1989. A non-technical book that makes gem identification possible for anyone—even without a science background. A "must" for beginners, and the experienced may pick up a few tips, too. Practical, easy to understand.

————.*Engagement & Wedding Rings,* Woodstock, VT: Gemstone Press, 1990. Everything you need to know to select, design, buy, care for, and cherish, your wedding or anniversary rings—his and hers. Beautiful photos of rings from 15th century to present.

Miller, Anna. *Cameos Old and New.* New York: Van Nostrand Reinhold, 1991. A fascinating and invaluable resource for cameo lovers. Beautifully illustrated.

Nassau, Kurt. *Gemstone Enhancement.* Woburn, MA: Butterworth's, 1983. Possibly the most comprehensive and understandable book available on gem enhancement.

Pagel-Theisen, V. *Diamond Grading ABC.* 10th Edition. New York: Rubin & Son, 1990. Highly recommended for anyone in diamond sales.

Pough, F.H. *The Story of Gems and Semiprecious Stones.* New York: Harvey House, 1969. Good for beginning and amateur gemologists.

Read, Peter G. *Gemmology: A Textbook for Students.* Oxford: Butterworth-Heinemann Ltd., 1991. One of the best new books for the student of gemology.

Sauer, Jules. *Emeralds Around the World*. Rio de Janeiro: Amsterdam Sauer, 1992. A new, exciting approach to an intriguing subject, for layman and specialist alike.

Scarisbrick, Diana, Ed. *The Jewelry Design Sourcebook*. New York: Van Nostrand Reinhold, 1989. A spectacular visual survey of jewelry from the ancient world to the present day. An invaluable reference for gemologists, jewelry makers, designers and collectors.

Schumann, W. *Gemstones of the World*. Translated by E. Stern. New York: Sterling Publishing Co., 1977. This book has superior color plates of all of the gem families and their different varieties and for this reason would be valuable to anyone interested in gems.

Sinkankas, John. *Emerald and Other Beryls*. Tucson, AZ: Geoscience Press/Harbinger House, 1982. A classic work on the beryl family.

Sofianides, Anna S., and George E. Harlow. *Gems & Crystals*. New York: Simon & Schuster, 1991. Features 150 stunning full color photos of 400 different gems and crystals from the collection of the American Museum of Natural History.

Ward, Fred. *Emeralds*. Bethesda, MD: Gem Books Publishers, 1993. Fascinating coverage of history, lore, and famous emerald mine. Superb photos.

Webster, R. Revised by B.W. Anderson. *Gems*. 4th Edition. London: Butterworth & Co., 1990.

————. *Practical Gemology*. 6th Edition. Colchester, Essex: N.A.G. Press Ltd., 1976. Both are highly recommended for the serious student of gemology, especially *Gems*.

Zucker, Benjamin. *Gems and Jewels: A Connoisseur's Guide*. New York: Thames and Hudson, Inc. 1984. Lavishly illustrated book on principal gems and "great" gemstones of the world, with fascinating historical facts, mythological tidbits, and examples of jeweler's art from widely differing cultures.

# Color Plates and Exhibits

All of the charts that appear here were especially designed and executed for use in this book; however, in some cases, charts from other publications were used as inspiration and reference. Grateful acknowledgment is given to the following for use of their charts as references:

The chart on page 57, "Sizes and Weights of Various Diamond Cuts," with permission of the Gemological Institute of America, from its book, *The Jewelers' Manual.*

The chart on page 58, "Diameters and Corresponding Weights of Round, Brilliant-Cut Diamonds," with permission of the Gemological Institute of America, from its book, *The Jewelers' Manual.*

The chart on page 91, "Diamond and Diamond Look-Alikes," with permission of the Gemological Institute of America, from its publication *Diamond Assignment No. 36,* page 27.

### Color Photographs

We wish to thank the following persons and companies for the color photographs appearing in this new edition:

#### Gemstones

Page 1   Fancy diamond "peacock," blue and pink diamonds, green diamonds courtesy of Robert Haack Diamonds. Photos/Sky Hall.

Fancy-color diamond floral brooch courtesy of Sotheby's, NY.

Assorted natural color diamond suite (top left) from the *Aurora Collection,* American Museum of Natural History, NY. Photo/Stephen Hofer.

Page 2   Star ruby courtesy of International Colored Gemstone Association (ICA). Photo/Bart Curran.

Selection of red and pink gemstones, and rhodochrosites, courtesy of Pala International, Inc.; Red beryl courtesy of Rex Harris. Photo/Sky Hall.

Page 3   Blue Paraiba tourmalines, star sapphire, and moonstones courtesy of International Colored Gemstone Association (ICA). Photos/Bart Curran.

Selection of blue gemstones courtesy of Pala International, Inc.; Chrysocolla, courtesy of American Gem Trade Association (AGTA), cut by Glenn Lehrer, AGTA *Cutting Edge* competition winner. Photo/Sky Hall.

Page 4   Selection of yellow and orange gemstones courtesy of Pala International, Inc. Photo/Sky Hall.

Topaz courtesy of American Gem Trade Association (AGTA). Photo/Natural Arts, Inc.

Sunstone courtesy of Ponderosa Mine, Inc. Photo/Bart Curran.

Sapphire, andalusite and cats-eye chrysoberyl courtesy of Krementz Gemstones; fancy-cut citrine with concave facets courtesy of American Gem Trade Association (AGTA), cut by *Cutting Edge* winner Richard Homer, American Lapidary Artists; yellow beryl courtesy of AGTA, cut by *Cutting Edge* winner Karl Egan Wilde. Photos/Sky Hall.

Page 5    Selection of green gemstones and tsavorite garnet courtesy of Pala International, Inc. Photos/Sky Hall.

Emerald-cut emerald courtesy of International Colored Gemstone Association (ICA). Photo/Sky Hall.

Laboratory-grown synthetic stones courtesy of Chatham Created Gemstones.

Period Art Deco jadeite brooch courtesy of Christie's, NY.

Page 6    Andamooka crystal opal, Andamooka matrix opal beads, and two free form black opals courtesy of Western Opal. Photos/Sky Hall.

Mexican opals and oval cabochon black opal courtesy of International Colored Gemstone Association (ICA). Photos/Bart Curran.

Page 7    Lapis sculpture by Michael Dyber. Photo courtesy of Ledge Studio.

Belt buckles courtesy of Elizabeth Rand Studio.

Intarsia box by Nicolai Medvedev, courtesy of E.F. Watermelon Co. Photo/Sky Hall.

Stone cabochons and beads: Photo/Sky Hall.

Page 8    Diamonds cut in classic shapes courtesy of MEFCO Inc. Photo/Sky Hall.

Quadrillion-cut diamond and diamond ring courtesy of Ambar Diamonds.

Dream-cut diamonds courtesy of Maico Industries. Photos/Rich Russo.

Royal-cut diamonds and photo courtesy of Suberi Bros.

**Jewelry**

Page 1    Platinum and diamond *Tension* ring by Steven Kretchmer. Design copyrighted. Ring patented, U.S. patent no. 5,084,108. Photo/Weldon Photography.

Platinum and diamond "heirloom" ring by Richard Kimball.

Collection of Edwardian jewelry: Photo/Sky Hall.

Platinum and diamond "ball" jewelry by Etienne Perret.

Page 2    Antique gold jewelry from the Collection of the British Museum. Photo reprinted with permission of the British Museum, London.

All other jewelry and photos courtesy of Barnett Robinson.

Page 3    "Moon and Stars" suite courtesy of Barnett Robinson.

Round curb-link necklace and reversible necklace courtesy of Abel & Zimmermann.

Center selection of popular chains and photo/Sky Hall.

"Makume Gane" bands courtesy of George Sawyer Designs.

Page 4    Gold and pearl earrings by Eric Russell.

Selection of pearls pictured at bottom of page, and "cross-shaped" pearls, courtesy of King Partners and A&Z pearls. Photos/Sky Hall.

All other photos courtesy of the Cultured Pearl Association of America, NY.

Page 5    Natural black color cultured pearl necklace courtesy of Robert Adams. Photo/Sky Hall.

Natural black color cultured pearl, ruby and diamond pendant/enhancer courtesy of Sultan Company. Photo/Sky Hall.

American freshwater *natural* pearls from the Collection of John Latendresse. American freshwater cultured pearls courtesy of American Pearl Company. Photos/Rich Mays.

Page 6    All jewelry courtesy of the designers pictured. Michael Good neck piece/photo by Ted Pobiner Studio; photo of Eric Russell's stacking rings/courtesy Eric Russell. All other photos, courtesy of the American Gem Trade Association (AGTA) and the *Spectrum* awards committee. Photos/Sky Hall.

Page 7    All jewelry courtesy of the designers pictured. Eddie Sakamoto's ring courtesy of Concept One. Susan Saunders' brooch courtesy of the American Gem Trade Association *Spectrum* awards committee: Photo/Linda Urban Photography.

Page 8    Top left: pair of rings with trilliant-cut diamonds courtesy of Mark Michaels; right, six contemporary bands courtesy of William Richey.

Second row: left, diamond band with marquises and baguettes courtesy of Kwiat, Inc.; center, "Tiffany" style solitaire courtesy of the Diamond Information Service; right, band combining fancy color and white diamonds courtesy of Fire & Ice.

Third row: left, trio of contemporary diamond rings courtesy of Scott Keating Design; right, trio of classic anniversary bands courtesy of Kwiat, Inc.

Fourth row contemporary diamond rings: left, courtesy of Bagley & Hotchkiss; right, courtesy of Coast Diamonds.

# Index